THE RESILIENT SOCIETY

'Can our political and economic systems be flexible enough to protect against large shocks but also enable us to bounce back after? Markus K. Brunnermeier addresses this question with originality and depth. As the world emerges from the pandemic and braces itself for more such shocks, this compelling book could not be more timely or valuable.'

ARVIND SUBRAMANIAN, former Chief Economic Advisor to the Government of India

'The global economy is at a crossroads. Transformational changes and attendant challenges abound: pandemics, policy normalization, climate change, cyber risk and digital finance, among others. In *The Resilient Society*, Markus K. Brunnermeier provides a coherent path forward to prepare for it all and recover robustly when future shocks inevitably hit. A must-read for Indian policymakers, businessmen and young minds as the country tries to bounce back from past shocks and deal smartly with an increasingly uncertain future.'

VIRAL V. ACHARYA, former Deputy Governor of the Reserve Bank of India

'A landmark book on resilience ... an indispensable guide to what we must learn from the pandemic and how to do better next time.'

ANGUS DEATON, 2015 Nobel laureate in economics

'In this book, Markus K. Brunnermeier thinks big about the long-term future, in light of the lessons we have learned from recent transforming events. A significant read for anyone taking a leadership role in the coming years.'

ROBERT SHILLER, 2013 Nobel laureate in economics

'Markus K. Brunnermeier, one of the leading economists of this generation, shows us how we can address crises more effectively in the future. This book will be an invaluable resource for scholars and practitioners looking to build a more resilient, just and productive society.'

RAJ CHETTY, William A. Ackman Professor at Harvard University and the Director of Opportunity Insights

'Provides a new framework for understanding resilience in finance and in the political economy. Lucid, clear and engaging, the book should be required reading for any economist or policymaker seeking a new way of imagining the craft of economics.'

GILLIAN TETT, Chair of the Editorial Board and Editor-at-Large, *Financial Times*

THE RESILIENT SOCIETY

ECONOMICS AFTER COVID

MARKUS K. BRUNNERMEIER

HARPER BUSINESS

An Imprint of HarperCollins *Publishers*

First published in 2021 in the United States of America by
Endeavor Literary Press
with support from the Peterson Institute of International Economics

First published in India by Harper Business 2022
An imprint of HarperCollins *Publishers*
Building No. 10, Tower A, 4th Floor, DLF Cyber City, Phase II
Gurugram, Haryana 122002
www.harpercollins.co.in

2 4 6 8 10 9 7 5 3 1

P-ISBN: 978-93-5489-576-0
E-ISBN: 978-93-5489-385-8

Cover design: Saurav Das

Printed and bound at
Thomson Press (India) Ltd

HarperCollinsIn

MIX
Paper
FSC FSC® C010615

This book is produced from independently certified FSC® paper
to ensure responsible forest management.

Contents

Foreword

As a result of the Covid-19 crisis, the world must address a critical question: How can societies be reshaped so that we can face inevitable, severe shocks with resilience? To answer that question, this book proposes a shift in our mindset and our social interactions. Rather than lethargically avoiding risks, we should proactively develop societies that are resilient to adverse shocks.

The Covid-19 pandemic has provided us with an opportunity to learn how to be better prepared for future crises, on a national and international scale. This book is my take on those lessons, specifically related to the economic challenges that societies around the globe now face and how we can prepare for the next shock. It presents an analysis of the immediate and long-term pandemic impacts on societies.

The aim of the book is to present the concept and principles of resilience in a structured way, and to make them available to a broader public. However, the book makes no attempt to be all inclusive, comprehensive, or fully rigorous. Rather it raises intriguing perspectives designed to encourage readers to think. Hopefully, the book will stimulate discussions among politically interested citizens who are keen to build a more resilient society.

Part I of the book outlines the concept of resilience and how our social contracts could be redesigned to make societies more resilient to unexpected shocks. Part II outlines four core elements of resilience management using the Covid-19 pandemic as the primary example. Part III addresses future macroeconomic challenges, such as scarring effects, high debt levels, and inflation. Part IV emphasizes global challenges. Each chapter stands on its own and can be read without reading the earlier chapters.

I draw from the insights of others, but the book presents my own analytical summary of the main tradeoffs and should not implicate others. In fact, this is a work in progress. Events are still unfolding. Hence, the book should be read as an interim synthesis.

Markus Brunnermeier

Princeton, June 2021

Acknowledgements

Special thanks go to Thomas Krön. Without his help and dedication, this book would have never found its light. His help was essential.

I have gained many insights from the top scientists and economists who presented at the Princeton webinar series "Markus' Academy" that I started in March 2020. Special thanks go to more than a dozen Nobel Prize laureates including, Paul Romer, Angus Deaton, Joe Stiglitz, Michael Kremer, Paul Krugman, Michael Spence, Bob Shiller, Jean Tirole, Chris Sims, Bengt Holmström, Bill Nordhaus, and Esther Duflo. I also wish to thank epidemiologist Ramanan Laxminarayan and historian Harold James. I'm grateful for the following top economists: Torsten Slok, Nellie Liang, Olivier Blanchard, Tyler Cowen, Joshua Gans, Penelopi Goldberg, Hyun Song Shin, Dani Rodrik, Daron Acemoglu, Jeremy Stein, John Cochrane, Larry Summers, Gita Gopinath, Darrell Duffie, Lisa Cook, Ken Rogoff, Raj Chetty, Veronica Guerrieri, Erik Hurst, Arvind Krishnamurthy, Richard Zeckhauser, Esteban Rossi-Hansberg, Luigi Zingales, Robert Hall, Emily Oster, Stephen Redding, Jason Furman, Nick Bloom, Adam Posen, Charles Goodhart, James Stock, Andy Lo, Lasse Pedersen, Monica de

Bolle, Iván Werning, Amit Seru, Alan Auerbach, Robin Brooks, Gary Gorton, Emi Nakamura, Antoinette Schoar, Alberto Cavallo, Philippe Aghion, Edmar Bacha, and Viral Acharya. My writing greatly benefitted from several current or former central bankers, including Bill Dudley, Philip Lane, Arminio Fraga, Raghuram Rajan, Jerome Powell, and Agustin Carstens. My gratitude also goes to Eurogroup President Paschal Donohoe and finance experts Barry Ritholtz and Liz Myers. I'm grateful for tech experts like Eric Schmidt. Special mention goes to Delaney Parrish and Kelsey Richardson who helped me establish the Princeton webinar series during challenging times.

Jean-Pierre Landau deserves special mention for his detailed, constructive feedback. I received helpful feedback from Joseph Abadi, Kartik Anand, Sylvain Chassang, Martin Mühleisen, Dirk Niepelt, Pietro Ortoleva, Jean Pisani-Ferry, Rohit Lamba, Ricardo Reis, Yannick Timmer, Sigurd Wagner, Jeromin Zettelmeyer, Hans-Helmut Kotz, and a reading group at the Bundesbank, as well as from four anonymous referees at the Peterson Institute for International Economics.

I also want to express my deep gratitude to Christina Xu and Mohan Setty Charity who diligently went through each chapter to improve early drafts. Don Noh deserves credit for collecting the data and creating the graphs in the book. I wish to thank my editor, Glenn McMahan, and James Clarke for his cover design for the American edition of the book and for his typesetting.

Finally, I would like to thank my wife, Smita, and my two daughters, Anjali and Priya, for their support during the Covid-19 period.

Introduction

The Covid-19 pandemic has made us feel fragile. As individuals, we discovered that we could suddenly be hit by a rapidly spreading, unknown disease. It upended our perception that medical progress would prevent such events. Societies around the world faced disruptions on an unprecedented scale. The pandemic paralyzed recreational activities, stretched public services to the limit, left the poorest and most vulnerable unattended, turned our homes into workplaces, stopped our kids from going to school, disrupted our family lives, and forced us to connect with friends through screens. And we lost many lives.

The pandemic has also given us reason to be confident in the power of medicine and technology. Indeed, we can only marvel at the speed and efficiency of vaccine discovery, which occurred less than a year after the virus was identified. But what about social fragility and vulnerabilities? Will our societies quickly recover, or will they bear permanent scars? Most importantly, will they be able to overcome similar shocks in the future? This book seeks to address that question.

The key concept in this book is **resilience**. The term refers to an *ability to rebound,* which is different than the idea of **robustness**, which is an ability to resist. Sometimes robustness is not the best way forward. Resilience is about being able to weather a storm and recover, as described in the famous poem by Jean de La Fontaine titled *The Oak and the Reed.*"[1] The oak is robust. It is mighty and looks indestructible in the face of normal winds. By contrast, the reed is resilient. Even light breezes bend the reed. But when a strong storm erupts, the reed declares: "I bend but do not break."

That phrase incorporates the essence of resilience. The reed bounces back when the storm is over. It fully recovers. The robust oak can withstand strong winds, but it breaks when the storm becomes too severe. Once it has fallen, no recovery is possible. Its lack of resilience prevents restoration. The reed, always in motion, might look vulnerable, but it is much more resilient than the oak.

This is a nice metaphor from nature, but it does not fully describe the challenges we face. There are, of course, purely "physical" pillars of resilience. For instance, in daily life we depend on the proper functioning of numerous networks and infrastructures. Just imagine life without telecoms, the internet, and roads. So, if we want those elements of our physical infrastructure to rebound after a shock, we might need to build them with redundancies, buffer stocks, duplications of structures, and added capacities. Doing so implies a possible need to sacrifice efficiency in exchange for greater resilience.

So far, societies have sought to manage production systems according to a "just in time" principle; that is, to maximize flows and minimize stocks, which is the objective of global value chains. By contrast, the concept of resilience leads us to emphasize a "just in case" approach, which would give us the ability to recover speedily after a shock. For that to occur, we must give priority to resilience, which turns redundancies into a virtue rather than a vice. Safety buffers are useful because they allow us to absorb shocks. A mindset of resilience provides a new way of looking at cost-benefit calculations.

Another way to understand the difference between resilience and robustness is to consider an electric circuit with numerous light bulbs. The most cost-efficient way to set this up would be a series circuit like those used in old-style Christmas tree lights. In this case, if one light bulb failed, the entire Christmas tree would turn dark. A more resilient alternative is a parallel circuit. In this case, each light bulb is connected to a main circuit, which is the norm for lighting a staircase. If the second-floor light bulb fails, the lights on the first and third floors stay on. The total cost of the wiring is higher because more wire is needed, but the parallel circuit is more resilient.

Resilience is also different than **risk**, which refers to the frequency and size of shocks. Resilience is about the *ability to react* after a shock hits—the ability to bounce back or, in formal terms, to "mean-revert." This ability to rebound implies the need to facilitate adaptation. If we are able to adapt and change, we will strengthen our resilience. With improved resilience, we will be able to take more chances and embrace more opportunities—because the shocks will be less detrimental.

Resilience is also an essential component of **sustainability**. In the absence of resilience, a society can become unsustainable. Severe shocks might push society over the cliff, leading to detrimental adverse feedback loops.

The Covid-19 pandemic has taught us that resilience requires more than individualistic thinking. A society relies on healthy collective functions, which are created (or not) by the quality of our **social contract**. This contract emerges from the recognition that our individual conduct will impact others. Economists call these impacts "externalities." Without a social contract, people often impose negative externalities on each other. As a result, some citizens become trapped or pushed close to tipping points. Taken as a whole, negative externalities increase social fragility and undermine resilience, particularly when a shock like the recent pandemic hits.

In this book, I argue that resilience can serve as the guiding North Star for designing a post-Covid-19 society.[2] This overarching principle can help us think about how to prepare society and foster cohesion that enables us to better react to future shocks. Throughout, I apply an economist's perspective on health and the social contract.

Granting to people the personal freedom they need to dream, experiment, strategize, plan, and possibly fail is essential for societal progress. It is my view that that this freedom is also essential for human dignity. However, people should not be trapped or fall into poverty. They should have the ability to rebound and try again after they have learned from their failures. Personal bankruptcy protection serves precisely that purpose. Hence, rather than shielding people from possible failure, society should encourage experimentation and curiosity while also making individuals resilient.

Implementing a Social Contract

This book addresses how a resilient social contract can be implemented, either by governments or via social norms. Authoritarian **governments** use outright force to limit externalities.

In open societies, governments have to rely more on the power of persuasion. Due to the Covid-19 pandemic, the pendulum might swing toward increased government intervention that could limit individual freedom. **Social norms** are another way to enforce the social contract and to internalize externalities. An example can be seen in Japan where, without government pressure, citizens have generally adhered to mask-wearing guidelines and social distancing recommendations because they fear social stigma.

Markets can also play an important role in aggregating the information that is dispersed in a society. If many people like a product, they will demand more of it and thereby push up its price, which signals firms to supply more.

All of these factors—social norms, government mandates, and the market—can play a role in implementing a social contract. That said, it is important to recognize that a society and its social contract will be more resilient if the contract's implementation can *flexibly respond* to shocks. Depending on the nature of the crisis, implementing the mix of social norms, government mandates, and the market will need to be adjusted. Making these adjustments will require careful discernment. Too much flexibility can be detrimental. People need to rely on a clear, consistent social framework in order to make predictions and plans with at least a modicum of certainty.

Therefore, it is paramount for us to understand how human behaviors change when shocks occur in waves, as has occurred during this pandemic. Managing a crisis requires information. To understand new situations, we need experimentation. Accurate communication is also essential, in part because it has such a powerful influence on human behavior. However, conveying factual information about public health guidelines during a pandemic, for example, is challenging. People struggle to grasp unobserved counterfactuals, such as the estimated number of Covid-19 deaths in the absence of certain public health measures.

Finally, any resilient response to a crisis needs to include a vision for the new normal. The book is designed to help readers think about the future. What will society look like at the end of a crisis? Where will we go next?

Long-Run Forces and Tensions

From a macroeconomic and financial perspective, we should recognize the reality of volatility while also developing the capacity to rebound (resilience). In other words, for us to attain long-run growth we will need to flexibly adapt and embrace disruptive technologies. Paradoxically, this resilient approach to shocks will be *less risky* than maintaining the status quo, which can lead to long-term stagnation.

Shocks like the recent pandemic can trigger two long-run forces during the post-shock recovery phase. On the one hand, the Covid-19 pandemic has induced technological progress and **innovations** in several areas of life. These new technologies might foster resilience and therefore provide additional capacity to adjust to future shocks.

On the other hand, there is a risk of long-term **scarring** that could undermine resilience. Workers who lost jobs might lose skills and struggle to return to the labor market. Disruptions within education systems might lead to human capital scarring. And finally, firms might suffer from debt overhang. If large debt burdens hold firms back from investing, the economy might suffer in the long run.

To remain resilient, we must avoid **financial market** havoc. Financial markets remained resilient in 2020 and early 2021. After an initial shiver in March 2020, central bank interventions rapidly removed the tail risk in markets and stabilized asset prices, resulting in a drop-and-rebound pattern similar to a whipsaw. As central banks contained the risk of widespread negative outcomes, firms benefited from lower interest rates as they raised much needed liquidity. In the future, this type of scenario might make the economy more resilient, but it might also lead to financial instability in the medium term.

Public debt typically soars in times of crisis, just as it has during the Covid-19 pandemic. The large fiscal stimulus programs have so far averted an outcome like the Great Recession, even though the pandemic has caused a much larger fundamental shock than what we experienced in 2008. Nonetheless, there are worries about debt sustainability and the long-term economic outlook. A society is only resilient if government debt is sustainable over the long run. Otherwise, the society will face a sizable risk of inflation and also a risk of deflation due to debt overhang. Until now, the US government debt burden has been bearable because of low interest rates and the safe asset status of government bonds. However, governments that are vulnerable to interest rate hikes might experience skyrocketing interest burdens. Remaining vigilant to these potential adverse jumps in debt markets is critical.

There is also a risk that **inflation** will display whipsaw dynamics over the medium term. In 2020, depressed demand lowered inflation rates; however, inflationary forces could be unleashed in the future. To foster resilience, central banks must remain alert to the danger of deflation traps and inflation traps. Like a high-speed race car with strong brakes, an independent central bank can boost the economic recovery while the economy remains in recession, or it can step on the brakes and tighten policy in times of rapid economic growth. However, at any time, a conflict of interest between the central bank and the government might emerge if tighter monetary policy increases the government's debt servicing costs.

A social contract is only resilient if society is fair and if **inequalities** are kept in check. In the case of the United States (at least), the Covid-19 pandemic has revealed the ways that inequality impacts all parts of society. Racial inequalities have become more apparent. We have seen the problem of unequal healthcare access and how that problem has heterogeneously affected different communities. The Covid-19 pandemic has worked like an X-ray machine, revealing the hidden challenges under the surface of many societies.

Global Resilience

Finally, this book will discuss how the world as a whole can enhance resilience. The Covid-19 pandemic has reminded us that we live in a global society and that we need global resilience. We have seen again how a contagious disease can rapidly spread throughout the world. Perhaps surprisingly, it is common for viruses to transmit from animals to humans. This happens on a weekly basis. But human-to-human transmission is much rarer for zoonotic viruses. Hence, banning wet markets, establishing early warning systems, and promoting early responses to outbreaks are critical to improve global resilience.[3] Such interventions might also be useful to detect mutations of SARS-CoV-2, such as the ones discovered in Southeast England and in South Africa in late 2020, or the Delta variant in India in the spring of 2021.

This need raises broader questions about the **international order**. As in previous health crises, or in the battle against climate change, all humans have recently faced one common enemy: Covid-19. However, international coordination has been a low priority since the early days of the pandemic. At the time of this writing, many countries are still working unilaterally to secure vaccine commitments.

Emerging and **developing countries** face particular challenges in retaining resilience while escaping poverty and middle-income traps. *Policy space* to respond to shocks is more limited in developing nations. For instance, lockdown measures during the Covid-19 crisis triggered starvation and other invisible deaths from missed immunizations for other diseases. Moreover, developing nations have limited *fiscal space* and that restricts their ability to foster resilience. Strained public finances leave little room for further stimulus should another crisis appear.

Looking ahead, international relations will play a crucial role in shaping the post-Covid-19 world. The latent power struggle between the US and China is likely to drag on in several areas, including digitization, cybersecurity, spheres of influence, and trade. At the same time, Europe will have to decide whether to align more closely with the US or play a more independent role relative to both China and the US. The pandemic has also highlighted the vulnerability of deeply integrated global value chains. In the future, supply chains might need to be more diversified to improve resilience despite slightly higher costs.

Last but not least, the principle of resilience is important in the context of climate change and environmental sustainability. We will face shocks and setbacks, but we need innovation to reduce emissions. Without that, society will be propelled toward irreversible, dangerous tipping points that make us more vulnerable. A single shock or unexpected event could push society over the edge to a point of no return, or into a state of ongoing deterioration.

Shocks can be caused by many factors, of which pandemics are just one. The Covid-19 crisis has clearly revealed that a failure to prepare for risks can have a devastating global impact, especially in societies that lack the resilience needed to face unforeseen circumstances. This highlights the necessity to consider the main theme of this book. When the next unforeseen crisis strikes—a large-scale internet failure, a cyberattack, a bioengineering experiment failure, a superbug, a catastrophic climate event—all of humanity will benefit if the social contract is designed to enable us to bounce back after we have been knocked off our feet.

PART I

RESILIENCE AND SOCIETY

How should resilience and a social contract guide our societies and the way we live together? We will dive into the details of that question in this section. Chapter 1 defines the concept of resilience and compares it with the related concepts of robustness, sustainability, and risk. Next, chapter 2 explores the implications of resilience for the social contract, especially how it can enable us to live together as a peaceful society, and how to make the social contract itself more resilient.

CHAPTER 1
Resilience and Its Cousins

A resilient society is able to react to and respond after a shock. Resilience even opens new doors to enhanced growth and sustainability.

A Definition of Resilience

A society can drift and change, but it will usually follow a trend—a smooth procession over time. Occasionally a society faces shocks that lead to deviations from the normal trend and expected outcomes. A shock can trigger abrupt changes in, for example, stock prices or the wellbeing of individuals.

Prior to a shock, we are typically aware that something could suddenly change, and we foresee possible future paths. Of course, the ex-ante view is blind to whether the shock will materialize.

We can only assign a probability to that event. Some shocks are extremely rare and improbable. Others are more likely. Some shocks are good and others are bad. Some future scenarios are dangerous, as we have seen during the Covid-19 shock. Others are completely unforeseen, or even unimaginable.

Shocks have two important features: amplitude and frequency. An ample shock causes more damage than a small one. The difference is shown in figure 1-1, where the shock is amplified in the right-hand panel.

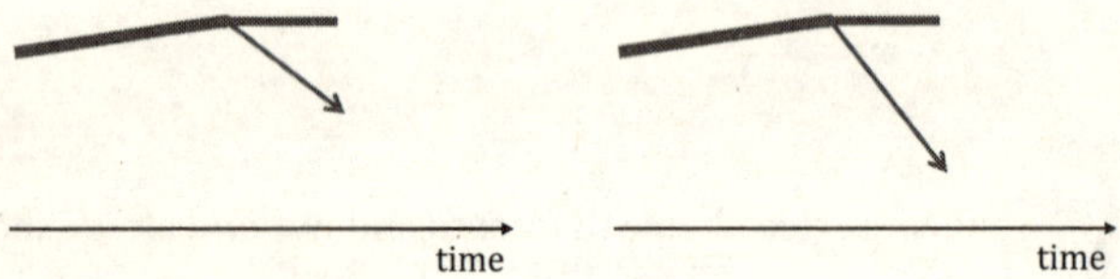

Figure 1-1: Each panel depicts the impact of a negative shock. The impact of the shock on the left-hand panel is smaller than the impact of the shock on the right-hand panel.

Resilience pertains to what happens after a shock has occurred. A long-lasting impact is known as a persistent shock, as shown in the left panel of figure 1-2. In contrast, a resilient process occurs when a society bounces back like a trampoline, as depicted at the right panel of figure 1-2. Resilience is, in formal mathematical language, a reversion back to the mean, back to the original conditions. In fact, the concept of resilience originated in the field of materials science. For example, a metal is resilient if, after it deforms under stress (the shock), it returns to its original state.

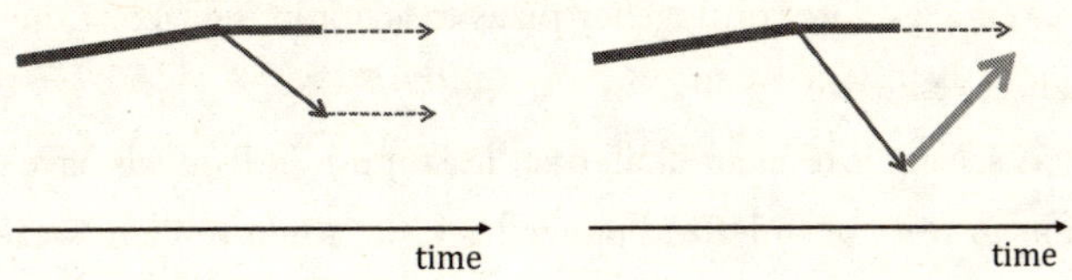

Figure 1-2: Both panels show the process extending after the shock. In the left panel, the shock is persistent. The right panel depicts a resilient process that bounces back.

The left panel shows a less ample shock, but the shock has a persistent impact. In contrast, the right panel depicts a larger shock, but with a more resilient outcome. The impact of the shock is only temporary, and the system partially bounces back. Stated in statistical terms, the parameter reverts back to its mean.

A more troubling scenario occurs when the impact of a shock becomes worse and worse, perhaps spiraling out of control. This is the opposite of resilience and is not depicted in figure 1-2.

Individual and Societal Resilience

The concept of resilience can be applied at an individual, societal, or even global level. Individuals are resilient if, after falling down during a crisis, they can make the right moves and bounce back to their feet. Whether a person recovers often depends on how she or he reacts after the shock's impact. This idea is also found in the social sciences, in which resilience pertains to the ability to adapt and react rather than panic. Importantly, resilient people are able to reinvent themselves, to be actively engaged in the rebound. Developing ex-ante contingency plans to adapt in the face of shocks enhances resilience.

A society is resilient if all, or at least most, individuals have the option to react in order to bounce back. In a non-resilient society, some people might never recover from a severe crisis. Temporary job losses might lead to permanent unemployment, firms might close forever, or large debts might hold back households for years. These people do not bounce back even if insurance cushions the fall. Societal resilience might also depend on interactions among individuals and on a society's preparedness for severe events, such as pandemics. Using simulations and stress tests to evaluate various responses to shocks can increase the preparedness and resilience of society. Overall, resilient societies are able to react in a coordinated way and institutions can be reinvented.

Small and Big Risks

Perhaps paradoxically, enduring a small crisis from time to time can be preferable to avoiding them at any cost. A crisis is an opportunity to make needed adjustments. Without adjustments, imbalances can build up over time. As large imbalances accumulate, the inevitable crisis will be more severe and the system will be less able to rebound. In contrast, a system with a higher frequency of smaller crises, each followed by a rebound, is more resilient and therefore less prone to risks than a seemingly stable system. This phenomenon is sometimes referred to as a volatility paradox. We should be most cautious when volatility is very low.

Risk Exposure Teaches Resilience

How does a society or individual obtain the capability and knowledge to adjust swiftly in order to bounce back? How can we foster resilience and strengthen people's capacity to flexibly adapt and react to shocks? One possibility is to learn to react during occasional smaller shocks. The human immune system is a good example. To develop antibodies and resistance against germs, the immune system needs to be exposed to them. If the immune system is isolated in a hyper-sterile environment, the body will not develop resilience. Upon leaving the sterile environment, the body will not be trained to fight germs, leaving it more vulnerable to infection. Similarly, many entrepreneurs have experienced failures, but those failures have led them to develop immensely successful unicorn business models. If there is resilience, setbacks can lead to improved insights and practices.

The same is true for whole societies. Experiencing a smaller shock can help a society better handle subsequent shocks. Taiwan has successfully managed its Covid-19 outbreaks because the nation learned how to implement contingency plans during the SARS outbreak in 2003.[4]

When individuals or societies are exposed to some risks, they gain an opportunity to develop resilience by learning how to adapt plans and then deal with similar risks in the future.

Robustness and Redundancies

Robustness

Robustness, unlike resilience, is about the ability to resist shocks without adapting. A robust system performs well and continues to operate as normal—in most circumstances. Like the oak, a robust system can withstand the impact of most shocks, but it breaks in extreme circumstances. The more robust a system is, the costlier it is to operate because more safety buffers are needed. Total robustness that covers all contingencies (i.e., zero fault-tolerance) is typically nonviable.

In contrast, resilience is the capacity to withstand shocks in a dynamic way. Like a reed, it gives in, adapts, adjusts, and then bounces back. Resilience can cover more contingencies and therefore survive shocks that break through the "robustness barrier."[5] Resilience involves "giving in" slightly so as to lower the costs—a core premise of resilience. Therefore, developing resilience can be economically more efficient. The choice is between a costly, sufficiently robust solution and a less expensive resilient approach that constantly adjusts to each situation.

Another analogy illustrates the difference between the two concepts. A robust skyscraper that can unwaveringly withstand any storm would need a massive quantity of materials, which would make it expensive to build and potentially so heavy that it could not hold its own weight. A resilient skyscraper, instead, sways a little in the wind. The Willis Tower in Chicago can sway up to three feet from side to side on a windy day.[6] This type of resilient construction enables higher and lighter constructions with modern glass facades.[7]

Redundancies and Buffers

Redundancies are safety buffers. They are crucial for both robustness and resilience. However, the types of safety buffers needed for each are distinct. Robustness requires redundant backups for each unit and each task that might face a shock. If one fails, an immediate replacement is necessary. In contrast, a resilient system handles shocks by regrouping resources after temporary withdrawals. Agility, flexibility, liquidity, and general education are key to a resilient system's redeployment after a shock.

An optimal approach is to integrate resilience and robustness. For example, if a shock forces a person into a trap or makes it difficult to rebound, redundancies that foster robustness are the right answer. For shocks from which a person can regroup and adjust, it is economically wiser to have re-deployable redundancies at hand. Finally, societies and individuals should have generic redundancies that prepare them for unforeseen shocks, the so-called "unknown unknowns." Flexibility and agility are paramount in order to cover a broad range of unforeseen threats.

Resilience and Sustainability

The concept of resilience can also be linked to the concept of sustainability, which is the focus of this book's chapter on climate change. A development is sustainable if it can be maintained in the long run.

Resilience is essential for sustainability. It prevents a person or society from falling off a cliff after being hit by a shock. However, resilience alone is insufficient for sustaining development. If a society has underlying factors that cause slow and constant deterioration, the future will be dire and unsustainable.

Paradoxically, taking on some risks with resilience might be the only way to make the path sustainable. Imagine a room that is flooding as water pours in through the backdoor. If nothing is done, the whole room will soon be completely filled. One option would be to allow water to escape by opening another door. However, there could also be even more water outside that door. Although there is complete uncertainty in this situation, doing nothing would be unsustainable. Some risk-taking is needed.

In many cases, the only way to make a process sustainable is to embrace technological disruptions. These disruptions could lead to temporary shocks, but with clever and creative reactions the process could become resilient enough to bounce back after each shock. Progressing through these disruptions might be the only way to achieve ultimate sustainability and its necessary ingredient, resilience.

Growth with Resilience

At first sight, it might seem that resilience can only be achieved at the expense of growth. Intuition tells us that the faster a society grows the more fragile it could become. Growth creates tensions in "just in time" supply chains, it necessitates many quick adjustments in the workforce, and it puts strain on capacity utilization.

That intuition is misleading. To the contrary, a resilient society will enjoy stronger growth over the long run because it will better absorb shocks. For that reason, a resilient society is better equipped to take risks. And risk-taking is an essential driver of growth. A prominent explanation is "Schumpeterian creative destruction." Promoting innovation, which possibly disrupts whole economic sectors, leads to higher growth on average. However, it also makes the economy more volatile as new entrants displace incumbent firms. As long as the economy is resilient, it will bounce back from temporary disruptions. If, however, resilience is lacking (e.g., after a financial crisis) and a recession leads to a permanently lower growth path, then risk considerations deserve much more attention.

Investment, innovation, entrepreneurship, and R&D all involve risk-taking—and society often benefits. Think of the risks embraced by the CEOs of the German startup BioNTech, Ugur Sahin and Özlem Türeci. They reconfigured their entire company to search for a new mRNA vaccine against Covid-19 in January 2020.[8]

This type of innovation can subsequently boost economic growth, which, in turn, provides more resilience. As the economic bicycle moves faster, it becomes more resilient to dangerous side winds. However, in many circumstances, risks materialize and heavy losses ensue. If those losses cause irreversible damage, if risk-taking puts the survival of the economic entity in danger, then it is better to take fewer risks and potentially accept slower growth in the long run.

Risk versus Resilience

Before a shock occurs, society faces risk. Referring back to figure 1-1, the ex-ante risk depicted in the left panel is smaller than the one in the right panel because the possible shock is smaller. This assumes that the shock for both panels is equally probable. In reality, shocks can be more or less likely, or more or less frequent. For instance, the temperature or a stock price can remain stable for some time and then suddenly move up or down. In the language of statistics, amplitude and probability distribution can be combined into a single measure called the "variance."[9]

Thus, we face a fundamental choice in relation to managing risk. The first is **risk avoidance**. In this case, the society organizes itself with the primary objective of reducing the frequency and size of shocks. Social rules and norms are built to reduce the risk exposure of individuals and groups. One might refrain from certain activities or insist on exclusion of liability in order to minimize risk exposure.

There are two problems with the risk avoidance strategy. First, it could discourage intrinsically risky activities that might yield great societal and economic benefits. In fact, a society should desire such risk-taking. Otherwise, companies might not reap the full benefit of R&D investment. If underinvestment in risky R&D is the norm, individual firms might not have sufficient incentives to innovate, which might reduce societal benefits. A second problem with the risk avoidance strategy is that it could fail. However hard we work to limit exposure to risk, some risks could materialize in totally unexpected ways. The Covid-19 pandemic, of course, is a case in point.

An alternative might be preferable in the long run. This second approach is based on the **acceptance of risk** but in a framework of institutions, rules, and social processes **that ensure resilience**. If successful, it would foster risk-taking and growth while protecting the society if potential dangers materialize. Strong resilience yields major benefits when the shocks are exceptionally strong. A striking example is the cohesion that the Japanese society sustained after the Fukushima disaster in 2015, which proved to be a terrible combination of a natural disaster—the tsunami—and a human-caused catastrophe.

The point is this: As economic activity becomes increasingly complex and inherently risky, resilience can and should become a key growth factor.

Resilient Risk-Taking through Limited Liability

If a society is able to rebound after failure, then it will continue to encourage risk-taking. This simple insight has many public policy implications. One important policy approach is limited liability, which is often presented as the innovation that started capitalism. Limited liability is a means of sharing downside risks across a society, providing a form of resilience. Limited liability incentivizes risk-taking by limiting downside risks. With limited liability, the maximum loss for an entrepreneur is capped. As a consequence, an entrepreneur will have enough resources to rebound even if she fails.[10] When the downside risk is restricted to the size of an initial investment, the entrepreneur might as well engage in a project that offers more upside.

On the private level, personal bankruptcy usually allows households to discharge parts of their debts. The remainder is paid back until they emerge debt-free, usually after a couple of years. This provides people with a ladder to climb out of personal bankruptcy in the medium run. Limited liability mechanisms insure individuals against negative tail risks while ensuring individual resilience.

Of course, to fine-tune limited liability is a balancing act. On the one hand, it should stimulate R&D investments; on the other hand, it should avoid excess risk-taking, especially in the realm of financial speculation.

Figure 1-3 illustrates two growth paths. Each line could represent the possible cumulative returns of a mutual fund, or long-run growth in an economy, or the growth trajectory of a start-up. (At this point, the discussion will generally apply to all these examples.) If decision-makers focus only on avoiding risks, resulting in a low-volatility scenario, then the straight-line trajectory would be appealing. It has no volatility, but fairly substantial growth. The other line presents a scenario of higher growth, but at the cost of significant volatility. People who are very risk-averse would pick the straight line.[11]

However, it's important to recognize that the more volatile path remains highly resilient. After every decline, the path fully bounces back and grows. A resilient strategy would focus on strengthening the underlying factors that support resilience *in the midst of volatility.* Over the longer term, the higher growth rate will accumulate and an exponential gap between the two processes will emerge. Thus, figure 1-3 succinctly captures how risk minimization can forego large gains, whereas resilience management might lead to superior outcomes.

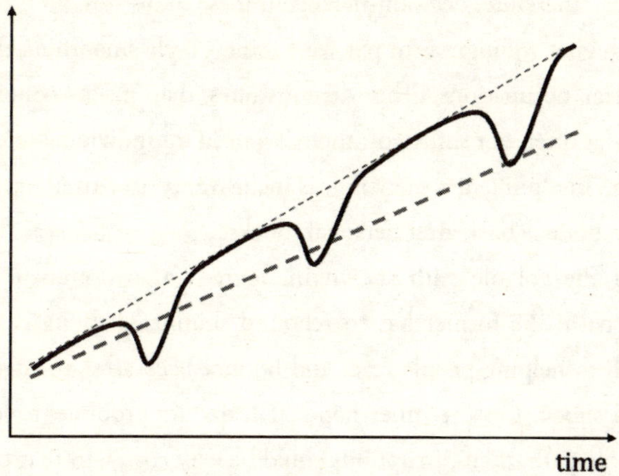

Figure 1-3: Risk avoidance path (straight line) vs. a volatile but resilient path.

A concrete example of this distinction is the economic analysis of business cycle costs. How much should we be willing to pay to eliminate business cycle fluctuations? An analysis by Nobel Laureate Robert Lucas suggests that we should pay very little. Stated differently, sacrificing some long-run growth to eliminate business cycles would prove costly. Of course, Lucas's analysis takes the rebound for granted, and he does not address the topic of how to design a resilient economy. In contrast, a risk-minimizing person would be willing to pay a substantial cost and to incur lower long-run growth to eliminate fluctuations (see the straight line in figure 1-3). But this approach completely neglects resilience. For many years, the US economy steadily bounced back from every recession. It was very resilient until 2007, at least.

Aggregate numbers obviously obscure significant heterogeneity. Occupational groups in disrupted industries can be hit hard by recessions. Therefore, decision-makers in these industries often have a much higher willingness to pay for business cycle smoothing than noncyclical occupations. This demonstrates that macroeconomic resilience is often not sufficient; there is a need for individual micro-resilience. In a resilient society that is inclusive, every citizen has the ability to bounce back after personal shocks.

For the volatile path shown in figure 1-3 to dominate the straight path, the former has to rebound. Limited liability is one approach to helping people react and bounce back after an adverse financial shock. On the other hand, if **traps** are prominent along the volatile path, then disruptions could be very costly. In that case, adopting the straight path (less volatile) will seem more reasonable.

Exogenous growth models all simply assume resilient paths. In many endogenous growth models, constant innovations can lead to a higher growth path. There are also endogenous growth models that exhibit traps where resilience fails, such as when the economy falls into a poverty trap or middle-income trap. More generally, as shown in part 3 of the book, we will see that financial crises often lead to non-resilient outcomes; they push the economy toward a permanently lower growth path. Recessions caused by external shocks, such as the Fukushima nuclear catastrophe in Japan, often have more resilient outcomes (at least from a purely economic perspective).

Mutual Reinforcement between Resilience and Growth

A society is more resilient if the *pace* of change does not outstrip the *capacity* to change. Consider an analogy of a cyclist riding into crosswinds. If the cyclist is riding at a healthy speed, the bike can resist sudden crosswinds; it is resilient. Likewise, disruptive changes that put certain parts of society under stress are more difficult to master if the economy fails to grow. Ultimately, a society that boosts inclusive growth stabilizes the social contract itself, culminating in a virtuous cycle.

There is also a danger. If a cyclist rides too fast, his or her vulnerability will increase. Riding at high speeds will diminish the cyclist's ability to avoid a pothole, potentially leading to a crash. Once a biker falls and incurs an injury, it will be more difficult to ride again. And so, change and technological progress must avoid leaving people behind. We will come back to these thoughts in the chapters that discuss innovation and inequality.

To achieve growth, societies must be able to take risks in order to innovate. However, risks could materialize. If they do, those negative situations should not be allowed to destroy individuals or the society. That is why resilience matters. It enables individuals, groups, and societies to take risks and yet rebound when risk-taking does not work out.

Societies have other ways to deal with risk. For instance, they can try to mitigate risks by opting for slower growth. They can also insure people. Insurance is a process by which risks are pooled and/or transferred to others. But insurance raises difficult issues of moral hazard. It can lead to excessive risk-taking or a bad allocation of risk in the economy. A resilient society naturally finds the optimal level of risk to achieve its objectives. It does not protect its members from every risk, nor does it seek to fully eliminate risk. Rather, it explicitly aims to endow its members with the *ability to rebound* if and when risks materialize. This leads to a totally different approach to welfare and public policy.

CHAPTER 2

Resilience and the Social Contract

Imagine a group of people who act only on the basis of their immediate needs and self-interest, without ever considering the effects of their actions on others. Such a group would be violent and unstable. It would be the law of the jungle. Any shock or hazard would be amplified, often irreversibly, by those who try to pass the impact of the shock to others. The law of the jungle can improve life for a few people, but it can ruin life for society as a whole. In fact, we would not call such a group a "society."

Moreover, the law of the jungle exposes a society to permanent danger. Societies subsist because they have mechanisms—collectively called a "social contract"—that prevent shocks from spiraling into self-destruction. A social contract should encompass all the forces and mechanisms that contribute to a society's resilience.

Philosophers of the Enlightenment, such as Thomas Hobbes, John Locke, and Jean-Jacques Rousseau, reasoned about the emergence of social contracts. Hobbes postulated that if people were to live in a pre-social "state of nature," or a world without social order or laws, then they might not shy away from violating the wellbeing of others. For example, nothing would stop them from stealing someone else's belongings or taking advantage of them. For this reason, the basic assumption of behavior in economics, encompassed in the *homo economicus,* is based on Hobbes's view that humans are egoistic and will do whatever they can get away with. In contrast to the Hobbesian assumption, which also underlies classical economics, Locke and Rousseau were more optimistic about humans. They emphasized that humans are fundamentally good but might be corrupted by society. More recently, behavioral economics has studied altruism and attitudes about fairness.

To overcome the bad outcome of the pre-social "state of nature," humans can come together and agree on an implicit **social contract**. These contracts can be at the family, community, firm, national, or global level. They can assign people's individual rights and enable them to better react to shocks. In short, a social contract defines levels of individual freedom. It can dramatically change the playing field.

Along which dimension of wellbeing—economic, societal, or individual—should the social contract exhibit resilience? All of these dimensions are important. Above all, the social contract itself needs to be resilient. A social contract is of little use if it cannot sustain an external shock. Indeed, a society is not resilient if its social contract easily disintegrates.

To better grasp the links between social contracts and resilience, it is useful to first refer to "externalities," a concept familiar to economists that can be used in a broader social context.

Externalities and the Social Contract

Externalities designate spillover effects. They arise when actions by one individual indirectly affect other people. A classic example in economics is a firm that pollutes a river thereby imposing a negative externality on people living downstream. Besides the externality, an additional consideration is important: How can the person on the receiving end of an externality react to the hardship? For example, she could react by using a water filter, or she could do something that passes the danger on to others.

In the Covid-19 world, three striking examples of externalities immediately come to mind. First, masks have protected the health of those who wear them and those around them: a positive externality to others. Moreover, everyone can see who is not wearing a mask, which allows others to react and stay away from non-wearers.

Another example is social distancing. When people choose to reject social distancing recommendations, they put others at risk of infection. This negative externality can be mitigated in many circumstances by taking protective, though often costly, countermeasures.

A third example—refusing to be vaccinated—limits the benefits of vaccines and puts others at risk, causing yet another negative health externality. In this case, it is difficult to know whether someone has been vaccinated; thus, it is difficult to react in situations that involve many strangers.

In addition to these individual-level externalities, countries can also create externalities that spill over to other countries. Since January 2021, with Covid-19 spreading out of control in many countries, the number of virus variants has increased. There is a risk that the virus could evolve to a point at which current vaccines become less effective or even ineffective. Countries that do not contain the virus might therefore impose negative externalities by providing a breeding ground for new variants that might spread around the world.

Contagion as a Form of Spreading Externalities

Virus contagion illustrates how negative externalities can start with one person and then impact many others. In epidemiology, virus spread is often measured by using the reproduction rate R0, which relates to how many new people an infected person will infect. If R0 exceeds 1, then on average each infected person would infect more than one person and the virus would spread across the population.

The implications of exponential virus spread are treacherous. As sometimes occurred in this pandemic, Covid-19 incidence numbers started to rise slowly, which might have appeared to be linear growth. But after a couple of weeks, the exponential growth became apparent and the case numbers exploded.[12] In such cases, resilience only kicks in when the externality slows down and when those who incur the externalities have a better defense mechanism, such as social distancing or vaccination. Importantly, virus spread might not be uniform across a population. It might spread from one age group that is less careful to other age groups, for example.

Figure 2-1 provides a striking illustration of these externalities during the summer and fall of 2020 in Germany. In July 2020, the virus was largely contained. It then started to rise again, driven by the behavior of people in their twenties. During calendar weeks thirty-five to forty, the virus spread slowly but clearly through all age groups up to the nonagenarians. This pattern clearly illustrates how young people spread externalities to older populations over time. Infection rates remained very high for the elderly, who also had a substantially higher death rate.

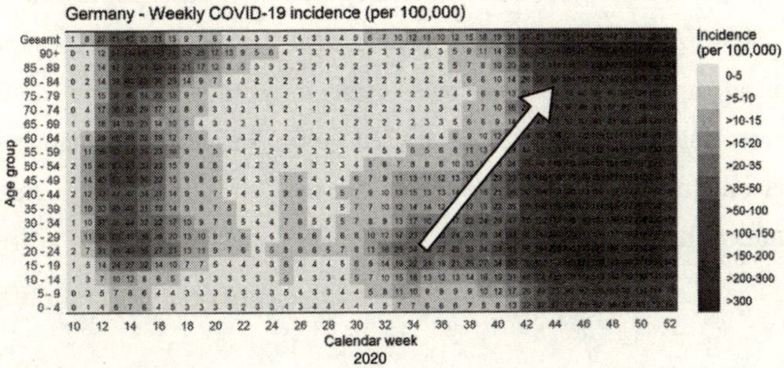

Figure 2-1: The spread of Covid in Germany in 2020 across age groups. Source: Robert Koch Institute 2020

Externalities also exist across population groups and can even be induced by politics. In India, migrant workers in larger cities who contracted Covid-19 from rich travelers were forced by the lockdown to give up their employment. To avoid starvation, they had to return to their home villages. This migration spread the virus around the countryside.[13]

With these examples in mind, we can see that resilience kicks in when externalities are contained, for example through immunity. In basic SIR contagion models, resilience comes from herd immunity—assuming that recovery from the sickness leads to permanent immunity. The predominant barebones epidemiological model, the SIR model, demonstrates how a virus can spread among a susceptible population (S) and gradually infect (I) most of the population before those people recover (R). The key parameter in this model is the reproduction rate of the virus, the R0, which measures how many new people an infected person will infect. If each infected person infects more than one person, the outcome would be an exponential spread of the virus. As the fraction of recovered people rises over time, the fraction of susceptible people declines. As a result, the sick people cause fewer externalities. The spread of the virus slows down. Herd immunity kicks in, which drives resilience. When each infected person infects fewer than one person on average (R0<1), the virus dies out slowly and society bounces back.

Feedback, Trap Externalities, and Tipping Points

Resilience, or the lack thereof, is often about how people react or are able to react to shocks. "**Trap externalities**" rob people of their resilience—their ability to bounce back after a shock. For example, if an employer fires a worker who subsequently cannot afford to send her children to school, her children's potential will be severely compromised. The children will have almost no way to react to the shock. Such outcomes resemble the oak tree in Lafontaine's fable. Once the oak tree has been uprooted by a storm, it dies.

The reaction of someone who has been exposed to an externality can lead to destabilizing feedback loops and to weaker overall resilience. In other words, people might cumulatively inflict externalities onto each other and therefore cause a deterioration in the society's equilibrium and resilience. We call those situations "**feedback**

externalities." A classic example is a bank run. If many bank customers withdraw their money on one day, they destabilize the bank and cause a negative externality. It the actions of those people incentivize others to withdraw money as well, more "feedback externalities" would ensue. Ultimately, this process could result in a full-blown bank run, which would force the bank to suspend withdrawals because banks typically would not have sufficient deposits.

From an abstract perspective, the hoarding of face masks is like a bank run. A store might have enough face masks to supply one for each potential customer, but hoarding would cause the store to become illiquid in relation to face masks.

Both types of runs illustrate the large effects of feedback externalities. The few individuals who cause a bank run or hoard masks can induce negative externalities on many other people. Economists attribute these types of feedbacks to so-called "strategic complementarities." Hoarding behavior is illustrated graphically in figure 2-2. Suppose that some people, including person A, purchase more toilet paper than typically needed. As a result, there will be less toilet paper available for others, including person B in the figure below. Person B suffers from a negative externality. Observing this, others might infer that toilet paper is scarce, so they also purchase more toilet paper. Now person A suffers from an externality that he or she caused. As toilet paper becomes quite scarce, person A will hoard more and person B, in reaction, might also acquire more toilet paper. At some point, when all toilet paper has been purchased, the loop stops. Externalities combined with feedback loops are the real "resilience killers."

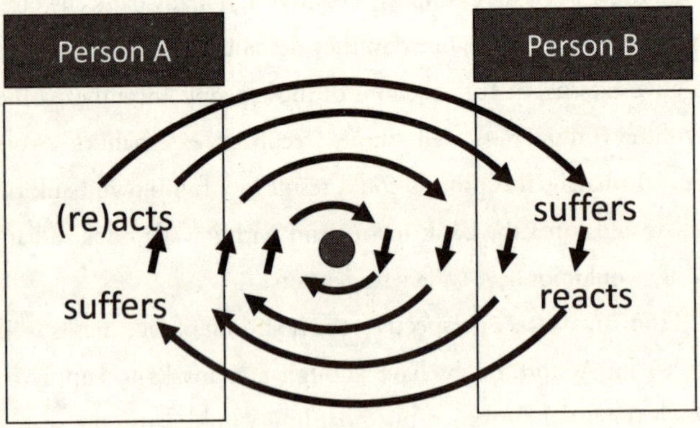

Figure 2-2: Feedback Externality Loop.

The opposite of a destabilizing feedback loop is known as "stabilizing dynamics." These dynamics arise when a person who has been exposed to a negative externality reacts like a **maverick**. She either does not buy toilet paper, despite her fears, or she returns the extra she has purchased. However, once a feedback loop gets going, a few mavericks alone will not be able to stop it. A government intervention will be needed.

More profoundly, the potentially devastating effects of adverse feedback loops have been recognized for millennia. Ancient societies implemented "eye for eye, tooth for tooth" laws of retaliation precisely to contain violent adverse feedback loops. Without such laws, one incident might trigger another retaliatory incident of even larger proportions, and that might trigger even more retaliation. A "tooth for tooth" stops this loop after the first two steps. However, a better approach would be to compensate the other person with livestock (or money) for the lost tooth.

Tipping points occur when feedback externalities kick in. Tipping points are serious "threats to resilience." Societies should identify and avoid them. Once a tipping point is crossed, resilience is lost. For example, a small trigger could push a society suffering from latent discontent beyond the brink. The society could disintegrate and end up in civil unrest. Once violence breaks out, returning to peaceful coexistence is a difficult process.[14]

In many cases, it is difficult to know when a tipping point might be crossed. Everything might look stable until the tipping point is reached, leading to rapid deterioration. Tipping points make social dynamics highly nonlinear.

Paradoxically, the social contract itself will become more resilient if *some* decline in individual or aggregate wellbeing—perhaps caused by an externality or shock—is absorbed and those individuals are able to bounce back. In other words, if individuals and societies can remain far from tipping points, the outcome will be more stability and less disintegration.

Social Contract and Containing Externalities

The resilience of societies is anchored in social contracts, which serve at least two purposes: containing externalities that members of society impose on one another and insuring against natural shocks. Without a social contract, people are free to impose negative **externalities** on each other.

In the absence of any social contract, externalities will abound. Because a social contract sets limits to admissible individual behaviors, it helps people avoid trap externalities and it stops feedback externalities. However, social contracts could be perceived as restricting individual freedoms. To address externalities caused by others, a social contract might limit people's actions. During a global pandemic, for example, externalities abound and raise intense questions about personal freedoms. Should individuals have the freedom to infect others? What should limit this freedom and why? Should we have the freedom to go to a political rally even if this action might spread a deadly disease? Or should we limit personal freedoms to protect the vulnerable? In relation to resilience, externalities that influence how people react to spillovers deserve special attention.

Insurance and the Social Contract

Shocks from Mother Nature

There is a second rationale for a social contract besides containing externalities and enabling positive reactions: to uphold people who are exposed to natural shocks and the externalities caused by mother nature.

Adverse shocks come in many forms. To the extent that these shocks are idiosyncratic—that is, different from person to person—the lucky ones can insure the unlucky. Every year some people get sick while others do not. We cannot know exactly who will get sick, but we know that the individual cost of sickness will be quite high because treatments are expensive. However, because few people in the population will be sick, the average cost per citizen will be relatively low.

A reasonable solution in these cases is insurance, which is designed to spread the costs for all. Everyone pays an insurance premium. In exchange, the individual costs of sickness are partly covered. Effectively, the healthy subsidize the sick. Everyone pays a small bill rather than some people being forced to pay a large bill while others pay nothing.

An insurance contract can be part of a social contract, or it can be a formal agreement via an insurance company. Some forms of "insurance" are based on social norms. For example, after a natural disaster, people typically help each other, even when they are not explicitly obliged to do so by law.

To better understand why social contracts are needed to protect people from natural shocks, remember for one moment that we were behind a "**veil of ignorance**," similar to our condition before birth. Behind that veil of ignorance, we do not know where people will be born or what their individual talents and weaknesses will be. Such is the hypothetical economic situation imagined by philosopher **John Rawls**. In that context, would we want to insure the weakest members of society, not knowing who they will be, in the event of a future large natural shock, such as a pandemic? Many would agree that we should provide some insurance. This was the essence of the pre-Covid-19 social contract. But, behind the veil of ignorance, most people would choose less-than-perfect insurance in order to preserve incentives for individual effort.

Insurance provides a hedge against the risks of a car accident, but it does not guarantee a reversion to the mean. The effectiveness of insurance also depends on society's heterogeneity and **diversity**.

In a highly homogeneous society, everyone sustains similar shocks, so there is a narrow scope for cross-insuring each other. A more heterogeneous society with diverse preferences might be better suited for social insurance. If everyone in an economy works in manufacturing, they will all be similarly affected when a negative shock occurs. If instead some people also work in the service sector, a shock to manufacturing would not affect everyone equally; therefore, the service workers could implicitly insure the manufacturing workers.

Diversity ensures that a society has the flexibility to withstand shocks. On the other hand, people in a more homogeneous society are more *willing* to insure each other. The recently departed Italian economist Alberto Alesina argued that the European social security system is more developed than the US system because people within each European country are more homogenous than within the US. In short, diversification is not possible in a society in which all agents are homogeneous and face the same shocks. Diversity makes diversification possible. In other words, monocultures tend to be vulnerable. A forest that consists of only one type of tree might fully die out if a disease to which those trees are susceptible emerges. A mixed-tree forest can weather shocks much better. Diverse cultures also tend to have more creativity and out-of-the-box thinking. A diverse society is more likely to benefit from mavericks.

Adverse Selection and Moral Hazard: Risk versus Resilience

Diversification via insurance reduces individual risks and

therefore enhances resilience. But insurance is not a miracle solution. Insurance is plagued with so-called adverse selection and moral hazard problems. Adverse selection occurs because sicker people usually have a higher willingness to obtain health insurance. Thus, insurance companies might end up with only high-risk clients. The answer for private insurance companies is to "skim the cream," to insure only the least risky individuals. This leads to a breakdown of insurance for high-risk groups. As a result, private healthcare insurance tends to fail, and public health coverage becomes necessary for people who are marginalized by the private sector.

There is also a problem of moral hazard: People behave differently once they are insured. Insurance protects against risk, but it might also discourage effort, a problem often mentioned for generous unemployment insurance schemes.

In contrast, resilience has less of a moral hazard problem. A resilient society offers people ways to better respond to shocks. For example, a resilient unemployment scheme does not focus purely on offering unemployed people cash compensation for lost income; rather, it places the emphasis on reskilling the unemployed so they can bounce back. Importantly, for those who suffer a shock, a resilient approach is to encourage people to actively engage in the rebound process. By requiring effort, we can reduce the moral hazard concern. In my personal view, another aspect is even more important. If people achieve a personal comeback, they rightly feel proud about their achievement, and this fosters dignity.

Approaches to Implementing a Social Contract

How does a society implement a social contract? One approach is **government enforcement**, which can be administered at the national and regional levels. Implementation can take two forms: authoritarian or open society.

Some countries, such as Japan, internalize externalities via strong **social norms**. Even without government intervention, many people comply with mask mandates, social distancing, and other public health measures. Fear of social stigma serves as a powerful disciplining device.

Another common way in which a society organizes is through **markets**. The price system, for example, is a powerful orchestrating tool for an economic system. But markets are not perfect. While coping well with small shocks, they might be destabilizing in the wake of a large crisis and therefore offer little resilience.

Balancing between these different ways of organizing human interactions is critical in the quest for improved resilience. A society is most resilient if the form of implementation can adjust to the environment it faces.

There are trade-offs among these forms of implementing a social contract. Each approach to ensuring resilience has its own advantages and drawbacks. Citizens self-police **social norms**, and so these norms are not as heavy-handed as government regimes. They are bottom-up and extend much farther into all corners of society. However, they are not very responsive to changing environments.

Strong **government enforcement** is top-down, which makes it possible to implement coordinated action across a region or nation. Governments, if they are able to communicate the rules, can easily adapt to new circumstances. Spillover effects are minimized in the presence of a clear and efficient governance structure. One drawback of top-down regulation is that governments often lack the detailed information needed to implement optimal rules. During the initial phases of the Covid-19 pandemic in China, information flow from local and regional authorities to national ones was slow. This led to adverse feedback loops, which might have impeded the speed of the government's response. Other countries, such as Tanzania, lost precious time when its leaders failed to communicate the seriousness of the pandemic.[15] In addition, government implementation might be driven by lobby groups and corruption rather than benevolent objectives. Another problem is government surveillance, which increases the risk of authoritarianism.

Markets are another way to implement the social contract. With this approach, markets often collaborate with government enforcement of property rights. The big advantage of markets is that they aggregate information and typically foster innovative and creative solutions. There are ongoing economic debates about the resilience of markets when left to their own devices. Markets contribute to resilience in "normal times," but they might break down when confronted with large unanticipated shocks, regime changes, and uncertainty. Markets, especially financial markets, can be caught in spirals and runs that lead to permanent decline. Economists from various economic schools disagree as to whether the macroeconomy reverts back automatically after recessions. The Real Business Cycle theory dismisses resilience concerns whereas the Keynesian school argues in favor of policy interventions to orchestrate a quick rebound. The concept of resilience is clearly relevant to the analysis of financial markets and macroeconomic policies.

Implementation through Social Norms and Conventions

The Implicit Social Contract

I briefly discussed social norms above, but the topic should be addressed further. Although often ignored, especially by economists, social norms and conventions affect most decisions; thus, they are important parts of a social contract. In contrast to a national constitution and the legal codex governing a society, social norms are not legally binding. They are not enforced by governments, rules, laws, or regulations. People implicitly adhere to this type of social contract.

Social norms can facilitate integration in society by fostering a sense of community. However, strict social norms can limit exploration and risk-taking. Mavericks are usually not welcome in societies that are heavily governed by social norms. Yet it is those who pursue idiosyncratic, often futile, but sometimes groundbreaking ideas who are the key drivers of innovation. They make the social contract sustainable in the long run.

Many people argue that Asian countries handled Covid-19 outbreaks successfully because of their widespread use of technology. However, Japan kept the disease in check without employing many advanced technologies. Figure 2-3 shows that it also did not impose stringent lockdown measures.

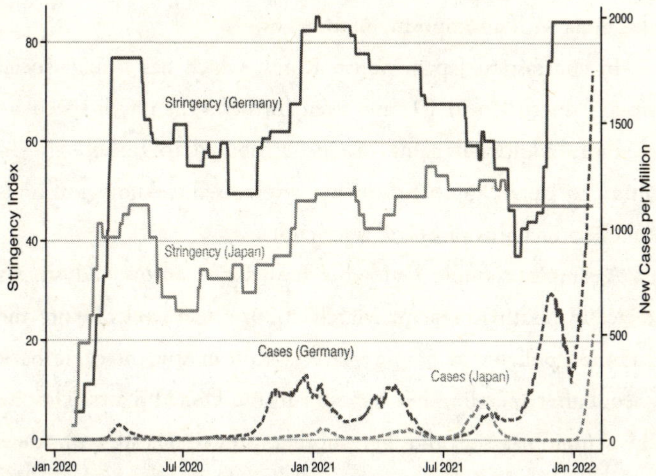

Figure 2-3: Covid cases have been significantly lower in Japan, despite lower stringency measures than, for example, in Germany. Source: Our World in Data 2021

How is it that **Japan** did much better at controlling the pandemic than Germany and the US despite having less-stringent public policy measures? Implicit social norms arguably played an important role. There is a strong culture of adherence to social norms in Japan. Social norms can be powerful. The negative reaction of peers affects people's behavior. People in Japan proactively and voluntarily put on their masks to avoid being reprimanded or suffering social stigmatization.

Likewise, nobody in Japan has spelled out how government leaders should behave if suspected of financial misconduct or extramarital affairs, but Japan's culture of public shame is reportedly so strong that cabinet members have committed suicide in these instances.[16] Some observers have noticed that Japan's cohesive social structure enabled its people to live through a nuclear disaster in Fukushima without imposing martial law.

In contrast to Japan, South Korea, which has similar social norms, reduced Covid-19 cases even further. One might speculate that those additional gains can be attributed to technology. In contrast to Japan, South Korea extensively used technological tools to track coronavirus cases and trace contacts.

A simple example highlights how social norms and stigma interact in South Korea. In March 2020, a few weeks before the quarantine policy was put in place, a Korean student came back to Seoul after spending her semester in the United States. Despite mild symptoms, she and her mother pressed ahead with their originally planned trip to Jeju Island, a popular vacation spot for Koreans. When her Covid-19 test came back positive and it became known to the Jeju province and the merchants that the family had visited, the Jeju province immediately filed a $100,000 lawsuit for damages. The mainstream media and Naver (the Korean equivalent of Google) rushed to report the story. Large parts of the public were outraged with the student's family. This account demonstrates the overwhelming weight that the Korean public puts on protecting the welfare of the overall society relative to protecting the "freedom" of individuals.

Even within a country, the norms governing social behavior can differ. In some parts of the **US**, such as the Northeast, people will frown on someone who is not wearing a mask even if there is no mask mandate. For fear of receiving negative reactions from peers, many will wear masks even if they are not legally required to do so. In other parts of the US, however, wearing a face mask only garners strange looks.

Despite their implicit power, social norms have several disadvantages. Social norms can suppress dissenting opinions and mavericks can be sidelined. Nobody clearly questions and searches for the best intervention or comes up with alternative new solutions. Nobody has to take responsibility for the decisions.

Additionally, changes to social norms are not easy to implement, especially in the short run. Usually, they are the result of decades or centuries of social evolution. Social norms reinforce old habits and customs. After large shocks, such as the recent pandemic, we might need faster intervention.

Common Identity

A **common identity** is crucial for sustaining implicit social norms. Individuals freely stick to this type of social contract because they have a desire to identify with a group. An economist would say they "derive utility" from being part of a group. Identity is a way to internalize externalities and ultimately bolster society's resilience to outside shocks. Creating a common identity in a diverse society is a critical yet difficult task for many governments.

After the Apartheid regime, South Africa was on the brink of being torn apart. As depicted in the movie *Invictus*, Nelson Mandela used the 1995 Rugby World Cup in South Africa to create a stronger sense of community between black and white South Africans. His instrumental effort was certainly helped by the fact that South Africa's multi-ethnic rugby team achieved its first World Cup victory. The 2019 Rugby World Cup victory by South Africa had a similar effect.

We care about others. We do not live in a society of purely self-interested individuals, so our **sense of community** is critical. In times of crisis, a sense of solidarity can bind people together in community. In the spring of 2021, for example, neighbors in New Delhi cooked for each other during India's devastating second wave and organized neighborhood help for families of Covid-19 patients. A crisis can help internalize the myriad externalities, a point that will permeate this section.

Implementation through the Government

According to Hobbes, government is essential for protecting the public. Locke instead emphasized the role of the people to deliberately desire their government, in light of the benefits they would receive. Rousseau believed that the primary role of government was to enforce the social contract.

Governments can change laws and regulations after crises occur, which allows for a coordinated response. Rather than debating whether government should be larger or smaller, we will start by analyzing possible government policy approaches.

The government has three ways to implement policies. First, it can impose strict authoritarian rules. To prevent infection externalities during a pandemic, a government can opt for a strict lockdown that effectively prohibits non-resilient behavior. Second, the government can tax certain behaviors, such as going to a crowded bar. The tax raises the price of these activities and thus internalizes the externality. The third approach is to assign and guarantee property rights. If these rights can be traded, people can pass them on to others who value them more in exchange for other benefits.

Surveillance versus Privacy

A first approach is to impose a social contract via government **force**, rules, and regulations. To internalize the externalities, the government can impose lockdown policies, forced vaccinations, or rigorous social distancing. Government interventions require enforcement and hence some higher authority. The government, or ruler, can simply outlaw certain activities and then impose fines or incarcerate people who do not comply. In France, not wearing a mask in public places can entail a €135 fine (about $160).[17] These policies correspond most closely to enforcement with a "stick."

Governments could mandate vaccinations. An obvious concern with forced vaccination is that it might undermine trust in a vaccine. In many advanced economies, a substantial fraction of the population (up to 50 percent in France) report that they do not want to be vaccinated. Forced vaccination might amplify mistrust in vaccines even if it succeeds in raising the number of vaccinated people.

If implementing the social contract strongly relies on government rules and force, policy implementation will require some level of **surveillance**. Mandatory quarantines for travelers can only be efficient if they are enforced; otherwise, free-riding incentives will dominate. Even if enforced, however, there will be tradeoffs between privacy and more efficient Covid-19 containments.

The contrast between surveillance and privacy is illustrated by the various approaches to contain Covid-19 in China and Western democracies, where privacy attitudes differ substantially. Social premises in these cultures are exemplified by their technological approaches to Covid-19 containment. China implemented an app-based color system. At the entrance of buildings, citizens had to scan their phones before being granted entry. Green on the phone app indicated that the person was not infectious and therefore allowed to enter. On the other hand, Germany launched a Covid-19 app with decentralized data storage and voluntary compliance. The app alerted citizens who came close to a person who had been infected, but there was no central quarantine enforcement in those cases. The adoption of these digital tools by the wider population critically hinged on citizens' trust in their respective governments, with those **trust** levels being relatively low in many countries.[18] The German app did not prove to be very effective.

Subsidies Instead of Prohibition

Another way to change behavior so that people do not impose externalities on others is to put a price on the externalities.[19] A government could impose a **tax** on people who reject vaccination, or it could subsidize those who accept the vaccine. Rather than preventing externalities via strict rules that prohibit non-vaccination, the tax approach puts an implicit price on the externality. People who are strongly opposed to receiving a vaccine could decide not to get vaccinated, but there would be a price to pay for that privilege.

Ensuring Property Rights

The economy only works well if rules are well-established and property rights are clearly assigned, tradable, and enforced. The latter requires a government to step in. The assignment of property rights grants individual freedom, but it naturally limits the individual freedom of others. The state can clearly assign property rights to minimize externalities. But to whom should the government grant these rights? How should it regrant individual freedom?

If some rights are tradable, then people can engage in free decision-making via market interactions. The question of property rights extends to other types of permissions. For example, in the US or France, no proof of a negative Covid-19 test or vaccine has been required to enter a restaurant. In Germany, one of these proofs had to be provided as of June 2021. This made a huge difference for people who were vaccinated but still fearful about catching the virus. By knowing that everyone around them had either tested negative or had been vaccinated, they could be more comfortable with eating out.

Federalism and Resilience

Around the world, the Covid-19 pandemic has tested the relationship between federal governments and more decentralized nodes of power within states, counties, and cities. A guiding principle for the centralization or devolvement of power is the subsidiarity principle. According to this concept, each task should be assigned to the smallest layer of government that can effectively deal with it. New parking meters in your hometown should be administered by municipal administration, not the state or federal government. Conversely, your local mayor is unlikely to effectively handle your home country's foreign policy. Instead, the federal government should handle it.

Crises change circumstances, which requires adjustments to the social contract. When implementing adjustments between social norms, governments, and markets—and within the government sector—powers should either be devolved or centralized, depending on circumstances. Critically, any changes to the balance of power should adjust flexibly to circumstances. Resilient subsidiarity remains flexible and avoids getting stuck or trapped by institutional arrangements.

In the context of the Covid-19 pandemic, the advantage of federal structures is their **flexibility** to address the heterogeneous spread of the disease across a country.[20] Compared to central authorities, local politicians have a better feel of the pressure points. Tensions played out in September 2020 during the second pandemic wave in France. When politicians in Paris decided that Marseille, one of the hot spots of the renewed outbreak, should impose the closure of bars and restaurants, the move was met with resistance by local small business owners and local politicians who deemed it to be an excessive sanction ordered by people without knowledge of Marseille's situation.[21]

Another advantage of federalism is **backyard competition** and the possibility of local experimentation. However, federalist states are typically slower to respond because numerous local government agencies have to manage Covid-19 outbreaks. Also, variations in local rules can confuse citizens who often think the rules are unfair.

The appeal of central rules is that everyone knows the rules for every location. Germany decided to adopt centralized rules at a time when local lockdowns were about to be reinstated during the attempted reopening in March 2021. This created tension for local politicians who faced strong opposition to a new tightening of rules. Indeed, some local politicians quickly deviated from some nationwide guidelines.[22]

Empirically, it is unclear whether the Covid-19 pandemic has exposed a failure of federalism. Germany and South Korea reacted effectively in the early phases of the pandemic, but other countries (e.g., the US and Italy) struggled.

Implementation through Markets

In an open society that relies on informed, innovative, and creative responses to shocks that avoid spirals and feedback loops, market mechanisms must be involved in implementing a resilient social contract. For one, market mechanisms that foster competition and level the playing field reduce the concentration of power. New entry and innovative breakthroughs are more likely in competitive markets. Therefore, incumbent firms are under constant threat of being displaced. Perhaps paradoxically, disruptions make the system more flexible and adaptable, which contributes to greater resilience. A system that is constantly in flux can more easily adapt than a non-resilient, rigid system.

Self-Stabilizing and Destabilizing Markets and the Value of Price Information

Markets react quickly and are **self-stabilizing**. They are resilient when faced with small or medium shocks. As the world evolves, markets adjust and drive change. They typically ensure an efficient but not necessarily fair allocation of resources. Markets, in collaboration with government, can play an essential role in supporting the social contract.

As initially stressed by Ludwig von Mises, the price of goods **signals** their relative abundance or scarcity. In March 2020, soaring prices aggregated dispersed information and signaled the scarcity of and need for face masks. This induced existing manufacturers to scale up production, and it encouraged new firms to enter the market. The magic of the price system allows for many economic actors to coordinate, often at the global level.[23]

On the other hand, when markets are left alone to deal with large or extreme shocks like the Covid-19 pandemic or wars, they are destabilizing. They make things worse, and perhaps permit society to spiral out of control. In contrast, governments can manage large shocks by adjusting taxes and transfers. Moreover, they have a superior ability to ameliorate shocks over time and redistribute resources among people.

Markets tend to work well for goods and services, but they are less reliable in relation to the allocation of risk. Asset markets are subject to speculation and bubbles, which can destabilize the market and interfere with the efficiency of allocations.

Fairness and Markets

Finally, the market raises questions about **fairness**. Owners of firms that produce face masks or medical equipment, such as ventilators, make a windfall gain when their goods are scarce, when demand unexpectedly soars, and when other suppliers cannot enter the market in time. This causes a fairness tension: An unexpected price increase causes some random windfall gains that are not shared with other members of society. Although those windfall gains seem unfair, the free-market price signal might be an important incentive for more firms to enter the market.

Markets are not perfect. They are also subject to tensions between immediate and long-term objectives. Medical drug development exemplifies this tension. By the time a drug or a vaccine has been developed and approved, large ex-ante fixed costs have already been incurred, and therefore production should be scaled up for the whole population. From an ex-ante perspective, however, these monopoly rents are needed to offset the initial R&D expenses. For this reason, governments grant exclusive intellectual property rights in the form of patents.

A Responsive Social Contract for Resilience

Each of the three approaches to implementing resilience—social norms, government enforcement, and markets—comes with distinct tradeoffs. Stricter social norms lead to a self-policing society. Less government enforcement is required as citizens endogenously comply with norms, even in the absence of explicit rules. Yet, it can be difficult to rapidly change social norms when needed, and diverse societies can struggle with establishing common norms.

Government can more effectively adjust and adapt in a coordinated manner, but government might lack the information needed to implement effective interventions. Authoritarian governments typically have the power to act swiftly to threats in a coordinated fashion. However, they too might lack needed information that is dispersed among many citizens.

Markets are better information aggregators, but they can be destabilizing during extreme shocks.

So, in terms of implementing a social contract, what is the optimal mix between social norms, government, and markets? It is always a combination of the three approaches. In reality, markets need a functioning state to, for example, enforce property rights and create a level playing field that gives everyone ex-ante the same opportunity. Each society needs to find the right balance to implement a social contract. Figure 2-4 illustrates this idea, with the dot representing society.

A Responsive Implementation Mix

Importantly, resilience rests on a society's ability to shift and adjust the optimal mix of implementing its social contract when circumstances demand it. The society should be responsive and willing to accept changes, but also able to return to the ex-ante status after the temporary threat recedes. Rather than remaining statically in one place, a resilient society is able to adjust within the triangle (in figure 2-4) as circumstances demand. Being able to move the blue dot is in itself a critical factor of resilience. A society that prospers on mutually accepted social norms but can accept temporary increases in state powers is naturally resilient. This is challenging for the state. It must be ready to act when needed but stay passive when circumstances do not demand intervention.

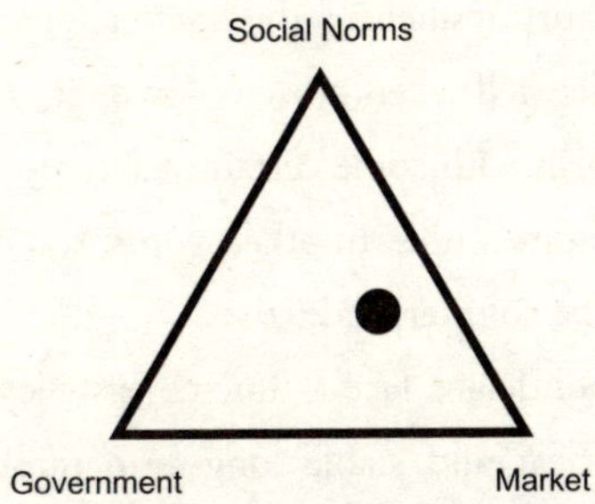

Figure 2-4: Tradeoffs between the three implementations.

A good example during the Covid-19 crisis was the US deployment of "war powers" to boost vaccine development. This move demonstrated that the government could spend large amounts of resources while also cooperating with the private sector through public-private partnerships (PPP). Operation WARP Speed in the US devoted around $10 billion to vaccine development and an additional $1 billion to Covid-19 therapeutics in order to reduce the spread of the virus.[24] Similarly, Germany spent the equivalent of $445 million for BioNTech to boost its vaccine project.[25] Moreover, individual freedoms were suspended during the worst phase of the pandemic. A truly resilient society is one in which the government cannot permanently grab power; rather, as a threat recedes, so does government power. Life returns to the ex-ante status quo.

Ex-ante vs. Ex-post Resilience

Robust institutions, constitutional laws, and **rules** might limit flexible responses to a crisis shock. When circumstances change radically and are difficult to foresee, an ability to adjust enhances resilience. On the other hand, extreme flexibility and constant change can also hurt resilience; the implementation of a social contract only works well when citizens "own" it. They do so more easily if they can plan with some certainty and are not confused by constantly changing measures. In other words, too much **discretion** for politicians can be counterproductive.

As a result, politicians face a time-consistency problem. They need to promise clear and stable long-term measures. Doing so boosts ex-ante resilience. However, when circumstances change, politicians need to deviate from the promise and reoptimize, as far as the institutional framework will allow it. This ability to adjust enhances ex-post resilience. A society's institutional framework can help to balance this tradeoff between ex-ante and ex-post resilience. In addition, institutional guardrails can help to push back against some politicians' tendencies to be overactive, to be seen as "doers" and strong crisis managers.

A responsive social contract can ensure a more resilient society and more resilient individuals. Importantly, a social contract should also ensure its own resilience by incorporating fairness, equal opportunities, and social mobility. We will revisit this theme in chapter 12.

PART II

CONTAINING THE SHOCK: THE CASE OF COVID-19

The Covid-19 pandemic foreshadows many of the future challenges the global community might face. Other possible challenges could result from bioengineering mishaps, climate catastrophes, or cyberattacks. Crises embody the exact opposite of resilience if they spiral out of control, as often occurred during this pandemic. Exponential spread of the SARS-CoV-2 virus and its variants, combined with insufficient preparedness for large pandemics in many countries, made it difficult for governments to coordinate a rapid and targeted response to stabilize the situation, gain time, and bridge the gap to a long-run solution.

The chapters in this part of the book outline how to contain the source of a crisis. Important elements include understanding human behavior and gathering information. We need to fine-tune policy responses and communication while developing proper ways to work toward a new long-run normal.

In order to contain the source of a shock, one has to understand how people behave in response to crises. People's reactions are not driven only by selfishness; they are also motivated by psychological elements, such as fear and anxiety. Crises can shift as people's attitudes change, which can influence policy measures. If people are under the illusion of resilience—for example, falsely believing that a crisis is over—then the outcomes of a shock will be different.

The Covid-19 crisis has taught us that the often-argued tradeoff between protecting human health and economic wellbeing only exists if one takes a myopic perspective. From a dynamic perspective, physical health and the economy go hand in hand. Reducing economic activity by imposing a lockdown immediately improves health outcomes and future economic outcomes—because the pandemic will be brought under control faster. For society as a whole there is **no tradeoff**. Effectively fighting the disease enables a faster economic recovery.

Chapter 4 highlights the importance of **information** and experimentation. Information is necessary to develop targeted measures that are designed to reduce and control the cost of containment measures. Depending on the situation, policymakers could follow one of three pandemic containment strategies. First, they could aggressively seek to prevent their nations' exposure to the virus until a long-term solution becomes available. This approach was followed by New Zealand and Australia during the Covid-19 pandemic. As island countries, they found it much easier to readily control who entered the country. Australia's borders shut down in March 2020 and the earliest reopening was envisaged for mid-2021.[26] The second strategy consists of aggressive virus suppression. By keeping the number of daily cases low, perhaps with a weekly incidence of ten cases per one hundred thousand inhabitants, information gathered through contact tracing and quarantines could effectively break infection chains. Japan, for example, initially and successfully experimented with such measures. The third strategy is more relaxed. The goal is to keep the number of severely infected patients below the capacity of hospital ICU facilities; that is, to prevent the healthcare system from becoming overwhelmed. With this approach, the virus nonetheless circulates quite widely.

Note that these three strategies require different types of information, and they are subject to multiple tipping points. For instance, contact tracing has been ineffective when incidence numbers are too high. The threshold at which contacts can no longer be traced represents such a tipping point. Aggressive virus suppression attempts are needed to keep society far from these tipping points so that the spread of the virus does not revert toward exponential growth.

Chapter 5 focuses on the important role of **communication** and trust. Effective communication that fosters a sense of community and ensures that all citizens do their part can effectively complement testing and tracing strategies.

Finally, chapter 6 outlines how any resilience strategy must include long-run solutions that allow society to **return to the new normal** after the threat is finally overcome. In a sense, it is the timely return to normality that constitutes resilience. In the Covid-19 crisis, some countries, like Sweden and the UK, thought the long-run new normal would occur when herd immunity kicked in. However, this turned out to be illusory because people who had been infected and recovered did not become permanently immune, and because Covid-19 often produces long-lasting health effects, the so-called "long Covid." The more promising approach to attaining a long-run new normal was large-scale vaccination, which is another form of herd immunity. Some countries, such as the US, put most of their efforts on promoting speedy vaccine development. Many Asian countries managed the first elements of the resilience strategy rather well, with innovative information gathering and clear communications. But they put less emphasis on vaccine developments than the US and Europe. In short, they underestimated the importance of having a clear vision of a new normal that any successful resilience strategy requires.

An additional element of a long-run new normal could be a mechanism that incentivizes countries to report contagious health emergencies early on. Currently, countries do not have such incentives. Reporting an emerging pandemic in one's own country can lead to large economic losses because other nations will try to shield themselves. As a consequence, countries with small outbreaks might wait before reporting them to the international community. They hope that the small outbreak will disappear on its own, even though the outbreak could evolve into a large pandemic. For this reason, a global mechanism that compensates countries for implementing early lockdowns to contain pandemics could be powerful. Akin to an insurance program, it would provide financial compensation for countries that report local outbreaks and implement public health measures.

CHAPTER 3

Behavioral Responses to Waves and Resilience Illusions

Individual behaviors and responses to crises are critical along all stages of resilience management. Human behavior can potentially amplify or even preempt the effects of policy. People might wear masks voluntarily in the absence of mask mandates. In contrast, people could rebel against mask mandates and thus weaken the effects of specific policies. Therefore, understanding people's attitudes and behavioral biases is an essential component of implementing containment measures, especially during the first stage of a crisis response.

The Covid-19 crisis evolved in three phases, with some variation in timing from country to country. Each phase reflected a different behavioral tale. In March 2020, individual behavior was dominated by fear. Without precise knowledge about how the virus spread or how lethal it would be, many people retrenched from as many contacts as possible, prioritizing their own safety. But humans are social beings. As the first wave eased in some parts of the world, a resilience illusion set in. Many people believed that society had become resilient to Covid-19 and that normal life would soon return. This belief was an illusion.

By the fall of 2020, we had much better knowledge about the disease. But the resurgence of the virus was not met with appropriate adjustments to individual behavior. Fear of the virus ceded to pandemic fatigue. During the spring of 2021, we witnessed a third wave, which coincided with large-scale vaccine rollouts. Why didn't people adjust their behavior? This phenomenon is widely known as the "last-mile problem." Organizations, groups, and individuals often struggle to carry through in the final stages of a project. The last Covid-19 mile was accompanied by a third round of lockdowns, particularly in some European countries. In some emerging economies, such as India, Sars-CoV-2 mutations that were more contagious emerged in the spring of 2021.

Before discussing the pandemic's waves, I will elaborate on SIR models—the dominant epidemiological models—and how modifications to these models should increase resilience.

SIR Models with Behavioral Response

The predominant bare-bones epidemiological model, the SIR model, portrays how a virus spreads among a susceptible population (S) and gradually infects (I) most of the population before those people recover (R). The key parameter in this model is the reproduction rate of the virus (R0), which measures how many new people an infected person will infect. If each infected person infects fewer than one other person on average, the virus will slowly die out. On the other hand, if each infected person infects more than one person, we will see exponential virus spread.

Large **behavioral externalities** related to a virus can strongly affect contagion rates and therefore have direct implications for epidemiological modeling. Once R0 exceeds 1, a tipping point is crossed. Due to exponential growth, the virus spirals out of control as an adverse feedback loop sets in.

This process only comes to a halt when almost no one is susceptible to infection. At that point, the pandemic slowly peters out. In other words, resilience only comes when herd immunity is achieved. The policy recommendation based on these models is to flatten the curve below ICU capacity by implementing social distancing measures and lockdowns.

However, the infection curves predicted by basic SIR models—if they ignore behavioral adjustments—might be misguided. In practice, Covid-19 peaked much earlier and among a much lower share of the infected population than standard SIR models predicted. Resilience was achieved and the exponential growth of the disease was subdued. But it was not herd immunity that suppressed the spread of the disease. In fact, as of this writing, herd immunity is still far off in all countries. Instead, what slowed the virus spread was behavioral change. For this reason, SIR models need to incorporate **behavioral responses**.[27]

Once behavioral responses are considered, the reproduction rate of the virus tends toward 1.[28] When the reproduction rate is below 1, people often relax their precautions. That causes the reproduction rate to rise again. As the reproduction rate rises above 1, people again seek to curb the outbreak by adapting their behaviors. In the physical sciences, this leads to what is known as a steady state.

A risk minimization approach would aim to further reduce R0 down to zero. If that could be achieved and R0=0, it would mean that the virus had effectively died out and there would be no risk of new outbreaks. In contrast, a resilience approach would allow some shocks to emerge. R0 would be reduced below 1, which would be sufficient for the virus to remain contained. Even if local flare-ups occurred, the virus would not spread widely. It would die out as long as R0 remained below 1.

Tale 1: Covid-19 Fear

In the early days of the pandemic, fear of the virus dominated every nation. Figure 3-1 depicts the evolution of economic activity (measured as the change in spending relative to January 2020) by comparing two US states, Wisconsin and Minnesota.[29] Wisconsin locked down a little earlier, but it also reopened much later. Strikingly, this shows that fear of the virus led people to shut down the economy before official lockdowns were imposed.[30]

As people in Minnesota observed what was happening in neighboring Wisconsin, they adjusted their behaviors without much regard to official lockdown announcements. Conversely, when Wisconsin reopened, the consumption patterns of Wisconsinites was not unlike the patterns in Minnesota. The key drivers of the spending collapse in the United States were not lockdowns; rather, households endogenously started to practice social distancing and they reduced consumption in contact-intensive service industries.

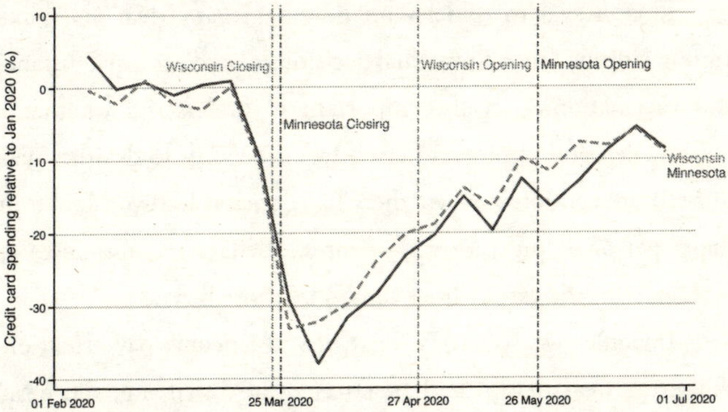

Figure 3-1: Consumer spending across the two states in the US, Wisconsin and Minnesota, which had different lockdown policy, but nevertheless similar economic activity in spending. Source: Opportunity Insights 2021

Much of this **decline in spending** was driven by **high-income workers** who worked remotely while being cautious about the virus.[31] Spending fell significantly more for the top 25 percent of households by income than for the bottom 25 percent. This suggests that shifts in preferences and risk perceptions drove the economy more than reductions in purchasing power.[32]

Economists Austan Goolsbee and Chad Syverson from the University of Chicago reached similar conclusions when comparing US counties in states that shutdown with neighboring counties in states that remained open. People in counties that remained open reduced their foot traffic.[33] These observations demonstrate the crucial role of fear, and they help to explain why Sweden and Denmark, for example, faced relatively similar economic fates despite having vastly different pandemic responses.[34]

Society's Fear: Aggregating Anxiety

It is crucial to understand how aggregated fear and anxiety among citizens drives individual decisions regarding social distancing and vaccination. It is also important to understand whether one person's decision to protect herself from the virus leads other people to be more cautious, or whether that decision leads others to relax their personal protection measures. Behavioral responses will interact with the externalities caused by those behaviors.[35]

Imagine two scenarios. First, if most people pay attention to the virus, wear masks, and practice social distancing, the positive externalities stemming from those widespread protective measures will reduce the incentives for other individuals to follow suit. In this way, the actions of others act as **strategic substitutes** for the actions of other individuals. If that effect dominates a situation, more people will choose moderate anti-virus measures. In other words, the actions of some people can dampen the individual responses of others. Ultimately, externalities are mitigated but not eliminated.

However, there is also an **information component** to individual behavior. As people practice social distancing, for example, it signals that Covid-19 is dangerous. As a result, one person learns about the severity of the virus from the actions of others. Then that person might increase his social distancing habits without any explicit announcement by the government. In this scenario, each individual's actions can trigger a cascade of adjustments in the lives of others, resulting in strong virus-protection measures. This scenario's outcome admittedly assumes **strategic complementarities** (mutually reinforcing factors). The outcome would be mitigated if heterogeneous agents modeled different behaviors and communicated different information. Nonetheless, individual actions are amplified as they influence the behaviors of other people.

Strategic complementarities are amplified in the presence of information echo chambers, such as modern social media. The theoretical idea goes back to DeMarzo, Vayanos, and Zwiebel.[36] Individuals do not realize that information bounces back to them.[37] In the case of a pandemic, if person A practices social distancing and causes person B to do the same, then they each interpret the other's behavior as a signal to treat the virus seriously. This is a textbook example of **feedback externalities**. Person A incentivizes person B to practice social distancing, which in turn causes person A to double down on her effort. This feedback loop converges to produce widespread social distancing, perhaps describing what occurred in March 2020.

In the context of the Covid-19 pandemic, lockdowns might have played a crucial signaling role because of these information externalities. They likely became communication tools that signaled the seriousness of the crisis. Pursuing an "awful action" might have raised awareness about the gravity of the public health crisis.[38] One example is the Indian lockdown, which was announced just four hours before it took effect. This rapidly implemented, strict lockdown served as a signal to capture the population's attention.[39]

Fear can be a powerful mechanism to induce behaviors that prevent the spread of a virus and thus foster resilience. But because strategic complementarities are so powerful, societies might overreact and destabilize the system. As US President Franklin Roosevelt stated in his first inaugural address, sometimes the "only thing we have to fear is fear itself."[40]

Aggregating Anxiety with Super-Spreaders

Heterogeneity across the population merits additional consideration. Covid-19 has been driven by super-spreading events and super-spreaders, the people who infect many others. Super-spreaders typically work in contact-intensive jobs, or they are fearless and imprudent. They might bring harm on many others, but it is not easy to instill fear and prudence in them. Thus, they can increase aggregate anxiety throughout a population.

Resilience from Heterogeneous Types

Despite all the fear of Covid-19 in the initial months of the pandemic, societies have always needed some fearless, caring people to perform essential work, such as in healthcare or in supermarkets. Heterogeneity in the population with respect to fear therefore sustains resilience.

Alternatively, we might incentivize people to take up essential jobs by paying higher wages. However, this might incentivize the wrong type of selection. We would not want super-spreaders to work in health-care roles, after all.

Tale 2: Covid Fatigue and the Resilience Illusion

Anxiety during this pandemic did not last forever. As the situation rapidly normalized during the summer of 2020, as demonstrated for example by Europe's low infection rates, behaviors changed. When cases suddenly exploded in September and October 2020, few behavioral adjustments could be observed. People in Europe continued to flock to outdoor dining and hold private parties regardless of the health risks. What had happened? The fall wave was much more characterized by Covid-19 fatigue, denial, or even fatalism. Similar developments were observed during India's second wave in the spring of 2021. Large religious gatherings and political rallies facilitated the rapid spread of the new Delta variant and previous individual protection measures were often scaled back.

People tend to be optimistic. They quietly derive anticipatory utility from the expectation of good outcomes. The German saying, "*Vorfreude ist die schönste freude*," means "anticipatory joy is the greatest joy." People want to see things in a rosier light. Therefore, a person's beliefs might be optimistically distorted.[41] Unfortunately, expectation mistakes can be costly because they induce people to base decisions on distorted views of reality.

There is also a "realism force" that pushes even overly optimistic people toward realistic expectations. **Optimal expectations** balance these two opposing forces (optimism and realism). However, the realism force can be dampened if the government imposes restrictions on individual behavior by imposing lockdowns and other targeted interventions. Similarly, the realism force can be subdued if, because of externalities, outcomes are governed by others and not by one's own behavior.

On the whole, these optimistic expectations can explain the substantial worsening of Covid-19 during the fall of 2020, especially in Europe. Countries such as Poland and the Czech Republic that mostly dodged the first wave were among the hardest hit by the second wave. The fact that there were bustling ski resorts in Germany during the winter holidays in 2021, despite hotel and restaurant closings, also illustrates pandemic fatigue.[42]

An alternative hypothesis about the resurgence of Covid-19 in the fall of 2020 is **seasonality**. Other coronaviruses prior to Covid-19 all tend to display a strong seasonal pattern. They ebb during the summer months before reemerging during the winter.[43] One possible cause for this pattern is stronger UV light in the summer. Beyond seasonality, average temperatures have also affected the spread of Covid-19. Behavioral adjustments to colder temperatures, indoor socializing in particular, favor the spread of the virus during the winter.

Tale 3: The Last Covid-19 Mile

In early 2021, vaccines became increasingly available in advanced economies. An end to the Covid-19 crisis emerged on the horizon. By adhering to public health measures for a couple more months, societies could theoretically buy enough time to vaccinate large swaths of their populations. This would pave the way for a gradual relaxation of pandemic restrictions. Instead, many countries, especially in Europe, but also in India, witnessed a third wave in the spring of 2021.

As mentioned earlier, this is sometimes referred to as the last-mile phenomenon. People often have a difficult time carrying through once the end of a task is in sight. By the spring of 2021, most steps to control and eventually overcome the pandemic had been taken. But more patience was needed. Announcements about successful vaccine developments, starting in November 2020, elevated hopes for a rapid return to normal. As a result, public pressure to ease restrictions grew.

The last-mile phenomenon challenges resilience. A resilient public health strategy might fail because people find it hard to carry through until the end of a pandemic. As populations become careless, strategic complementarities can reverse. As some neighbors become less concerned about the virus, others might relax their own precautions too.

Regional Differences

Many countries around the globe endured a first pandemic wave in the spring and summer of 2020. Then a stronger second wave occurred in the fall of 2020. During those periods, we saw large regional differences in the numbers of cases. Regions in the US that had the highest incidence of Covid-19 in the spring, for example in the Northeast, were *relatively* spared in the fall. In absolute terms, the fall resurgence still matched or surpassed the spring numbers, but regions that had largely avoided the first phase saw the most dramatic second phase in the fall of 2020. South Dakota had barely ever recorded one hundred new Covid-19 cases per day until mid-August 2020. By November, that state was hitting peaks of two thousand new daily cases, which was one of the highest overall infection rates in the US.[44] In Germany, the eastern province of Saxony became the worst hotspot in December 2020 after having been largely spared in the spring of 2020. The large cities (Leipzig and Dresden) posted the lowest incidences in the fall, whereas the spread of Covid-19 in more rural areas was driving infection rates higher.[45] Conspiracy theories such as QAnon found fertile ground in those regions.[46]

More generally, the initial spread of Covid-19 often occurred in urban areas, in part due to international travel. But in the fall of 2020, the virus was spreading broadly within countries, sparing no regions. The third wave in the spring of 2021, like the second wave, also did not spare any regions. More contagious variants of SARS-CoV-2 helped to drive these resurgences.

CHAPTER 4

Information, Testing, and Tracing

Information is crucial for any cost-efficient crisis-containment strategy designed uphold society until a new normal kicks in. But during a crisis, people often must act under the fog of the unknown. And in the case of the Covid-19 pandemic, as more information about the disease gradually became available, we often had to make U-turns.

In the absence of any information, people must develop an untargeted bridging strategy between the initial crisis and a new normal. Doing so in the fog of the unknown can be extremely costly. Due to a lack of information, governments initially had to impose general lockdowns. A more resilient and sustainable solution, such as quarantining only infectious people and those most vulnerable to serious illness, could not be implemented because we lacked adequate information.

However, gathering information can be challenging, especially during a new shock like Covid-19. Experimentation and developing new tests are typically key ingredients of any information gathering strategy. US President Franklin Delano Roosevelt tried out several policy tools during the Great Depression, and Federal Reserve Chairman Ben Bernanke experimented with various policy tools during the financial crisis of 2008. During major, world-changing events, such as a pandemic, standing still is typically not wise. It is better to adapt and to experiment in order to partially clear the fog.

In this chapter, we will explore tools for gathering information in order to design effective bridging strategies that preserve resilience. As in the rest of the book, we do this by drawing from Covid-19 experiences.

General Lockdowns versus Targeted Lockdowns

The economic costs of a general lockdown are gigantic. The US alone was losing about $80 billion per week in May 2020.[47] Beyond the immediate costs, there was a danger that the economy would not bounce back to a balanced growth path. In 2008, the cost of not returning sooner to the previous growth path was $1.2 trillion per year.[48] In other words, delaying a recovery increases the risks of deep and permanent growth losses. In the context of a pandemic, these considerations raise the following question: Can we design a targeted lockdown to save more lives while achieving better economic outcomes?[49]

Benefits of Targeted Lockdown Strategy

Superior information allows governments to develop targeted lockdowns. Imagine if we could easily identify infectious people, even asymptomatic people. In that case, effective isolation of those people would go a long way toward keeping the virus under control. In addition to reducing contagion, such a strategy would also lower the economic costs relative to a universal lockdown. We could quarantine only the infectious people while imposing relatively few restrictions on everyone else.

However, in the absence of perfect information, we do not know whom to quarantine. One practicable version of the semi-targeted lockdown consists of restricting the movements of non-working-age people. This is a simple way to limit immediate economic damage. Another option is to ask vulnerable populations, such as the elderly and those with preexisting health conditions, to remain at home.[50] This would substantially lower the death rate.[51]

Costs of Testing Programs

A semi-targeted lockdown of infectious people relies on information about who is infected and also infectious at any given time. This requires a testing program. What are the costs of an extensive testing program? They are strikingly small compared to an uninformed general lockdown. Assuming a test costs $20, which seemed reasonable in the spring of 2020, testing the entire US population would cost roughly $7 billion. Nobel laureate Paul Romer recommended the idea of testing about 7 percent of the

US population (twenty to twenty-three million people) on a daily basis.[52] The weekly costs of such a large-scale testing program would be around $400 million, a minuscule figure compared to the $80 billion in weekly economic losses caused by a general lockdown. This calculation supports moving to a targeted lockdown supplemented by extensive testing. People with positive test results could be temporarily isolated thereby interrupting transmission chains. The reproduction rate (R0) could fall below 1.[53]

Testing Can Lead to Emboldened Behavior

Another cost of testing is that it can change individual behaviors. Any Covid-19 test can produce false negatives. In these cases, people infected with the virus receive a negative test result.[54] Moreover, depending on the type of test, it can take days to receive a result. Thus, an infectious person might unwittingly spread the disease until the test result arrives. False negatives and delayed test results can induce careless behavior by people who feel secure but who are in fact spreading the disease. When that occurs, it kills resilience. At the onset of the pandemic, the strength of such effects was not known. That lack of knowledge motivated researchers to learn from large-scale testing and the behavioral adjustments that people made. This illustrates the importance of gaining empirical evidence that can better inform policy decisions.

Types of Information for Targeted Lockdowns

Targeted lockdowns, those that focus on specific groups in a population, might involve quarantining only infectious or vulnerable populations. But to narrowly identify those people, we need to collect specific and pertinent information. Testing with a post-infection antibody test, a rapid antigen test, or a PCR (polymerase chain reaction) test can help single out infectious people or help to measure a population's proximity to herd immunity. The infected people and their contacts—at least those who can be identified via contact tracing—can be quarantined. This approach is similar to the forty-day isolation of sailors during the plague in the Middle Ages.

Types of Information

The information needed for a targeted lockdown depends on which people are targeted. There are at least two options: to focus on those who are most vulnerable to serious illness or to focus on super-spreaders, those who infect many other people. Thus, the government either needs information about people who are most likely to suffer from negative health externalities, or about those who spread the externalities, the super-spreaders. Depending on which part of the population a government seeks to identify, different information will be required.

Types of information	Vulnerability (externality exposes receiver)	Spreader (externality caused by spreader)
Free	Age, preexisting health, nurses	Nurses, travelers from risky areas
Costly	Antibody test	Antigen test Tracing

Table 4-1: Classification of different types of information. Age is a good indicator of vulnerability. This information is freely available. The same applies to health worker status. In contrast, tests are costly.

Different Types of Tests

There is an important tradeoff between types of tests. PCR tests are very precise, yielding close to zero false negatives.[55] But they are most precise in patients who are already beyond the high infection phase, after the viral load has reached its peak. Although less precise than PCR tests, at least in terms of identifying the presence of the virus, rapid antigen tests are better suited for detecting actual infectiousness. Thus, they are critical for an efficient Covid-19 containment strategy.

Tracing, Efficient Testing, and Targeted Enforcement

Testing and contact tracing are employed to gather the information needed to effectively implement targeted lockdowns. However, these two methods offer different levels of precision. Testing provides a precise signal (the false-positivity rate is low), but results can be delayed.

Contact tracing could serve as a preliminary tool **before testing**. When tests are scarce, contact tracing becomes more valuable. If public health workers can identify people who have higher risks of infection, they can focus testing efforts on those individuals. The contacts of infected people are precisely those who will have a higher infection risk and might therefore require a test. Targeted testing is effective at breaking down infection chains, but it does not necessarily reveal the true prevalence of Covid-19 in the entire population. If that is the object of interest, widespread random testing would be required.

In China and a few other Asian countries, contact tracing via **mobile apps** has been very effective. Before people can enter a building in China, they must scan their phones. Access is denied to those who are known to be Covid-19 positive, or those who have been in contact with an infected person. Taiwan's strategy has focused on locking down those individuals who are most likely to be infectious and then tracing their contacts by using cellphone signals. Students returning from abroad, among others, have had to quarantine for two weeks. The country has used triangulation to track cellphone systems and surveil quarantine compliance. However, some unintended consequences have occurred. For example, when student Milo Hsieh's cellphone briefly ran out of battery, four government agencies contacted him within an hour to check his whereabouts.[56] Although Taiwan's "electronic fence" has kept the country safer, worries about privacy have persisted. A low-tech tool that facilitates contact tracing is a contact diary. It is less effective, but it increases privacy.[57]

Being able to test extensively and use contact tracing to track down more Covid-19 cases is a tremendous advantage that contributes to building economic resilience. However, two tipping points present a major challenge for contact tracing. First, if the reproduction rate (R0) exceeds 1, the virus begins to grow exponentially. The second tipping point is reached when the virus incidence rate gets too high. At both points, contact tracing becomes infeasible, at least without the technological solutions that many Western societies have shunned because of privacy concerns.

In Germany, the weekly incidence rate had long been determined as more than fifty per hundred thousand inhabitants. That incidence rate was later lowered to thirty-five. Once that threshold is crossed, contacts can no longer be effectively traced and the virus could spiral out of control. Thus, a resilient policy requires different and stronger virus containment measures to fend off adverse feedback loops if a tipping point is crossed.

Another effective tool is to enable between-group distancing, such as forming bubbles or so-called "pods." Forming bubbles or pods reduces the spread of the disease by encouraging people to only meet with others in the same group. Testing and contact tracing can further amplify the benefits of age-targeted lockdown policies.[58]

Privacy and Stigma

Contact tracing, particularly with mobile apps, also raises concerns about the value of privacy and the potential stigmatization of infected people if their health status becomes widely known.

Information Sharing and Privacy

Information sharing among government entities and the private sector can greatly facilitate the implementation of any targeted measure. However, measures that single out particular groups might intrude on privacy.

Asian countries have been particularly effective with information sharing. For example, when a person tests positive in South Korea, the local government receives reports about the patient from the hospital. The government is entitled to gather the patient's hospital records, mobile GPS records, credit card history, and camera recordings from nearby buildings. The information, including the patient's history of merchant visits, can be widely disclosed across the local population within the patient's county. Information about the patient is disseminated daily through a government-generated warning text. People in the same county can also access this information through the Korea Disease Control and Prevention Agency website. Also, people who had visited any of the merchants together with the patient are notified through text and receive a recommendation to get tested. Privacy concerns led the South Korean government in October 2020 to restrict information about individual cases.

Stigma and the Fear of Testing

These privacy and stigmatization concerns mean that governments need to walk a fine line. If people are afraid of getting tested because of privacy concerns or because they fear social stigma, then these social forces can weaken a widespread testing strategy.

In particular, the stigmatization of sick people can spur adherence to pandemic rules, but it can also produce the opposite effect. For example, a Covid-19 outbreak at a childcare facility would have huge externalities. Parents of the infected children would have to quarantine and all parents of any child in the day-care center would need to make alternative plans if the facility closes. Thus, any parent who sends a child to a Covid-19 test might "cause" a large inconvenience for all other parents. They in turn might stigmatize the parent whose child tested positive. In that case, the fear of stigma would disincentivize getting tested and lead to potentially nefarious consequences. The virus might spread across the entire day-care center, even though it would have been simple to contain ex-ante.

In summary, information is paramount for developing a feasible containment strategy that is designed to sustain a society until a new normal is realized. It is important to understand that asymptomatic virus transmission, assortative contacts, seasonal effects, and the impact of the virus on children are critical inputs into optimal policy.[59]

CHAPTER 5

Communication: Managing People's Worries

In the previous two chapters, we stressed the importance of individual behavior and information to define and implement a feasible bridging strategy. Social learning and feedback externalities could powerfully amplify behavioral responses to Covid-19. Therefore, information communicated by influencers and the government is critically important. Effective **persuasive** communication, which requires a base level of trust, is key.

Using communicative tools resembles a walk on a tightrope. The government might want to **foster some anxiety** to convey the severity of a health crisis, but it also wants to **avoid** widespread **panic**. A balance between creating fear and preventing a panic must be sought.

First, the government can convey objective information to the population, helping people to align their initial views with the facts about the disease. For example, German Chancellor Angela Merkel discussed the importance of focusing on R0 and that the margin of error on R was small. She said that the difference between R=.98 and R=1.02 is a choice between gradual decline versus the exponential growth of infection numbers. To the extent that better-informed citizens can more easily take appropriate actions regarding the crisis, communication can be a central element of building resilience. But communication can also further work through a range of non-government channels.

Fostering a Sense of Community

On one end of the spectrum, the rapidly implemented lockdown in India (within four hours) helped to signal the severity of the Covid-19 crisis and arguably stirred up some fear. As previously mentioned, some believe the lockdown served a **signaling role**. This interpretation of the lockdown (being used to create fear) points to a Machiavellian feature. On the other end of the spectrum, governments can tailor communication to foster a **sense of community,** to convey the idea that all citizens are in one boat. Rather than using fear to trigger the population into containing the virus, the sense-of-community approach uses a "warm glow" that encourages people to comply with restrictions for the common good. In economic models, altruism arises when an individual's utility depends on the utility of others.[60] In plain English, people care about each other.

To create a shared sense of identity, communication on multiple channels can be beneficial.[61] New Zealand's Prime Minister

Jacinda Ardern was widely applauded for addressing audiences on channels as varied as "parliamentary statements, daily briefings, Facebook Live broadcasts, and podcasts."[62] Good communication provides a resilient long-term anchor to people's expectations.

Additionally, using influencers to amplify the government's message can be effective. In India, Bollywood actresses and actors released videos showing compliance with measures to stem the pandemic, which can have a powerful amplifying effect on their followers.

At the intersection of these two channels, many politicians likened Covid-19 to a war thereby triggering a sense of community (similar to "rallying around the flag") and fear.[63] **As in war times**, sustaining morale is critical to keep the population mobilized in the fight against the spread of the disease.[64] In the context of the Covid-19 pandemic, all of humanity has faced a common enemy. That fact could be used effectively to form a common cross-national message, or to divide nations into subgroups that fight each other.[65]

The Role of Credibility in Communication

Whether the government effectively uses communication to persuade a population hinges on **trust** in the government and, more broadly, in science.[66] Information bubbles can shield some citizens from critical information. Given the daily information overflow, too much information can cause news to be overlooked or dismissed. Covid-19 was a topic large enough to allow critical information to penetrate those bubbles and to reach global and diverse populations.

Covid-19 Statistics

The notion that statistics can be repurposed to support different partisan agendas has gained significant traction ever since journalist Darrell Huff's classic book *How to Lie with Statistics* was published in 1954.[67] This possibility is unfortunate because the reliability of statistics is essential to convince the general public to accept and practice public health measures.

One example of society's need to trust science and statistics can be seen in relation to **Covid-19 death statistics**. It is not obvious what constitutes a Covid-19 death. Did a person die because he contracted Covid-19 or did he die of other causes while having Covid-19?[68] Furthermore, all-cause mortality typically falls in recessions and presumably even more during a lockdown, because accidental deaths decline.[69] In addition, Covid-19 might have had a "harvesting effect" by which "deaths get packed into the Covid-19 months" as people with short remaining life spans die of Covid-19. Despite seeing a shocking short-term spike, the overall, long-term mortality rate might appear less frightening.[70]

During this pandemic, some confusion arose around testing. Many asked questions such as: Does more testing lead to more Covid-19 cases? Obviously not. The cases are still in circulation even if they are not discovered by tests. If people are not tested, they might unknowingly infect more people. Therefore, over the medium term, more testing will likely decrease the total—albeit unobservable—number of Covid-19 cases. However, in the short run, the number of known cases rises because more people are being tested. As previously stated, negative stigma can prevent people from being tested or from reporting cases. This has a similar distorting effect on our perceptions of statistics.

Communicating Science

Scientific communication can be powerful in these circumstances. In an experiment, messages by Abhijit Banerjee, a Nobel laureate in economics, were broadcasted to communities in India during the Covid-19 pandemic. Adherence with public health measures, such as reporting symptoms, increased significantly after this trusted source conveyed important information.[71] Credible communication can therefore bring people onboard and enhance resilience.

Fighting Conspiracy Theories

These sometimes-subtle considerations, paired with distrust in science and statistics, have fueled **conspiracy theories** during this pandemic. Examples include the false ideas proffered by QAnon or by the misinforming movie *Plandemic.* Curiously, QAnon has spread in a manner similar to the virus. Despite its much less polarized multiparty system, Germany is now estimated to be the country with the second highest number of QAnon adherents after the United States, where the conspiracy theory group originated.[72] One ongoing challenge will be to maintain social cohesion in the presence of these conspiracies.

Gaining Credibility by Offering the Counterfactual

Dynamic crisis communication often requires credible communication of **counterfactual scenarios**. People have a limited understanding of counterfactual scenarios. A counterfactual approach to communication involves asking questions such as: What would have happened if there had been no lockdowns or social distancing measures?

Figure 5-1 depicts the excess weekly death numbers in Germany from January 2020 onward. The shaded area shows the range between the maximum and minimum number of deaths each week from the pre-pandemic years 2016 to 2019. Many conspiracy theorists used these numbers to claim that the Covid-19 crisis was a hoax since the death rates were, until the fall of 2020 (week forty), not truly excessive compared to historical data. Starting in the fall of 2020, the figure shows clear evidence of excess deaths. Of course, without any virus containment measures, the counterfactual death numbers would have largely outnumbered the actual numbers, as well as historical averages.

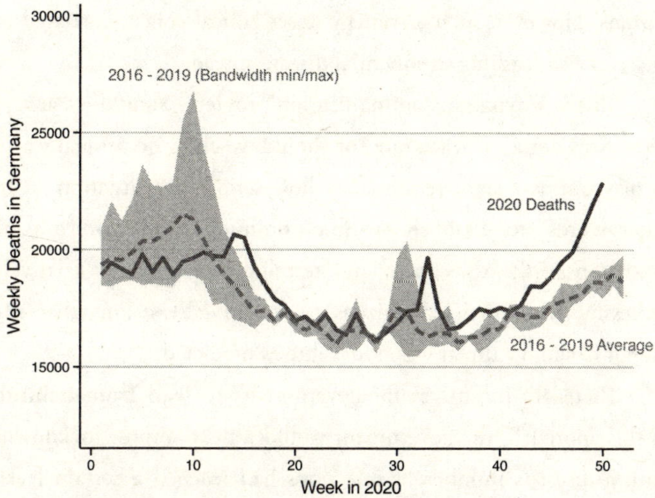

Figure 5-1: Weekly overall deaths in Germany, to illustrate the excess death rate due to Covid-19. Source: Statistisches Bundesamt 2021

How should policymakers communicate if people find it difficult to understand the counterfactual? In the context of the pandemic, one counterfactual would be related to how many deaths might occur in the absence of lockdowns. That would depend on how strictly the government applies its lockdown rules over time. Paradoxically, if a lockdown is extremely strict and the infection rate remains very low, the low infection rate might cause criticism and fuel conspiracy theories. People might think there is no problem and then falsely claim that the government had imposed lockdowns for nefarious purposes. If the government loses credibility, the people might look for ways to circumvent lockdown rules. If that occurs, the only way to credibly communicate the seriousness of the threat might be to occasionally let the crisis slightly erupt. In this way, the counterfactual scenario could be made apparent to less-informed citizens. However, such a strategy raises ethical concerns related to the risk of unleashing exponential disease spread.

This is a dynamic communication problem. Should we always allow for a certain "death rate" or should we allow occasional waves to play out as a stark reminder of how serious the situation is? In other words, to establish credible communication, governments must constantly experiment and test limits. Germany's relatively successful lockdown led citizens to spread false claims that the overall Covid-19 threat was not as dire as predicted.

There are incentives for governments to **lead from behind**. In this approach, the government would wait to impose lockdowns until a disease's number of infections had reached a certain level. The argument is that if a lockdown is implemented too early, the effort might become a victim of its own success. An early lockdown would no doubt prevent many bad health outcomes, but that might lead uninformed citizens to doubt the need for lockdowns. This is not conducive to strengthening resilience.

Similarly, a **foreign country that ignores** the Covid-19 threat, as occurred in Brazil or Sweden, **helps the communication** efforts in other countries. The negative outcomes in nations that mismanaged the pandemic have clearly revealed counterfactual scenarios. In economic terms, countries with weak policies have had a positive externality on the communication efforts in other countries.

Vision and Narratives

Should a political leader reveal a longer-term vision or keep it private? There is no simple advice for that type of strategic consideration. Revealing a vision publicly can invite backlash and criticism. But if leaders keep plans private, they can be attacked for lack of clarity. An example of walking the tightrope between inviting too much criticism and appearing too vague is Mario Draghi's London speech, the famous "whatever it takes" announcement. It projected a clear commitment to keeping the euro area intact while being sufficiently vague as to not invite criticism.

Franklin D. Roosevelt's approach during the Great Depression also highlights a possible approach. His administration tried various policies and looked for effective remedies to the crisis. At the same time, FDR made clear that he was caring for people and projecting a sense of pragmatic security.[73]

"Those who tell the stories rule the world." That quote is varyingly attributed to the Hopi, a Native American tribe, or to Plato. Whatever the case, **simple stories**, including economic models, can paint an easily understood picture of reality, which in turn makes it easier to persuade the population. But stories can be oversimplified, or they can distort the relevant context. From an economic point of view, the key tradeoff is between the internal and external consistency of models and stories. Information with internal consistency is presented with fully rational agents and logically coherent reasoning. But the model presented might not perfectly reflect reality. On the other hand, presenting information with an emphasis on external validity will more closely match reality, but that often makes the model too complex for a general population to comprehend.

As the world becomes more complex, tradeoffs between **oversimplification** and **inclusion** are amplified. Conspiracy theories are a good example. They present a straightforward view of the world designed to "rationalize" a diverse set of facts that might otherwise overwhelm people. Thus, the complexity (and uncertainty) of the Covid-19 pandemic provides one explanation for the rise of conspiracy theories in 2020 and 2021.

Controlling the narrative is also crucial. Where did the virus originate? Whose fault was the outbreak?[74] Some people have blamed China for insufficient reporting during the initial phases of the pandemic. Meanwhile, China, to avoid being the world's scapegoat, has tried to show that its system has handled the crisis better than other countries. We will return to China's face-mask diplomacy in chapter 14.

CHAPTER 6

The Role of Vaccines in Designing a New Normal

An important component of any crisis response is to develop a long-run and sustainable new normal. Resilience ultimately kicks in when society can gradually implement the necessary measures for that to occur.

In the case of the Covid-19 pandemic, herd immunity was initially seen as one of the long-run solutions, especially in Sweden and for a while in the UK. However, that was never a viable option, for three reasons. First, there has been significant evidence of long-lasting adverse health effects among Covid-19 survivors.[75] To pursue herd immunity therefore exposes many people to health problems from which they might never fully recover, the so-called long-Covid. Second, immunity to Covid-19 is likely to be temporary, so herd immunity might never be achieved at all. Third, new virus variants continue to emerge. Thus, the only viable option has been to develop vaccines.

Unprecedented scientific efforts have been devoted to

Covid-19 vaccine development, especially in the US and Europe. A process that normally takes a decade or longer culminated with the first vaccine candidates being deployed in large numbers within a year. Asian countries emphasized the containment elements of a resilience strategy, but they focused less on another element of the resilience strategy: the return to the new normal.

Due to the superior efficacies of several new vaccines, the spread of the virus and the death rates in many countries have been declining (at the time of this writing). Vaccinating about 60 percent of the population may be sufficient to bring R sustainably below 1, the threshold at which the virus would disappear by itself. In light of the current pace of vaccine production and distribution, some people hope that the pandemic might be over by 2022 in most of the world. However, it is possible that a vaccine could be highly effective against severe disease and death but have little effect on possible asymptomatic transmission of the disease. In that case, a far higher proportion of the population would need to be vaccinated to end the pandemic. Early data on the Pfizer-BioNTech vaccine indicate that it also lowers contagious transmission. However, the degree of this effect is not yet well understood.[76] Moreover, if new variants can dodge vaccines, some of our hopes could be dashed.

A broader lesson is that we can proactively build resilience for the next virus. Because it is common for animal viruses to transmit to humans, the risk of pandemics will continue after Covid-19 has been controlled. If we can improve pandemic preparedness, it will be a major step toward greater resilience.

The Cost-Benefit of Vaccines

The cost-benefit reasoning about testing and contact tracing applies to vaccine development even more. The marginal benefit of a vaccine can be approximated by the product of the marginal increase in the following factors: the probability of successful vaccine development; the $375 billion monthly economic costs in the US alone; and an assumed six-months advance in vaccine development. The marginal cost of a vaccine, depending on the type, is roughly $1 of production cost per dose multiplied by the total number of units produced.[77] Now we have to take into account the fungibility of capacity. A vaccine factory can be repurposed relatively quickly to produce another vaccine. So, for each vaccine designed to vaccinate eight billion people, the cost would be $8 billion.[78]

The mRNA vaccines, such as the Pfizer-BioNTech and Moderna versions, are an order of magnitude more expensive than other types, with prices alleged to be around $15 per dose. But the basic conclusion of cost-benefit calculus remains the same due to the large economic costs of lockdowns. Early on in the pandemic, discussions ensued about whether the EU should purchase the more expensive mRNA vaccines or the cheaper alternatives that would become available later. The potential cost savings of the cheaper options were minimal compared to the economic costs of a longer lockdown.[79]

Vaccine Development: Redundancies, Diversification, and Resilience

There are two ways to **incentivize vaccine development**. The first is to grant a company temporary monopoly rights, which guarantees a high profit margin if the vaccine is successful. The second approach is for the government to provide insurance against losses arising from failure.[80]

Firms withhold important private information about their vaccine candidates. Therefore, economist Michael Kremer, in May 2020, proposed an eighty-twenty funding scheme. The government would assume at least 80 percent of the costs for developing vaccine manufacturing capacity and private firms would have 20 percent "skin in the game." In return for the funding, governments would have an option to purchase the vaccine if it proved successful.[81]

Three principles should guide vaccine development. First, redundancies ensure there is more vaccine capacity than actually needed. This safeguards society against the failure of some vaccine projects. The second critical principle is diversification. By diversifying efforts across various vaccine technologies, we can reduce the correlation of the projects. More diversity increases the likelihood that some projects will be successful. Finally, resilient vaccine development ensures that they will be easily adapted to stop the spread of possible new virus variants.

Redundancy and Diversification: Developing Vaccines in Parallel

Vaccine development is risky and might fail, so multiple vaccines need to be developed in parallel.[82] Governments initially knew very little about which vaccines would most likely be successful. For this reason, many governments purchased vaccine commitments from several companies (figure 6-1). They ended up with more vaccine doses than their populations needed.

In May 2020, it was estimated that it would take fourteen vaccine trials to have a roughly 90 percent chance of developing one successful vaccine by the fall of 2021.[83] The number fourteen was based on the cross-correlation across various vaccines. Vaccines with similar technologies are highly cross-correlated, so developing an additional vaccine that is similar to the existing ones provides less diversification than adding a vaccine candidate that is based on completely different technology.

From the government's perspective in May 2020, the potential availability of numerous vaccines would fuel a standard diversification motive. Vaccines rely on four **broad sets of biotechnologies:** genetic mRNA (Pfizer, Moderna, Curevac, Sanofi); viral vector (Astra Zeneca, Johnson & Johnson, Sputnik); whole-virus vaccines (Sinovac Biotech, Sinopharm, Covaxin); and protein-based (Novavax)). **Diversification** requires purchasing commitments from companies that produce different vaccine types, and it goes one step further than pure redundancy. Indeed, most countries in figure 6-1 pursued such a strategy, although whole-virus vaccines were largely absent from many countries' portfolios.

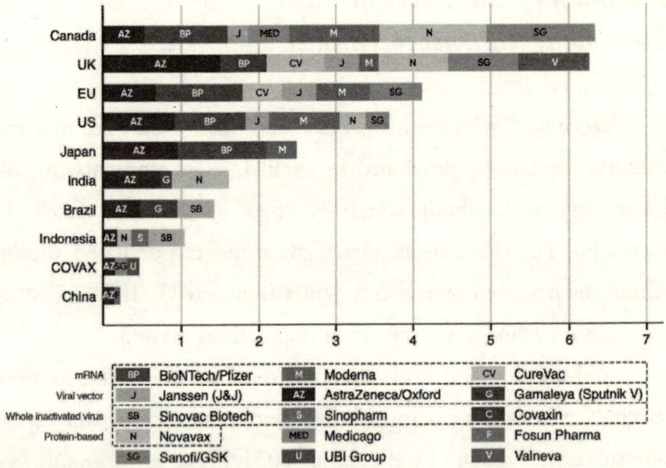

Figure 6-1: Redundancy, diversification, and resilience in vaccine ordering. Source: Bloomberg 2021

The emergence of virus mutations in late 2020 and into 2021 brought to light another consideration related to diversification. As of April 2021, we did not know which vaccines would be most effective against these mutations. So, it is important to diversify across vaccines and study their efficacies against each variant.

Internationally Coordinated Vaccine Funding

Financing strategies could in principle be developed with an international scope. For example, each country could contribute approximately 0.15 percent of GDP to help develop vaccines. At least initially, there would be strong incentives to join such a funding program because countries want to hedge the risks of failure related to their own vaccine candidates.[84] An alternative to a worldwide strategy would be lighter forms of cooperation in which the domestic government provides funding to foreign firms to build excess capacity.[85] COVAX serves as an example of an international initiative that has attempted to coordinate vaccine financing.

Paying for a Vaccine with Data

Economic transactions are routinely conducted by exchanging money for goods or services. However, when it comes to international vaccine distribution, some countries have been rewarding vaccine companies with data. **Israel**, which by late-January 2021 was the world leader in vaccination rates, had been sending weekly data reports about its vaccination efforts to Pfizer-BioNTech. These reports have included demographic data about vaccinated citizens.[86] It should be added that Israel is also paying a higher price per dose than the European Union, for example.

Vaccine Trials

Paradoxically, the failure of Covid-19 containment measures in certain parts of the world can render **vaccine trials** easier. Large-scale trials usually work by vaccinating tens of thousands of people with either the vaccine or a placebo. Researchers then compare infection rates across the two groups. However, the number of Covid-19 cases in Brazil and the US surged so high that the treatment and the control groups had sufficient virus exposure to test the efficacy of each vaccine candidate. In fact, by the second half of 2020, Latin America had emerged as a hot spot for vaccine trials because of high infection rates and because so many volunteers were willing to participate in vaccine trials.[87]

Vaccine Distribution

Once a vaccine is available, ethical questions abound. Which countries should be served first? Who within each country should be vaccinated first? The lack of international leadership on this front makes these questions particularly acute.[88]

International Distribution

A simple thought experiment helps to clarify the international considerations. Suppose two countries, A and B, each successfully develop a vaccine. Should each country give its domestic vaccine to its citizens or swap half of the vaccine with its neighbors? Standard risk-aversion arguments would support the latter. Suppose one of the two vaccines has side effects. Using an equal mix of both vaccines ensures that 50 percent of the population will not suffer side effects. Such considerations might, however, be difficult to communicate.

International spillovers must also be considered for vaccine allocation. Health externalities from emerging and developing countries (EMDEs) have impacted advanced economies due to production chain linkages and because of international travel, including tourism.

Many EMDEs face a choice between a rock and a hard place. The tradeoff is particularly amplified by the fact that EMDE countries cannot expect to receive preferential treatment as they procure a sound vaccine later on. We will return to the specific challenges faced by EMDEs in chapter 13 and to the topic of vaccine export controls in chapter 14.

Within-Country Distribution: Whom to Vaccinate with Which Vaccine?

On the national scale, there are two possible scenarios. First, if demand exceeds the number of available doses, there will be vaccine scarcity. Second, there might be an abundance of vaccine if demand is limited, perhaps because many people are afraid of unknown side effects. Additionally, the wrong types of people might want a vaccine. They might be people with high private benefits and thus have a high willingness to pay for a vaccine—as compared to the most vulnerable populations.

How can a government centrally allocate scarce vaccine resources? Assuming for now that people do not change their behavioral responses, we see a critical distinction between the receivers of externalities—the vulnerable populations—and the spreaders of those externalities, notably super-spreaders.

The government might give high priority to vaccinating **critical workers**, such as medical staff who provide critical services. Prioritizing **high social value** workers, particularly those with extensive occupation-related exposure to the virus, could also be prioritized.

A seemingly obvious solution would be to offer early vaccination to people who are most **vulnerable** to death caused by the virus. Vulnerable populations have strong private incentives to get vaccinated, so they might not need much additional "nudging" by the government.

However, the vulnerable are likely not to be the most socially active people. Although vaccinating vulnerable populations protects those individuals, the effort would not do much to reduce the spread of the disease. In stark contrast, the benefits of vaccinating **super-spreaders** would be manifold. That approach would protect the super-spreaders and also break the entire chain of additional Covid-19 cases associated with them. Vaccinating additional super-spreaders would help to lower the reproduction rate to less than 1, the **tipping point** below which the virus slowly recedes and dies out.

Perhaps counterintuitively, the social gains of first vaccinating super-spreaders might exceed the social gains of first vaccinating the most vulnerable populations, depending on the parameters.[89] Eliminating the infection externalities caused by super-spreaders would help the vulnerable more than giving them a vaccine early. However, there is the question of how to identify supers-spreaders. Some proxies might be young age or workers who do not work from home. But super-spreading is partly a biological feature, making it difficult to identify these people ex-ante.

In contrast to the vulnerable, super-spreaders might have far fewer private incentives to get vaccinated than the total social value of their vaccinations. This could create a case in which the government has a difficult time to "nudge" super-spreaders into being vaccinated. Moreover, super-spreaders might be much harder to identify.

Alternatively, one could prioritize people with a high private value of life. If the value of life is infinite, the elderly who are most at risk should be vaccinated first. But if the value of life is proportional to income or years of life, then the younger should be vaccinated first. Thus, ethical considerations are intricately linked to the economic cost-benefit analysis. A final aspect to consider is the standard economic motive of consumption smoothing. Old people cannot be compensated with a "future vacation" because they have a short remaining life expectancy. Young people can intertemporally smooth their consumption over a longer remaining period of life. If they did not go on a vacation in 2020, they might be able to go in 2021, 2022, or even 2025. This argument can further support the case for vaccinating old people first.

Another strategy employed in Indonesia consists of vaccinating the working-age population.[90] This approach aims to reduce the economic fallout of the crisis by enabling workers to work securely once they have been vaccinated.

Behavioral Responses

Behavioral responses play an important role in controlling the spread of a virus. If the vaccine is of high quality, with close to 100 percent efficacy, behavioral responses will not matter because the vaccinated would be perfectly safe. However, the logic is quite a bit different if the vaccine only has, say, 50 percent efficacy. A vaccinated super-spreader who has a 50 percent chance of immunity might increase his social behavior and go to twice as many parties. In that case, the super-spreader is half as likely to spread the virus per party, but doubling the number of parties attended would effectively imply that his vaccination did not have any effect in terms of reducing the prevalence of Covid-19.

Varying Effectiveness and Strategic Reserves

Vaccines with **varying effectiveness** have received approval. Which person should receive which vaccine? The answer is not obvious.

Another factor governments must consider is whether to keep some vaccine units in reserve. Doing so would allow the government to quickly react if hotspots emerge later. Essentially, there is a dynamic tradeoff. Keeping more vaccine as a strategic reserve might lead to more hotspots in the future; however, these hotspots could be more effectively contained by establishing strategic vaccine reserves. The precise answer to the question will also depend on the extent of contract tracing and the availability of other treatments.

Parameter Uncertainty

All scenarios considered so far rely implicitly on a relatively high certainty about the parameters. Parameter uncertainty is a critical concern for robust optimization. If there is initial uncertainty about the vaccine's effectiveness or about possible side effects, it might be best to randomize some vaccine allocations across the population—to learn more about the vaccine's efficacy across various subpopulations.[91] Results from this initial learning process could be used to later enhance the vaccine allocation mechanism. Another option would be to learn more about these parameters by focusing on a small country like Israel where the past ten years of health data have been digitized.

Fighting Vaccine Hesitancy

In many countries, vaccine scepticism is widespread. Just over half of people in France reported that they would want to be vaccinated in November 2020.[92] Vaccine hesitancy rates might change once vaccines are more widely available, but the question of how to bolster vaccine support remains vexing. Herd immunity requires 60 to 70 percent of the population to be immunized.

One way to increase support for vaccination might be for politicians to be vaccinated early and in public. Joe Biden and Benyamin Netanyahu went down that road.[93, 94] But other world leaders, such as Angela Merkel had to wait in line in accordance with national vaccine plans.[95] It is not clear which approach is politically shrewder. Leaders hope to rally support for vaccination, but they might also stir discontent about preferential treatment.

Vaccine Passports

One relevant approach to incentivizing vaccines is to offer privileges to the vaccinated. A lively public discussion has emerged about whether companies or institutions can grant preferential treatment to people who can prove they have been vaccinated. As vaccination gradually becomes available to everyone, at least in Europe and North America, offering privileges can be an important tool for increasing vaccination rates.[96] Individuals could receive vaccine passports to prove they have been vaccinated. Several countries including the EU and China are now working on vaccine passport implementations.[97, 98, 99] Israel used them widely in March 2021, allowing the vaccinated to return to public life.

Vaccine passports or domestic implementations can powerfully enhance resilience in a way that facilitates economic recovery—because they solve an information problem. If only vaccinated people are allowed to return to public life, the information asymmetry declines. If all moviegoers, for example, feel relatively safe about their health, movie theater attendance could surge.

In conclusion, to contain the source of a crisis like the Covid-19 pandemic, we need a deep understanding of human behavior, including psychological biases, fears, and anxieties. Second, it is illusory to think that fighting a health crisis and stabilizing the economy are mutually exclusive aims; they are, in fact, interdependent efforts. Information and communication are paramount for reducing the costs of a containment strategy and bringing a crisis to an end. Maintaining trust and avoiding conspiracy theories is challenging, but we can improve trust by credibly communicating counterfactual scenarios. Finally, crisis strategy should include a vision for a long-run new normal, which ultimately leads to resilience.

PART III

MACROECONOMIC RESILIENCE

A resilient society depends on its ability to implement appropriate responses after a shock occurs, with the aim of reverting back to the previous growth path. Following the immediate containment response, society needs to build a bridge to a new long-run solution. A resilient social contract is critical in the process of stabilizing the economy, which in turn stabilizes the social contract.

The Covid-19 recession is the deepest recession since World War II. In March 2020, some observers worried that we would experience a crisis comparable to the 1929 Great Depression. Thankfully, that type of outcome was averted. The economy quickly rebounded. We saw significant resilience in the economy. What will the future look like?

This section explores the key macroeconomic questions related to innovation, scarring, financial markets, fiscal and monetary policy, and inequality. The emphasis is on avoiding traps caused by economic scarring during and after, for example, recessions.

It is important to understand the relationship between how an economy enters a recession and the ways it should be handled. Paul Krugman distinguishes two fundamental types of recessions: those caused by **internal** imbalances, such as unsustainable private sector spending or investments that need to be corrected,[100] and those caused by **external** headwinds.[101] Historically, the latter type of recession often occurred after a period of stark monetary tightening, and then the economy exhibited a quick employment recovery.[102] Another example is the recent pandemic-caused recession. Prior to the shock, the economic fundamentals were sound, which facilitated a rapid rebound.

In contrast, recessions caused by private sector excesses followed by a sudden major stress in the financial sector—called a "Minsky moment"—typically have been followed by a sluggish recovery.[103] An example was the 2007-2008 recession. In 2008, a highly leveraged household sector was particularly vulnerable to a revaluation of house prices while an undercapitalized financial sector offered little resilience.[104] As a result, the ensuing need for deleveraging led to a prolonged recession. If that distinction holds true, the 2020-2021 recession could look more like the recession in 1979-1982 with a "swoosh"-shaped recovery.[105]

Figure III-1 illustrates how growth might suffer for a long time. It plots Japanese real GDP since the early 1990s. We can see how the Japanese banking crisis and the 2007 global financial crisis led to a substantial reduction in the pace of growth. The economy was not resilient and so we pivoted to a lower growth path during the early 2000s.

There are also **two types of rebounds.** First, an economy can bounce back to the level of the previous growth path. Second, an economy can bounce back to the pre-crisis level *and* resume the subsequent long-run growth rate. In the long run, bouncing back to the previous growth rate (the slope of the dashed line) is more important. The Japanese economy never bounced back to the pre-banking crisis growth rate.

In contrast, the 2011 earthquake near Fukushima, which was a much larger fundamental shock, had almost no notable effect on the growth prospects (the slope of the dashed line). The Japanese economy proved to be very resilient in the face of the natural disaster and bounced back rapidly. The question is what type of shock the Covid-19 pandemic will resemble. Will it be closer to the financial crises or more like a natural disaster?

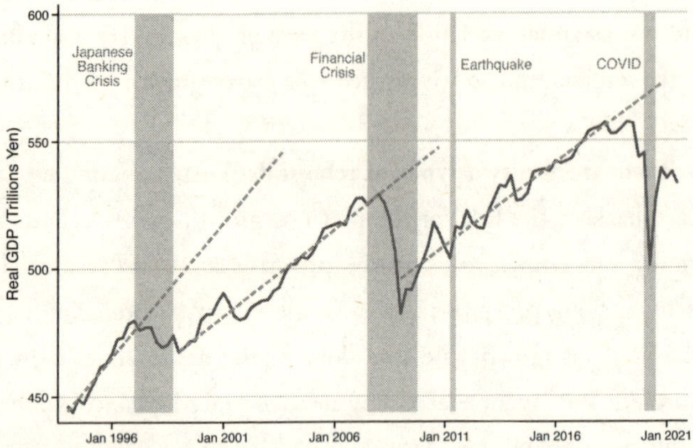

Figure III-1 depicts Japan's real GDP with linear growth trends (dashed lines). The two financial crises in the late 1990s and 2000s led to permanent drops in real GDP and (more importantly) GDP growth, while the exogenous shock by the Fukushima earthquake did not have long-lasting economic effects.[106]
Source: FRED 2021

Recessions also differ depending on which sectors are the hardest hit and which ones exhibit more resilience. In typical recessions, purchases of durable goods, such as new refrigerators or cars, collapse while non-durable consumption, such as haircuts or restaurant meals, remain relatively stable. This pattern, familiar to macroeconomists, has been turned upside down by the Covid-19 pandemic. The pandemic has had little direct effect on our ability to purchase **durable goods,** but it has increased the health risks of many nondurable consumption activities. As a result, contact-intensive sectors, often pertaining to nondurables, have been the most affected. Durables have been relatively less exposed to the direct impact of Covid-19.

Figure III-2 illustrates the year-on-year change in revenue

across all major industries in the US. Somewhat surprisingly, construction and manufacturing—two of the industries most affected by the 2008 recession—actually experienced large increases. On the other hand, the arts, entertainment, and accommodation and food services sectors dropped massively.

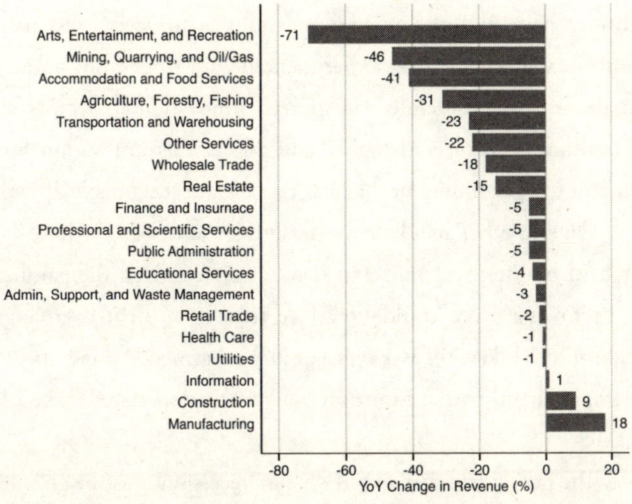

Figure III-2 shows the change in revenue across various sectors of the US economy. Source: Greenwood, Iverson, and Thesmar 2020

Hence, the Covid-19 recession has occurred in at least two directions, which is why it is sometimes called the K-recession. Firms that can easily offer goods or services online have benefited, as evidenced by the Nasdaq rally since March 2020. They represent the upper leg of the K. But business models based on in-person interaction or large crowds have suffered. Amusements parks, cinemas, and restaurants chains all belong to the lower leg of the K, at least at the time of this writing.

Total factor productivity (TFP) diverges between the contact-intensive and the contactless sectors, but if the pandemic lasts long enough, we could also see an innovation boom, which is discussed below. Is cross-sectoral reallocation desirable in the long run? We will explore that idea in the next section.

The dramatic changes that Covid-19 has imposed on our daily routines have also presented opportunities to revisit old habits. Most notably, people have experimented with work-from-home job situations. The pandemic has spurred innovation in sectors such as healthcare, retail, and higher education. This innovation boom might lift the economy in the long run toward sustainable growth.

On the other hand, many businesses and workers have been hit hard by the pandemic. Firms that only survived the pandemic by borrowing more could now face substantial debt overhang or bankruptcy. Likewise, workers could be harmed if long spells of unemployment worsen future employment prospects or cause a loss of skills.

The policy response to a K-shaped recession must be grounded in the special contingencies of the Covid-19 pandemic. Broad-brush stimulus has been inefficient. In a lockdown with closed restaurants, money from stimulus checks could not be spent at restaurants. The limited consumption possibilities (and insufficient precautionary savings prior to the crisis) led US citizens to save a substantial fraction of CARES Act stimulus payments.[107] An alternative and more targeted intervention would be to use digital coupons, with which the Chinese city of Hangzhou experimented.[108] People there received digital coupons on their phones, which in contrast to stimulus checks could only be used for consumption. Moreover, they had a fixed expiry date, which further incentivized short-term consumption. By restricting coupons to certain industries or certain parts of town, these coupons allowed for a highly targeted fiscal policy intervention.

Uncertainty has clouded the path of the pandemic recovery, especially considering the emergence of several virus variants. As a result, there has been a substantial **option value** for policymakers to maintain flexible policies that can be adjusted as the pandemic recession progresses. It has been important to "**keep some powder dry**" to avoid a "what have we done?" situation after the initial "whatever it takes" approach that was used in March 2020. This flexibility helps policymakers to avoid being caught in traps. Avoiding these traps bolsters resilience by helping policymakers retain the flexibility they need to adjust course as the situation unfolds.

CHAPTER 7

Innovation Boosts Long-Lasting Growth

As Microsoft CEO Satya Nadella stated in late April 2020, "We've seen two years' worth of digital transformation in two months."[109] Covid caused large **fundamental changes** in the **structure** of economic activity. The continued need for social distancing created an impetus for more innovation designed to help people adapt economic activities to pandemic pressures. Covid-19 has accelerated existing trends.

Large shocks can also shake up processes. If society was in a trap or suboptimal equilibrium prior to the current crisis, the Covid-19 shock has propelled us out of that trap and toward a new equilibrium. As we can see, a shock can release a society from a trap, unless it is permanent.

Leaps in **telemedicine** and **online education**, two sectors that have seen large price increases over the past decades, have facilitated the adjustment to Covid-19 contingencies.[110] Home offices, sometimes frowned upon before Covid-19, became the norm in

March 2020 for numerous workers—within weeks. In contrast to common wisdom, some people who worked at home have found that they are more productive than in a business office.

R&D expenditures, when compared to normal times, have fallen during this crisis. There are at least two reasons why. First, the R&D efforts of private firms involve large positive externalities. A Covid-19 vaccine, for example, benefits the drug developer and it generates widespread economic gains even though other firms did not bear the R&D costs of developing the vaccine. For this reason, underinvestment in research and development is often the norm. Society would gain much from increased research efforts, but from an individual company's perspective, the costs exceed the benefits—because social benefits are not internalized.

Second, successful research and development can lead companies to cannibalize their own existing products and business models. As an example, an automaker that develops a well-functioning electric car might need to cannibalize its existing business model designed for its combustion engine cars. We will address this issue later, along with coordination problems.

Finally, innovation is the main engine of long-run growth. An innovation boom might contribute to lasting long-run growth, which would make the social contract more resilient. A fast-growing economy with inclusive growth can more easily withstand the sidewinds that future crises might impose on the economy. On the other hand, if changes and trends accelerate too fast, many people could feel left behind. In this way, large shocks like the Covid-19 pandemic test the resilience of the social contract.

Speeding Up Preexisting Trends

By prompting innovation, the Covid-19 pandemic has increased the velocity of many preexisting trends. Home offices, online learning, and telemedicine (mentioned above) were all slow-moving trends that suddenly gained enormous steam when the pandemic forced us to rethink old ways. That presents a potential opportunity. Crises **shake us** in foundational ways that make us reconsider **entrenched habits**. As we are forced to experiment with new technologies and new approaches to daily life, profound improvements can emerge. The work-life balance might improve and technological innovation might speed up.

However, an economy is typically more resilient to slow change than to rapid transitions. If transitions happen too quickly, people can struggle to adjust and resilience can diminish. We emphasized earlier how a faster cyclist is more resilient to side winds. Yet, she is also more at risk of hitting a pothole. Likewise, if social change happens too quickly, many people will find it difficult to keep up, which can lead to social disruption. We would end up in a pothole rather than escape dangerous side winds.

For example, consider how the disintegration of manufacturing communities in many advanced economies, in the latter part of the twentieth century, shifted the economic epicenter to the service sector. More specifically, consider the mining workers in Germany. With the gradual decline of mining and the shutdown of most coal mines, the miners had to switch jobs and acquire new skills. For younger generations, this adjustment was easier. They could acquire new skills more easily and start new careers in non-mining sectors. For older mining workers, the process of change was much more complicated. Experienced coal miners could not become software engineers overnight. This shows us that some people need extensive time to retrain and learn new skills. Moreover, people are often reluctant to start something new.

A common dictum that worries many people is that twenty-first century workers will have to retrain many times. Due to structural shifts in labor markets, that is likely to be true. These structural shifts will also affect how workers should be educated, so that they can build personal resilience in a rapidly changing labor market. Training in highly specialized trades might make those workers less flexible in the wake of large economic changes. In terms of developing individual resilience, it might be more beneficial to develop malleable skills that can be flexibly employed across sectors.

Since rapid change can be hard for a society to handle, we need a more resilient society that can weather large shocks like Covid-19. But we also need more resilience to the slow-moving (and sometimes accelerating) trends that shape modern society.

Principles of Innovation: Cannibalization and QWERTY

Adopting new technologies typically comes at an initial fixed cost before the benefits become apparent.[111] Thus, changes are pushed into the future—unless there is a shakeup like a pandemic.

In addition to consumers' reluctance to adopt new technologies, businesses might also be reluctant to offer them, due to the cost of cannibalizing their existing technologies and business models. For example, Nokia, the world's largest cellphone manufacturer in the early 2000s, did not follow the smartphone trend and had to reorganize into a telecommunications infrastructure company. Another example is retail shopping at physical locations, which due to Covid-19 is now being substituted by online shopping. This shift in the mode of distribution was already under way, but the pandemic significantly accelerated it. Change has come at the cost of cannibalizing the initial store-centered business model of many retailers.

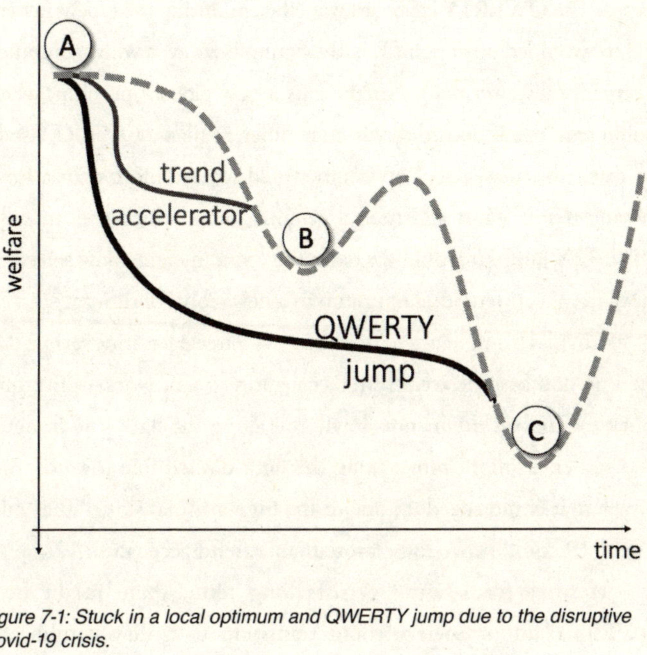

Figure 7-1: Stuck in a local optimum and QWERTY jump due to the disruptive Covid-19 crisis.

Another challenge for technological progress is the coordination of firms and citizens. A well-known example is the **QWERTY problem**, sometimes referred to as the chicken-and-egg problem. The QWERTY keyboard emerged in the nineteenth century as the only keyboard in English-speaking countries. It was based on the need to reduce mechanical breakdowns on typewriters (!) by minimizing the rate at which typewriter hammers crashed into each other. It is actually an inefficient setup for a computer keyboard, but the cost of switching is far too large.[112]

Figure 7-1 illustrates the challenge. When typewriters were first introduced, people experimented with various keyboards until the emergence of the QWERTY format became more popular than all other setups. The **QWERTY** keyboard was efficient during the typewriter era, and so we ended up at point B in the figure above even when computers emerged. However, point C represents a new global optimum, which would require a keyboard that is quite different than a QWERTY style. To reach this new global optimum would require more than a slow-moving trend. We would need a genuine jump, which we can call a QWERTY jump. It would shake up the economy and allow society to move from a current local optimum to a new global optimum.

Covid-19 might therefore have two effects on innovation. On the one hand, some trends are accelerating (e.g., work-from-home jobs).[113] The ball might not slowly roll along the dark line in figure 7-1; rather, it might move along the light dashed line toward point B, where it could speed up due to the higher initial slope. That said, Covid-19 could prove to be more than a trend accelerator.

If **work-from-home** persists long term, there might be a QWERTY jump. Society could transition to a new equilibrium (point C) with substantially more work-from-home arrangements than would have occurred had the pandemic never happened. In turn, the work-from-home shift might lead to a substantial productivity gain. As we discuss in this section, the shakeup induced by the pandemic might lead to a better long-run outcome.

Shaking Off Regulatory Shackles

Regulation can constrain technological advances. The Covid-19 pandemic has disrupted government coordination and regulation.[114] Some think that changes in these areas are not moving fast enough, given the large potential for improved social benefits, such as in telemedicine or AI.[115] The urgency of the crisis has induced changes that otherwise would have taken years or even decades to occur. We will return to the topic of telemedicine. For now, notice that the need for social distancing all but forced a rapid shift toward telemedicine, which has replaced some in-person consultations.

Regulation, however, interacts with innovation, especially in the digital age. If we over-regulate ourselves and stifle creativity, we might lose out on critical innovations. When regulatory bodies freeze the status quo, precluding innovation, we might never make new discoveries—not for lack of human ingenuity, but for lack of openness to new ideas.[116]

Examples of Innovation

There are many areas in which Covid-19 could continue to accelerate innovation. I address some of the primary innovation trends that relate to resilience in this section of the chapter.

Advancement in Life Sciences, Telemedicine, Vaccines

A prominent example of innovation that contributes to future resilience is vaccine development, particularly mRNA vaccines. The **mRNA technology** has been explored for years as a possible remedy against cancer. Now that mRNA technology has been successfully implemented, researchers see a potential boost to innovation in the genetics of individually targeted cancer treatments.[117] The mRNA technology also offers promise in the fight against malaria. Until 2021, only one vaccine against malaria has been brought to market, and its efficacy of 39 percent is relatively low. BioNTech aims to have a vaccine candidate with 90 percent efficacy at the clinical trial stage by 2022.[118]

Digitization also enhances health resilience by enabling better information gathering. For example, if health agencies are better equipped to collect data, future pandemic responses might be more effective. More flexibility also would allow us to reallocate health resources to where they are most needed.

In the longer run, artificial intelligence potentially offers huge potential benefits for medical diagnoses and treatments. Building on big data, artificial intelligence could assist in identifying cross-correlations before a patient sees a doctor.[119] Doctors would be better informed, and those diagnostic improvements would make treatments more efficient.

Telemedicine is rapidly becoming more widely used. Progress in health innovations is usually slower than in other areas because of privacy concerns and extensive regulations.[120] However, Covid-19 has rendered online consultations with doctors almost routine thereby loosening regulatory shackles.[121] Delivery of prescription drugs used to be an offline activity, but now Amazon, for example, can process and deliver prescribed medications to customers.

Management: New Hierarchies

The move to online meetings and conferences **overturns hierarchies** and the **dissemination of information**. Prior to Covid-19, many banks held key talks about M&As, for example, with only senior executives. However, these meetings have moved online since March 2020. Effectively, it makes no difference whether ten people are on a video conference call or one hundred. Now junior staff can be invited to these high-level meetings and learn firsthand from the senior employees. The advantages are manifold. First, junior staff are enabled to learn faster by observing how experienced staff members handle high-profile talks or negotiations; second, providing junior staff with early exposure to meetings probably boosts their motivation.

Online meetings also have an added efficiency gain. Top executives used to provide debriefings for staff members who did not attend meetings. This step can now be eliminated, which saves time and might facilitate the transmission of information. Taken as a whole, online meetings can essentially create a fast track for new recruits to become leaders.

Many processes have become increasingly democratized and the information gaps within the hierarchies of firms have been substantially reduced. To be clear, these changes do not indicate an increase of flat hierarchies. The hierarchical gradient might be preserved, but all members throughout a hierarchy's ladder can now have more equal access to information about specific business issues.

As a related matter, administrative meetings in institutions are increasingly conducted online. Prior to the Covid-19 pandemic, organizations relied on in-person meetings that usually required participants to travel.[122] These implicit barriers implied selection. Only some members could attend administrative meetings. Now everybody can participate online, listen to the issues, and contribute. There is a clear tradeoff: Although participation and attendance have been democratized, governance might become more complicated as more voices need to be heard. Of course, there are also other large drawbacks. Many of the informal but confidential meetings that occur during in-person meetings might not take place, for fear of being recorded on a video conference platform.

Work from Home

Covid-19 has dramatically altered attitudes toward working from home. Previously, working from home was considered to be somewhat unproductive, but it has rapidly become the norm for a substantial fraction of the workforce.[123] Work-from-home arrangements support resilience by giving more flexibility to workers who can be more easily reassigned or relocated. The pandemic has dramatically diminished the **stigma** associated with working from home.[124]

A less-explored topic is the impact of work-from-home jobs on impromptu social interactions. **Watercooler meetings**, coffee breaks, and random encounters in an office hallway are eliminated in the video conferencing world. Unlike many in-person office encounters, a video call requires an ex-ante purpose. On the one hand, the elimination of small talk might increase productivity by reducing activities that are not strictly considered work. Many executives have noticed that the efficiency of online meetings is better because they tend to be more focused. However, casual interactions might be critical to maintaining healthy work relationships or to brainstorming ideas about projects. Not every watercooler meeting is a waste of time. Instead, these interactions also serve the purpose of sharing information and discussing ideas. Additionally, there is often a hands-on component, even for white-collar work. For example, engineers often work collaboratively by using a whiteboard, and architects often work with physical blueprints and models. These activities are much more difficult to manage virtually.

How will working from home evolve in the future? A substantial challenge with home-based work is how to monitor employees and ensure they perform their tasks. Software exists to take screenshots of employees and their desktops, or to record keystrokes on a keyboard, but such surveillance raises questions about privacy.[125]

Monitoring performance will likely move from **input control to output control**. In this approach, managers check workers' outputs and evaluate them based on project completion. However, this brings its own problems. When tasks are clearly assigned to individual workers, output control is relatively straightforward, but when a team collaborates on a project, the output-control method might invite shirking.

Estimates suggest that only about 40 percent of US jobs can be done from home.[126] Moreover, these occupations are concentrated among high-skill workers. As such, the emergence of home offices might amplify preexisting inequalities as most home office workers are less affected by other slow-moving trends such as automation.[127] Ultimately, the necessity for interpersonal physical interactions or access to specific fixed equipment precludes many at-home jobs. Some activities, such as counseling services or customer relations, that are amenable to work-from-home situations might suffer from lower effectiveness.

Overall, the largest potential for home-office work is found in finance, insurance, management, and professional services. On the other end of the spectrum, manufacturing, construction, and agriculture have almost no work-from-home potential.

The available survey evidence supports these deliberations. Panels A and B in figure 7-2 illustrate how work-from-home arrangements are expected to persist in the future.[128] The first panel below reports the share of paid days worked from home during the pandemic, and the estimated number of days that employers will allow workers to work from home after the pandemic. Employers plan to permit employees to work from home for one or two days after the pandemic, but 30 percent of employees prefer to work from home for five days after the end of the pandemic (second panel below). So, a hybrid model might emerge in the coming years. Many workers might routinely work at home for a day or two and also spend significant time at their offices.[129]

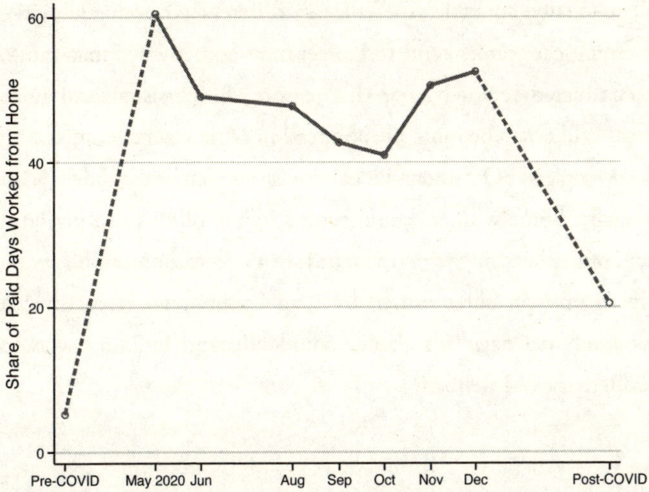

Figure 7-2: Panel A above shows the share of paid days worked from home (in percent) prior, during, and post-pandemic. Panel B below shows the desired number of paid days per week worked from home post-pandemic. Source: Bloom, Markus' Academy 2020

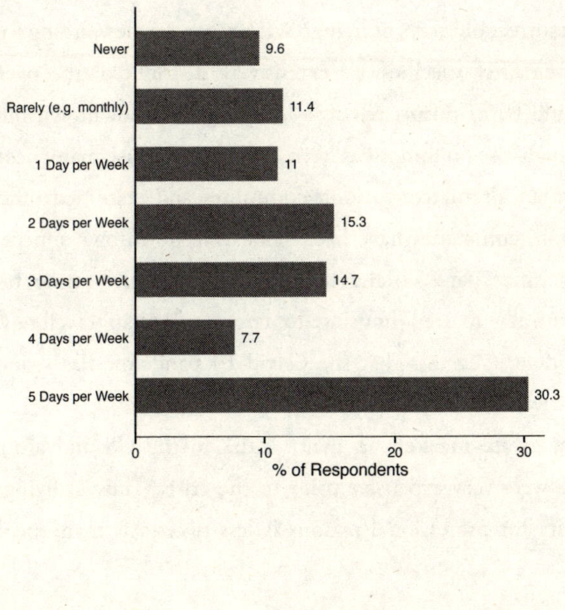

Globally, countries specialize in different economic activities. Emerging economies tend to concentrate on activities that cannot be conducted remotely. For this reason, the persistence of home offices is likely to be more pronounced in advanced economies.

Google CEO Sundar Pichai envisions a hybrid model for his company. Some workers could return to the office for a period of time, but others might permanently work from home. This would help to ease pressures caused by long commutes—often three or four hours per day. This change could substantially boost workers' productivity and wellbeing.

Urbanization: The Donut Effect

What impact might change in workplace preferences have on urban geography? Is the tendency to live in suburbs here to stay, or will we resurrect old ways of living? With more people working from home, even after vaccines are extensively distributed, the overall result could be a "**donut effect.**"[130] Demand for downtown office space in high-rise buildings has been declining because many people now have an alternative to long commutes and crammed offices. In addition, companies have been relocating downtown offices to suburban office parks. Many workers have been relocating from small, centrally located housing to larger suburban dwellings.[131] Some evidence suggests that the Covid-19 pandemic has reduced the attractiveness of "intense urban concentration."[132]

Real estate markets in major cities in the US and around the globe were very expensive prior to the crisis. Thus, if living in a large city for professional reasons is less necessary, many people might be lured by cheaper house prices to the suburbs or to rural areas, especially if social life in cities remains restricted.[133] As home office options remove geographic restrictions, many European couples with a dream of living in Italy's Tuscany region are seeing an opportunity to have that dream come true.[134]

California's Silicon Valley might also see a substantial overhaul. Sky-high housing prices and rents in San Francisco have long imposed a strain on companies to hire or retain workers in the Bay Area. With physical presence at work becoming obsolete, workers have begun to disperse into areas with more affordable house prices. Cities like Sacramento, Reno, or Boise have seen a surge in rents while demand has fallen for rentals in San Francisco and San José. These trends point to a potential larger shift with uncertain implications for Silicon Valley. Some worry that the economic spillovers from frequent interaction in geographical proximity will be reduced. But Silicon Valley could broaden its appeal by drawing in workers from outside the Bay Area so as to continue its spectacular growth.

As migration to the suburbs continues, there could be adverse consequences for centrally located retailers. Most people who work from home used to work in city centers. In his assessment of Manhattan alone, Nick Bloom predicts a 10 percent ($10 billion) drop in retail expenditures.[135] The move toward online shopping also has the potential to change the urban landscape. Many medium-scale cities in Germany, for example, see large retailers shutting down their stores and, in the US, the attractiveness of malls might shrink permanently.

Covid-19 has triggered a redesign of cities and public transportation. For example, New York added new bike lanes and closed certain streets to traffic. Lisbon, Barcelona, and Paris are adding dozens of kilometers of bike lanes.[136] It is not clear how these two forces—renewal of urban space and reversal of urbanization—will play out. At the turn of the millennium, the internet revolution and 9/11 led many observers to believe that big cities would suffer. However, the exact opposite happened, leading many to wonder why the impact of Covid-19 would be different.

Brick and Mortar vs. Online Shopping

Prior to Covid-19 there was already a trend toward online shopping. However, there were also some movements in the opposite direction. Amazon, founded as an online shop, moved into select brick-and-mortar locations and began offering an overhauled customer experience with automatic checkouts.

Traditional American retail chains, such as Neiman Marcus or JCPenney, were already under pressure prior to the pandemic. The rapid acceleration of a preexisting trend away from their core business models forced those chains into bankruptcy. Here again we see a K-type feature of the Covid-19 recession. Amazon hired one hundred thousand additional workers in the US during the pandemic to cope with additional demand. The shift toward online retail has bolstered resilience in relation to future pandemics, but it has simultaneously increased our vulnerability to a large-scale cyberattack, particularly in light of the fact that online retail is highly concentrated among a few large firms.

Online Learning

Similar to working from home, many people have perceived online learning to be ineffective. Some instructors have been concerned about students who are distracted in the classroom. Without the (perhaps modest) discipline that a classroom setting provides, these instructors have concluded that online education would be doomed or mediocre. Others have seen online education as a flexible way to serve the necessity of life-long learning, which contributes to resilience.

Despite these long-standing concerns, several trends emerged during the 2010s. Massive open online courses (MOOCs) such as Coursera, EdX, Lynda, and LinkedIn Learning have disseminated barrier-free education around the world. An internet connection can enable thousands of people to participate in these online education courses. In that context, the Covid-19 pandemic has again accelerated preexisting trends. Digitizing the classroom experience has been a major topic of discussion on boards of education for years. But the Covid-19 crisis forced the education system to move fully online within weeks, a trend that otherwise might have taken decades.[137]

The effects of this large-scale educational experiment will fuel an enormous body of research for years to come. The main questions are related to the importance of personal interaction and peer effects. How much do students learn from peers in the classroom? How much of that is lost in a virtual setting? At the higher education level, a related question is about the importance of networking activities. Is the quality of professional networks formed via virtual connections comparable to face-to-face networking?

Online education also offers distinct advantages. The opportunity costs for students are greatly reduced. Geographical constraints are eliminated. Working in Chicago while doing a part-time MBA on the West Coast becomes feasible, and without a daunting travel schedule. Furthermore, students enjoy guest lectures by famous speakers who might be reluctant to physically travel long distances for a short lecture.

To balance online education with the need for personal interaction, MBA programs are now offering hybrid solutions. For many years, Duke Fuqua's Global MBA has allowed students from around the globe to follow an evening MBA at their favorite time while offering occasional in-person meetings. MIT offers an online micro-master's degree in finance, which can be a gateway to acceptance into the regular master's degree in finance for the best performing students. The online micro-master's degree serves as a screening device to select the best of fifty thousand online students.

Another potential trend is a version of the **flipped classroom**. Lectures are often easier to conduct online, perhaps through prerecorded delivery methods. In comparison, small group interactions, such as sessions with teaching assistants (TAs) tend to be more beneficial when conducted in-person. Education models with in-depth online lectures, which are not much different than large-group offline lectures, could be complemented by small-group, in-person interactive sessions. This concept is not a twenty-first century innovation. Oxbridge and Princeton professors, for example, have long been conducting intensive-learning, small-group meetings with a handful of students.

As mentioned above, the growing prevalence of online education could facilitate life-long learning. As flexible careers replace traditional career paths, such as working for forty years in the same company, workers will need to learn new skills when changing jobs. Technological change also demands workers to be adaptable. Online training courses could complement in-person training. Life-long education and reskilling allow people to adapt and become more resilient to structural changes.

Digital Money and Data

The move toward online shopping also reduces the utility of carrying physical cash. Again, the Covid-19 crisis has accelerated the preexisting shift to digital payments. That does not mean that cash has disappeared. When physical stores and banks had to shut down, some people withdrew cash as a safe store of value in the initial weeks of the pandemic, a trend that was more pronounced in Europe.[138]

The traditional model of finance revolves around banks that take deposits and provide loans; meanwhile, the massive changes in the payments sector have only received limited attention. Chinese online payments platforms, such as Alipay and WeChat Pay, revolve fully around payments. Payments platforms can collect huge quantities of data. Those billions of transactions that Alipay collects over time are evaluated with machine learning algorithms to infer, as precisely as possible, the relationships between individual characteristics and default probabilities. Connecting payments data to a wide range of other individual characteristics greatly contributes to improving those predictions. Ultimately, customer information can be sold to banks or asset managers.

The world leader in digital payments is China where the ID

card, payments system, phone, and physical presence have all been centralized. In China, cash is basically superfluous.[139] As a result of the Covid-19 crisis, this transition is speeding up everywhere. Many emerging and developing countries have facilitated digital transactions with measures such as fee reductions or reduced regulatory requirements.[140]

Data from payments transactions is very valuable if it can be combined with other types of data from online platforms. It enables the creation of better recommender systems by using machine learning. Another application for this data is credit scoring, an area in which machine learning algorithms can compete with established credit bureaus.[141] The availability of large datasets in finance has been shifting informational advantages away from customers to service providers.[142] Traditionally, economists have assumed that an individual or a firm would know more about their probability of default than the bank. But with big data and machine learning algorithms, the bank can forecast default probabilities more accurately. Data from social media might also reveal information about which the individual is unaware.

Information is also critical for the business of insurance. Traditionally, insurance buyers know more about their own risks than insurance companies. As the informational advantage shifts away from customers, information rents are also shifting to platforms that process big data.

Other Digital Trends

Digital tools are being used to improve labor market matching as well. For example, during India's pandemic lockdown, many migrant workers returned to their home villages. They were reluctant to return to large cities unless there was work. A new digital business card service, similar to LinkedIn but for poor Indian workers, has facilitated more than one million successful job matches to date.[143] Such changes have helped workers adjust to the Covid-19 pandemic and thus will improve resilience during future crises.

Likewise, online tools such as LinkedIn have facilitated searches for new jobs. Research by the advisory firm Gartner suggests that many workers increasingly spend time using online job portals.[144] Workers whose home office efforts are not sufficiently recognized by their firms might be the first to leave as job vacancies surge at the end of the pandemic.

The ongoing widespread shutdown of social activities has also accelerated the move toward virtual interaction. Beyond traditional video games, online concerts, and streamed movies, numerous video call platforms have become hubs for leisure activities, such as a poker game with friends.

Deloitte's research reveals that "[one] third of consumers have, for the first time, subscribed to a video gaming service, used a cloud gaming service, or watched sports or a virtual sporting event."[145] Likewise, Twitch's livestreams of sports have reached record audiences.[146] South Korea has moved ahead of other nations in this area, with many people engaging in virtual reality experiences. In the future, people could find it increasingly difficult to focus for deep reading and intensive analytical tasks, which is impossible when people are simultaneously interacting with social media. Becoming addicted to video games or virtual life is another form of trap because it might impede people's ability to rejoin the labor force and bounce back after a shock.[147]

CHAPTER 8

Scarring

The absence of economic imbalances prior to the Covid-19 crisis, which is in sharp contrast to the housing bubble in the early 2000s, might suggest that there will be a more rapid recovery after the pandemic compared to a decade ago. However, the severity of the Covid-19 recession could lead to **long-term scarring** of workers and firms. Economic and financial scars hinder resilience. Deep scars might even trap the economy and lead to a long and persistent decline in economic activity. The pandemic has caused many businesses to close and has prevented others from operating at full capacity. Those outcomes have led other firms to suffer from temporary illiquidity, putting them at risk of insolvency in the medium term.[148] This is another crucial difference in relation to the 2008 financial crisis, when many efforts centered on restoring balance sheets in the financial sector instead of the nonfinancial corporate sector.

Severe crises can scar the economy along at least three dimensions. First, they can scar people by diminishing optimism and willingness to take risks. Second, labor markets might be scarred as human capital erodes during prolonged unemployment spells. Third, firms can be scarred by debt overhang, especially if bankruptcy processes are prolonged. All of these can hamper the economy and reduce the long-run growth rate.

Shifts in Optimism, Preferences, and Risk Attitude

Deep crises like pandemics are rare occurrences. The last major global pandemic was the 1918 influenza crisis (the Spanish flu).[149] The Covid-19 crisis has served as a powerful reminder that global pandemics are still a serious risk. Theories of rational **learning** predict that people will perceive the world to be riskier after a pandemic because they update their beliefs in relation to experiences.[150] As a result, they increase precautionary savings.[151] In that sense, higher perceived **risk and risk-aversion** could become separate drags on demand as the economy attempts to recover.[152] Historically, people who experienced the Great Depression engaged in less risk-taking behavior later. People who lived through high inflation during the 1970s had persistently higher expectations of inflation than later cohorts.[153]

Learning about the risk of black swans (unpredictable events) challenges the rational mind. When it comes to small probability events, behavioral biases abound. Countless experiments by Daniel Kahneman and Amos Tversky, two pioneers of behavioral economics, highlight how small probabilities are often fully ignored or disproportionately overweighted. Prior to the onset of Covid-19, people ignored the risk of pandemics. During this pandemic, many underestimated the risk of a subsequent wave, which undermined resilience. This phenomenon has been labeled the "resilience illusion." That said, in the near future, people will probably overestimate the likelihood of pandemics.

Over time, there can be a **cycle between** these **two biases**: an initial underestimation of tail risks followed by severe overextrapolation. The perceived risk of financial crises is typically distorted the same way. Despite the fact that financial crises regularly happen around the globe, they are often characterized as rare events. This is driven by **recency biases**. When a financial crisis happens, economic agents over-extrapolate beliefs so as to emphasize a substantial probability that a future financial crisis is imminent. But later on, if a sequence of favorable events happens, the risk is neglected. It then takes a large shock or a series of negative shocks for another belief revision to occur.[154] This bias suggests that scarring **might die out** over time and that **resilience might resume.**

Figure 8-1 illustrates another dimension of risk-aversion with the potential of long-run scarring. Survey respondents were asked to complete the following sentence: "After a vaccine arrives, I would return to pre-Covid activities . . ."[155] Only 27.5 percent of those surveyed reported that they would completely revert to their pre-pandemic lives. Avoidance of subways, taxis, crowded elevators, or eating out could continue for years to come, reshaping behavior and several economic sectors.

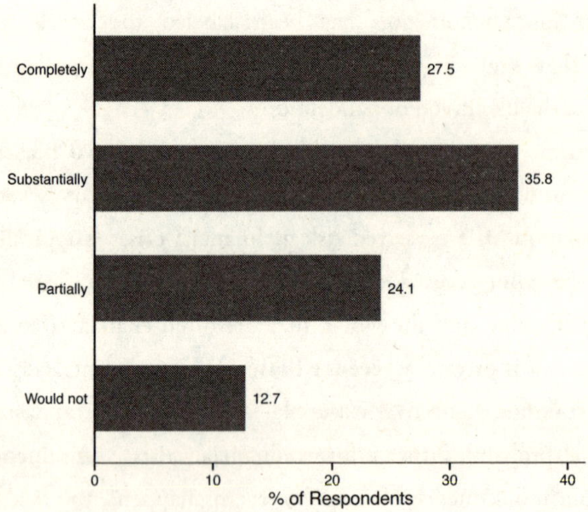

Figure 8-1: People's expectations to return to pre-pandemic activities after a vaccine arrives. Source: Bloom, Markus' Academy 2020

If increasing risk-aversion permeates normal everyday activities, more people could change their perceptions of future diseases as well. Until 2019, when people caught a light flu, it was common to "power through" and go to work without facing much social stigma. Now that people have become more aware of health externalities related to Covid-19, such behaviors may not be tolerated in the future. People who catch the flu now might be much more willing to stay home for the common good of their fellow office workers.

For older workers, the desire to avoid exposure to SARS-CoV-2 in the workplace is particularly strong. Because their stock market portfolios have usually performed well, despite the severe recession of 2020, they have found early retirement to be desirable and more affordable. This could trigger a paradigm shift in the wake of the pandemic. Rather than living to work, more people might be guided by a "live to live" approach.

Looking back in history, the Black Death plague in Europe during the fourteenth century profoundly reshaped the survivors' attitudes to life.[156] Some historians argue that this shift in preferences paved the way for the Renaissance. Survivors appreciated life more and wanted to enjoy their existence. During this time, the Medici family and others emerged as the first arts patrons.

Labor Scarring

Labor Match Scarring

As a result of the Covid-19 pandemic, the US unemployment rate jumped and then rapidly collapsed. But that picture is somewhat misleading. It should not be construed as a sign of strong resilience in the American labor market. Many workers were temporarily furloughed and then recalled once businesses reopened. This pattern merely underpins the extraordinary spike in unemployment rates over the first couple of months of the recession. If we look at the bigger picture, beyond the pandemic-specific forces, the unemployment recovery from this recession might look like previous recoveries. In fact, Bob Hall and Marianna Kudlyak document that US employment recovered steadily during each recession since the Great Depression at basically the same speed.[157]

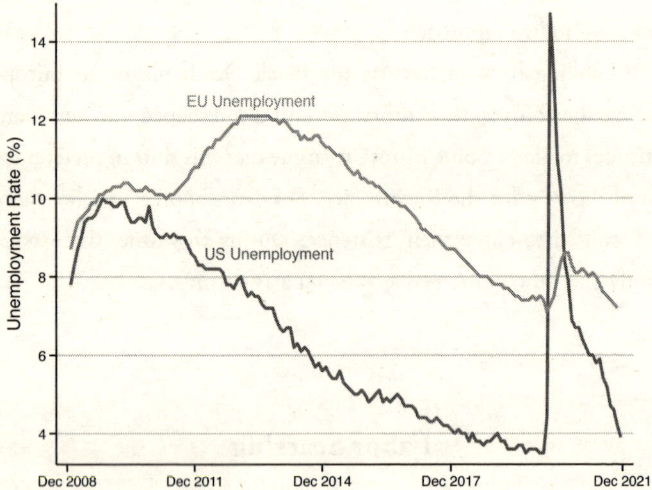

Figure 8-2: Unemployment rate in US and Europe. Source: FRED 2021

Figure 8-2 demonstrates how unemployment evolved in the US and Europe since the 2008 financial crisis. The spike in the US unemployment rate during the Covid-19 crisis is evident. While the US mainly relied on laying off workers and providing generous unemployment benefits, the European model centered around *Kurzarbeit.* This term means that workers retain their jobs, even while not working, and the government picks up much of the wage bill. (*Kurzarbeit* replacement rates are typically below 100 percent of the wage.) The long-run post-pandemic distribution of economic activity will determine which of these policy approaches is more successful. *Kurzarbeit* preserves **employment matches**, but it prevents the reallocation of labor, which is necessary for an economy to offer different jobs after a shock like the pandemic. European nations might discover substantial **hidden unemployment** if many of the jobs subject to *Kurzarbeit* do not return.[158] On the other hand, the US model of **strategic unemployment** breaks employment links and might lead to substantial labor market scarring.

Beyond preserving labor matches, *Kurzarbeit* also insures workers against macroeconomic shocks. They retain, for the most part, salary and other benefits. This approach achieves the social objective of providing insurance and resilience to workers.[159]

The key determinant for evaluating which approach is superior, in relation to providing long-run resilience, is the nature of technological progress. If there are large QWERTY jumps with new sectors emerging and existing sectors declining, the US approach would facilitate the reallocation of labor. In other words, if people permanently reduce the frequency at which they eat indoors at restaurants or shift permanently to more online shopping, *Kurzarbeit* might lock workers in declining sectors for too long. On the other hand, if a shock turns out to be short-lived, it would be preferable to maintain employment links.

Until June 2020, most employment gains in the US derived from rehiring former employees. This indicates the importance of preserving employer-employee links.[160] However, because the pandemic has been rather prolonged, support for workers and firms might need to shift toward facilitating reallocation across sectors. If the post-pandemic economy proves to be significantly different than the pre-pandemic economy, extensive subsidies to preserve employment matches would prevent the necessary reallocation of labor to new and expanding sectors.

Overall, there have been relatively few efforts in the US to protect employment links.[161] The main policy program aimed at maintaining the relationships between employers and their employees has been the paycheck protection program (PPP), which extended largely forgivable loans to employers on the condition that they designate the funds for payroll purposes. The program was poorly targeted; many loans went to large firms while education and research institutions, and state and local governments were marginalized.[162] It is also possible that the limited impact of PPP on employment occurred because many firms that took out the loans did not intend to lay off workers in the first place.[163]

Human Capital Scarring

Studies of college students have shown that the state of the economy in the graduation year matters substantially for how cohorts fare in the labor market, even years after they graduate.[164] Graduating from college during a recession leaves long-lasting scars on workers who for many years do not catch up to those who entered the labor market earlier. Similarly, being out of work erodes human capital. If they lose skills or fail to catch up with new trends, unemployed workers can face lasting labor market scars after losing a job.[165]

Hysteresis: The Delayed Recovery

Economists Olivier Blanchard and Larry Summers coined the term *hysteresis* in labor economics. It refers to situations in which labor markets do not fully rebound to previous unemployment rates before another crisis hits thereby leading to even higher unemployment.[166] More generally, in the physical and material sciences, hysteresis refers to a delayed recovery.

More recent work suggests that there might be hysteresis effects in the labor market, but the evidence is not conclusive.[167] Hence, labor scarring or technological shifts during recessions can lead to hysteresis effects in the labor market. These effects are defined as a significant delayed recovery from a recession, possibly associated with a higher long-run unemployment rate.

Firm Scarring

In the wake of the 2008 financial crisis, most government efforts in the US centered around supporting households, including many who had mortgage balances that exceeded the value of their houses after the housing bubble burst. The economy recovered slowly in many countries, particularly in Europe where the initial shock was followed by the euro crisis. In short, resilience was sluggish and only some emerging markets bounced back strongly. Unlike in 2008, the initial shock in 2020 primarily affected the firm sector, partly because the CARES Act in the US provided generous household support.

Debt Overhang

The Covid-19 crisis has been an unprecedented cash-flow shock for businesses, particularly in the contact-intensive sector. When cash flows dried up in March 2020, financial markets witnessed a "dash for cash." Firms began to draw down existing commitments on credit lines so as to build up liquidity buffers.[168] Credit lines allowed firms to borrow from a bank, usually with prespecified conditions and limits. The undrawn part of a credit line, which had not yet been borrowed, therefore represented an easily accessible buffer for companies when cash was quickly needed.

After the pandemic's initial impact on the financial decisions of firms, the danger of a second-round impact on real decisions emerged, most importantly in relation to real investments. Financially constrained firms without cash flows typically cut back on their investments, which is similar to how firms react when they foresee a cloud of uncertainty about the future of their business models.

Companies that are excessively leveraged after the pandemic will experience a long-term, persistent drag on growth, which is an impediment to resilience. **Debt overhang**, the overaccumulation of debt, creates an impetus for using cash flows to deleverage rather than invest. Holding back on investment will delay the recovery and increase the risk of long-run scarring.

Overall, measures that support firms and households are crucial. The multipliers of these policy interventions might be much larger than the usual Keynesian multipliers because relief measures preserve the capital stock of small and medium enterprises (SMEs) and the human capital stock of households.[169]

Small versus Large Firms

As the K-shape of the Covid-19 recession illustrates, the pandemic shock has affected various economic sectors in diverse ways. It has also impacted small and large firms differently.

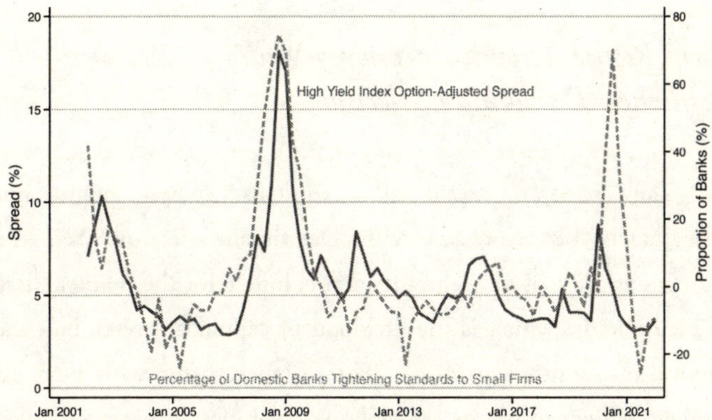

Figure 8-3: Financing conditions for large versus small firms. Source: FRED 2021

Figure 8-3 shows that credit spreads for large firms soared in March 2020. Then they returned almost to pre-pandemic levels. However, the lending standards of banks, which are critical for a small firm's cost of external finance, tightened considerably more during the initial phase of the Covid-19 crisis. The Fed's interventions in the corporate bond market stabilized the bond spreads, and subsequent bank profits also loosened bank lending standards. Thus, the K-recession across industries was partially mirrored in financing conditions across small and large firms. Small businesses, many of which were in the effected sectors, found themselves in a double-bind situation. They were unable to supply their services and they faced high funding costs from banks. Large firms in the US, much more than small firms, benefited from the Fed's corporate bond purchase programs, as discussed in the next chapter.

Firm Resilience versus Economy-Wide Resilience: Darwinian Selection

The corporate sector of a capitalist society might not immediately be associated with Darwinian selection. Yet, the permanent cycle of new entrants that compete for the market share of incumbents, which is the lifeblood of capitalism, resembles the survival-of-the-fittest principle. For instance, firms with business models challenged by the smartphone revolution either overhauled their product lines or disappeared. Kodak, for example, once the market leader in photography, missed the trends toward digital cameras and the shift from cameras to smartphones. In response, the company recentered its business model around digital printing services. This anecdotal evidence highlights the critical role of Schumpeterian creative destruction: New entrants challenge incumbent firms and drive innovation, and those innovations drive economic growth. In economies at the technological frontier, innovation continuously threatens leaders and forces them to continue innovating.

Figure 8-4 plots the fraction of public firms with negative earnings per share (EPS). To account for the fact that many startups report losses in their early years, the figure only presents firms that are at least five years old. At least 20 percent of mature US public firms commonly report a negative EPS. Part of this fraction is driven by smaller firms, but about 10 percent of large firms report a negative EPS each quarter. Moreover, the fraction of firms with negative earnings is increasing, mostly driven by smaller firms with accounting losses.

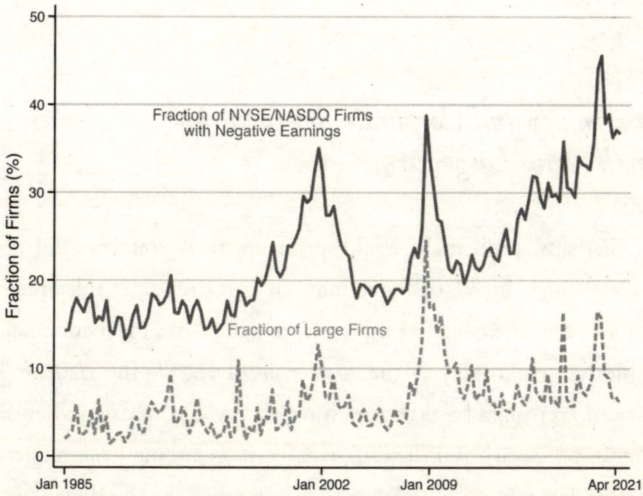

Figure 8-4: Fraction of mature firms (older than five years) with negative earnings. The solid line is the fraction of firms, older than five years, on the major American stock exchanges, which have negative earnings. The dashed line captures the same fraction but only on the sample of large firms. Source: WRDS, CRSP-Compustat 2021

Risk-taking is critical for a capitalist economy. If no firm in the economy had negative earnings, would it be time to rejoice? Probably not. This would most likely indicate a lack of risk-taking. Moreover, it is important to weed-out bad firms. Resources that are stuck in firms with grim future prospects eventually need to be reallocated to more productive firms. As highlighted earlier in the book, the economy bounces back faster through creative and disruptive innovation, even if that means that some firms will not make profits and exit the market. After the initial phase of the Covid-19 crisis, the US observed a record level of new business formation in sectors that are relatively pandemic-proof, including online retail.[170]

Bankruptcy and Corporate Restructuring: Small versus Large Firms

Perhaps surprisingly, bankruptcies in many countries did not increase much in 2020. Sometimes, as in Germany, bankruptcies have actually fallen due to a moratorium that relaxes the requirement to file for bankruptcy if the firm is insolvent.[171] The tradeoff is between averting a **bankruptcy wave** that would threaten a febrile economic recovery and the long-run losses stemming from reduced **creative destruction**. According to Schumpeter, creative destruction is the main engine of long-run growth. So, allowing too many **zombies** (unproductive firms) to survive might be good for the individual firms, but it can create a trap for the overall economy.[172] In other words, as banks roll over existing loans to protect zombie firms from realizing losses, resources get trapped in those unproductive firms. An excessive number of zombie firms undermines resilience by creating a persistent drag on growth.

These considerations connect to our earlier discussion on limited liability. On the one hand, limited liability provides downside insurance to entrepreneurs that can encourage risk-taking. But in the case of zombie firms, it can lead to inefficient continuations that hold back the entire economy.

This tradeoff also depends on the persistence of a shock. If it is temporary and the economy reverts back to its old equilibrium, a moratorium on bankruptcy facilitates the recovery just as *Kurzarbeit* preserves employment matches. But if the shock is long-lasting, a sustained need for resource reallocation and corporate restructuring will be needed.

Figure 8-5 sketches the normal process for US firms in financial distress.[173] There are two basic outcomes for a distressed firm: restructuring of debt and operations followed by continuation or liquidation. Both outcomes can be achieved formally through the bankruptcy court system or alternatively via private negotiations. The court option can be a powerful outside threat in negotiations with creditors.

Strikingly, 91.7 percent of firms that stop operating do not go through the bankruptcy court system. Insolvency does not always imply formal bankruptcy. For those firms that choose to file for bankruptcy, the vast majority (84.4 percent) file for Chapter 7 liquidation. For the remaining firms that file for Chapter 11, conversely, a bankruptcy judge decides whether they are sent into liquidation or into a reorganization and continuation process. The idea behind Chapter 11 is to reorganize the debt of financially distressed firms that are economically viable while liquidating firms that have no economic prospects.

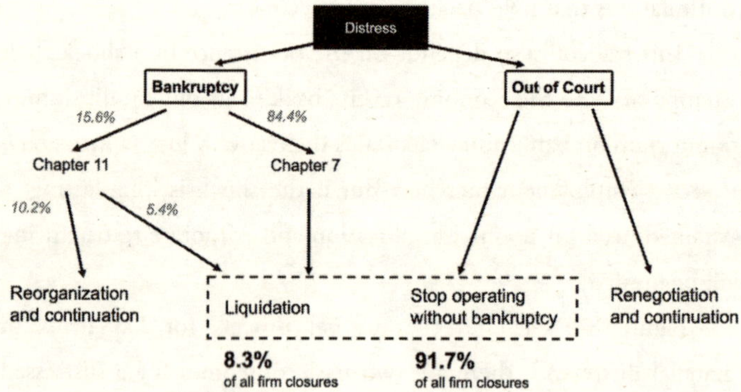

Figure 8-5: Overview of restructuring procedures of firms. Source: Greenwood, Iverson, and Thesmar 2020

Polarization in the corporate sector exists among large firms with ample cash buffers, which makes them much better prepared for shocks than weak capitalized firms with low liquidity, a group that includes many small and medium enterprises (SMEs).[174] In addition, large firms can easily be restructured under Chapter 11 while small firms often face the prospect of Chapter 7 liquidation.

This creates a rationale for bailing out SMEs to help avoid the erosion of firm value. In the absence of debt relief, firms would need to use scarce liquidity primarily to service debt rather than to maintain their workforces and capital, which would slow the post-shock scale-up of economic activity.[175] Many firms ultimately succumb to debt service obligations and end with Chapter 7 liquidation. This can lead to many inefficient bankruptcies in which firms with a post-shock high value could end up being liquidated due to liquidity shortfalls. Even for firms that manage to avoid liquidation, high debt can be a drag on operations during the recovery.[176] **Both channels hurt the economy's resilience.**

In contrast, bailouts for large corporations that can file for Chapter 11 bankruptcy are a waste of money because their shareholders are not essential for running day-to-day operations. The modern corporation is owned by shareholders who let management run the firm. In contrast, small firms are managed by the owner. Subsidizing large corporations only enables equity holders in those companies to delay a Chapter 11 filing longer than is socially valuable. This should not occur, especially when bankruptcy restructuring costs are relatively low.[177] Despite the inefficiencies, the bankruptcy system is nonetheless crucial, especially when we consider the surge in bankruptcy filings that accompanies most recessions.[178]

An additional complication is that bankruptcy courts might face increasing caseloads. There are two alternative approaches: either increase the capacity of bankruptcy courts or facilitate out-of-court restructuring.[179] The latter can be done by providing tax incentives to choose out-of-court restructuring. For instance, creditors who forgo some of their claims could receive a tax credit in return. Proposals along these lines emphasize risk-sharing. Part of the bill is shouldered by taxpayers, but creditors also shoulder some losses.

There are several ways to increase the capacity of bankruptcy courts, such as hiring new bankruptcy judges, hiring temporary judges, or reallocating judges to busier bankruptcy districts. Another option is to streamline the bankruptcy process.

In contrast to the US, many European countries have imposed bankruptcy moratoria, temporarily relaxing the requirement for bankrupt firms to file for insolvency. As a result, bankruptcies have been paradoxically low during the Covid-19 crisis. However, some fear that this approach could be the calm before the storm if zombie firms all start filing for bankruptcy once the moratoria are lifted.[180]

CHAPTER 9

The Financial Market Whipsaw: Central Banks as Guardians of Financial Resilience

Financial markets during the Covid-19 pandemic have demonstrated unprecedented resilience. A rapid downturn was followed by a recovery that led to record highs by the end of 2020. The rebound also culminated in record IPO issuances by the summer of 2020. This swift drop and rebound pattern is reminiscent of a whipsaw.

Explanations for why financial markets recovered much faster than the real economy include: low interest rates; the overweighting of large firms and tech companies in stock market indices; the strong performance of technology companies that benefitted from changes associated with Covid-19; central bank interventions that removed tail risk; and a potential stock market bubble, perhaps fueled by the rise of commission-free trading apps. I will explore all of these factors in this chapter.

In corporate bond markets, credit spreads—the difference between interest rates paid by risky firms relative to safer ones—drifted down from the initial panic. By the summer of 2020, a bond bonanza opened up. Fueled by record-low interest rates, firms refinanced their debts at an unprecedented scale. These patterns continued in early 2021. Both equity and bond markets saw unprecedented fundraising by corporations. High valuations in equity markets and low interest rates on corporate bonds have maintained incentives to raise capital for firms.[181]

Digital currencies such as Bitcoin displayed a similar financial whipsaw. After the drop in March, Bitcoin was up about 100 percent in 2020, followed by new record in early 2021.[182]

These whipsaws were aided by the rapid central bank interventions that occurred when financial markets wobbled in March 2020. Stabilization policy was powerful and contributed to the rapid rebound of financial markets—a striking resilience pattern in financial markets.

The Stock Market and Large Firms: K-Recession

When interest rates fall to record lows, it lowers the costs of raising debt in corporate bond markets and it further benefits the equity of firms. Lower discount rates—a lower opportunity cost of time—raise the value of future expected cash flows, which should increase stock prices.

March 2020 Drop

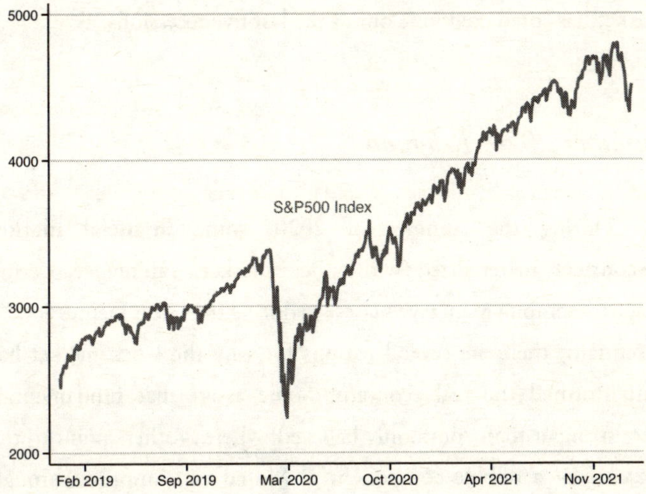

Figure 9-1: S&P 500 stock price index for US stocks. Source: WRDS, CRSP-Compustat 2021

Figure 9-1 plots the evolution since September 2019 of the S&P 500, which is a broad index representative of the US stock market. We can see that stock prices dropped more than 30 percent in March 2020 before gradually recovering during the rest of 2020 and into early 2021. One exception is the banking sector, which showed less resilience and only rebounded later in 2021. Since the latter half of 2020, stock prices remained high while the economy persisted in a deep recession with substantial involuntary unemployment during most of 2020. Stock prices are forward-looking and as such might be a better indicator of how the economy will do in the future rather than in the current moment. Bond prices tend to be superior predictors of economic activity in the short term. To cite an old dictum by Samuelson, the stock market is a good predictor in the cross-section of firms, but over time the stock market has "predicted nine out of the last five recessions."[183]

Summer 2020: Rebound

During the summer of 2020, some **financial market disconnect** materialized with stock markets rapidly recovering despite unemployment levels last seen during the Great Depression.[184] Essentially, there are several reasons for why the stock market has outperformed the real economy. Some assert that fundamentals were stronger than commonly believed, whereas others point to the presence of a bubble component.[185] Muted consumption through most of the Covid-19 crisis led to a large build-up in private savings, which were partially invested in asset markets.

First, there is a **compositional tilt** between the stock market and the overall economy. Contact-intensive firms are underrepresented on stock exchanges. In particular, many unlisted small and medium enterprises (SMEs) are not traded on the stock market. Moreover, stock markets have been driven by large stocks that carry disproportionate weight in indexes, and the large tech stocks have performed very well. Most notably, Amazon's business model has been an obvious winner during the pandemic.

Second, central banks have systematically removed tail risk across asset markets by purchasing a broad variety of assets. The Bank of Japan even purchases stocks and holds 90 percent of the Japanese ETF market.[186] The Swiss National Bank started purchasing US equities in an attempt to devalue the Swiss franc. In

2018, it owned more Facebook shares than the company's founder Mark Zuckerberg.[187]

Third, central bank interventions have likely played a role in the lowering of the discount rate during the Covid-19 pandemic. This drives up the value of stocks even if cash flows remain unchanged. In the simple **Gordon growth model**, it is the difference between the discount rate (*r*) and the dividend growth rate (*g*) that drives stock prices. (Remember that $P_0 = D_1/(r\text{-}g)$ where *D1* denotes the dividend.) Even if *g* had fallen slightly, this might have been overcompensated by an even larger drop in the real discount rate (*r*). Moreover, beliefs in a rapid V-shape recession without long-run scarring have likely contributed to medium-run expectations about fundamentals (*D1*) remaining stable.[188]

Fourth, an alternative set of explanations for the stock market's rapid recovery center around irrational exuberance. The **"fear of missing out on the recovery"** might have played a powerful role.[189] In 2008, the stock market first crashed but then strongly rebounded. Many investors who sold during the trough missed out on the strong post-2008 rebound and they did not want to repeat the mistake this time.

An increase in trading has also been associated with **trading apps,** such as Robinhood. These apps enable average investors to turn over their stocks each day, or even faster. As the spread of Covid-19 caused many gambling markets and casinos to shut down, the numbers of people using these apps surged in March 2020.[190]

Those who trade with apps like Robinhood have been associated with unusual phenomena. Based on tips exchanged on Reddit's online WallStreetBets forum, retail investors bid up the stock of videogame retailer GameStop by more than 100 percent on January 26, 2021. This caused large losses to hedge funds, which had shorted the stock.[191] Over the first twenty-nine days of 2021, GameStop's stock increased 1700 percent despite having a heavily retail-reliant business model that was badly impacted by ongoing store and mall closures. The frenzy extended further to other stocks, including to the movie theatre chain AMC, which was another heavily shorted stock. Most of these gains vanished quickly. Lasse Pedersen, who offered a detailed account of the events, linked these phenomena to meme-investing and predatory trading mechanisms. Predatory trading squeezes other investors and forces them to unwind their positions at unfavorable prices.[192]

IPO Boom

Bankrupt companies during this pandemic have managed to raise money, and startups have rushed to equity markets. Traditional initial public offerings (**IPOs**) involve an investment bank that oversees the process of a firm becoming publicly listed on a stock exchange. Traditional IPOs saw an unprecedented boom in 2020 despite the dire economic outlook. In fact, in nominal terms, the boom in 2020 surpassed the IPO frenzy at the peak of the dotcom bubble in 2000 (figure 9-2). The most burgeoning sectors have been healthcare, finance, and electronics. Some IPOs in 2020, such as Airbnb and DoorDash, saw first-day price increases not seen since the dotcom bubble, which is potentially an ominous sign.[193]

A new form of accessing public equity markets has emerged in the United States. IPOs are typically costly because investment banks receive fees amounting to about 7 percent of the offering.

An alternative that became more popular in 2020 is to access the equity market via direct stock market listings organized by a **special purpose acquisition company (SPAC)** thereby circumventing the traditional IPO process. A SPAC is a shell company that raises money for the purpose of acquiring and merging with another company that is seeking to go public. This process of going public through the backdoor has become increasingly popular, with a total volume of $70 billion in IPOs administered through SPACs in 2020.[194] The attractiveness of going public via a SPAC is not necessarily related to lower costs. SPACs tend to be a bit cheaper than IPOs, but they might require extra fees, including those related to various regulatory requirements.[195, 196]

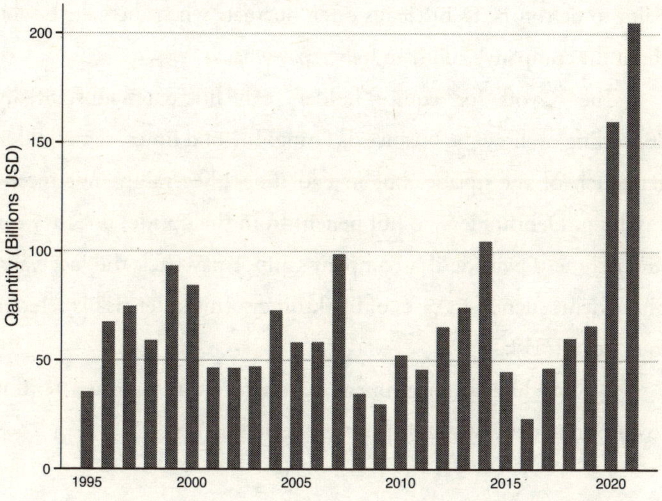

Figure 9-2: Volume of initial public offers in the United States by year. Source: WRDS, CRSP-Compustat 2021, SDC

Debt Markets

During the Covid-19 crisis, equity markets have shown extraordinary resilience. So have debt markets.

Equity claims confer partial ownership in a public company whereas investing in debt only entitles the debtholders to be repaid the amount they are owed without any direct say in the company's decisions. However, during times of financial distress, debtholders are reimbursed first, before equity holders receive anything. For this reason, debt is typically less risky. A distressed business is often able to service its debtors, at least partially. But there might not be much left for equity holders. Nevertheless, the value of a $100 debt claim by Google might still fluctuate in secondary markets when person A sells an outstanding claim to person B. Debt claims often fluctuate when there are doubts about the company's ability to fully repay what it owes.

The payoff for equity holders can fluctuate substantially, depending on how the business is faring. In good times, shareholders get much of the upside, but in bad times they might not receive anything. Debtholders do not benefit from the upside, but they can suffer some downside if a company cannot pay back the face value of the debt, such as in cases of bankruptcy. This latter risk is referred to as default risk.

We will look at government debt before turning our attention to corporate debt, which is privately issued by firms.

Treasury Market and Market Maker of Last Resort

Public debt is issued by federal or local governments. In the US, government debt securities are called US Treasuries. In Germany, the main government bond is called the *Bund.* In Japan, they are called Japanese Government Bonds (JGBs).

Textbook economic markets assume that buyers and sellers meet simultaneously and exchange goods, services, or assets against money. In practice, however, there can be a gap between the selling point-in-time when some party wants to sell, for example, a US Treasury and the buying-point-in-time when another investor wants to purchase that same security. To bridge the gap between these two points in time, a third-party **market maker** is needed to temporarily "store" the bond.

Historically, big banks assumed that role in the US Treasury market. They served as intermediaries between buyers and sellers by keeping large amounts of US Treasuries on their balance sheets. However, regulations after the 2008 financial crisis have required banks to have substantial capital to act as the market maker. These regulations have disincentivized them from assuming that role. They have preferred to engage in other activities that are less heavily regulated and that offer higher margins. Figure 9-3 illustrates the balance sheets of big banks. Capacity has remained stable since the 2008 financial crisis while the supply of Treasuries has steadily increased. Instead, over the past decade, hedge funds have stepped into the market-making segment.

In March 2020, the US Treasury market—one of the world's largest and usually most liquid financial markets—"choked" with the demand for liquidity. This required the US Federal Reserve to intervene as **market maker of last resort**—to restore resilience. No investor wanted to be the market maker because a pipeline effect overwhelmed the dealers. Although they were performing their role and expanded intermediation, the sheer volume of orders could not be intermediated quickly enough through their balance sheets.[197]

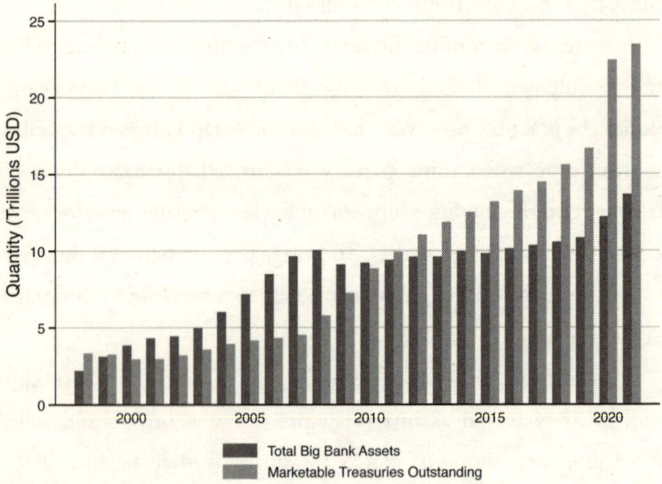

Figure 9-3: Growth of marketable US Treasuries (government bonds) outpace the assets of big banks. Source: Darrell Duffie, Markus' Academy 2020

Ultimately, the Fed purchased Treasuries worth close to $2 trillion. The intervention went beyond market making in that the Fed kept many of those bonds for the longer term as part of its quantitative easing programs. As the situation stabilized, government bond prices rose. But during the first weeks of the Covid-19 crisis, US government bond prices began to decrease.[198]

We can expect this market failure to happen again, and perhaps more often. As the US debt-to-GDP ratio continues to grow enormously, more Treasury securities need to be intermediated by the market.[199]

Darrell Duffie has proposed a Treasury market structure based on broad central clearing of trades. He has argued that it is inefficient to run the entire Treasury market through dealer balance sheets.[200] Broad central clearing would improve the safety of settlements in the market, through netting of purchases against sales for each market participant. This would reduce the amount of dealer balance sheets needed for a given volume of trade.[201] Such netting could be conducted by a central counterparty clearing house (CCP).

There would be three roles for the Fed to play in this proposed new market structure. First, the Fed would always be available to restore liquidity if needed. Second, and perhaps more controversially, it would provide last-resort intra-day liquidity to the central counterparty clearing house (CCP) against Treasury collateral. That is, the CCP would be able to borrow easily from the Fed using US Treasuries as collateral. Third, the Fed or the SEC would supervise and regulate the new CCP.[202]

Corporate Bond Market and the Central Bank as Tail-Risk Insurer

Corporate bonds are long-term fixed-income securities issued by a corporation. For instance, a company might promise to pay $100 to the bondholder in five years and collect $90 on the day the bond is sold. The per-annum yield of this particular bond at issuance is about 2 percent.[203] Thus, corporate bonds and government bonds function similarly. However, corporate bonds have higher default risk and are a less-valuable collateral. They are also less liquid, which means they are more difficult to pass on to others. In the US, this market is quite large, but in Europe and Asia, bank financing still dominates corporate bond financing.

Bond ratings are critical in this market. Rating agencies screen bond issuers and determine a rating for each bond. Highly rated bonds are referred to as investment-grade bonds whereas the remaining, riskier bonds are referred to as junk bonds.

In March 2020, financial markets were about to fall apart. The price of risk skyrocketed (figure 9-4) and international capital flows retrenched into safe assets, most notably into short-term US Treasuries. Volatility spiked in March, funding conditions tightened, and **corporate bond yields soared**, even for the safest companies.[204] Moreover, there were spillover risks. Many firms that were marginally rated at investment-grade (BBB rating) were held in the portfolios of Japanese or European investors. These investors often have investment mandates that only allow them to hold investment-grade bonds. Thus, a wave of downgrades among these firms could have spread internationally.[205] This description resembles the playbook of the 2008 financial crisis.

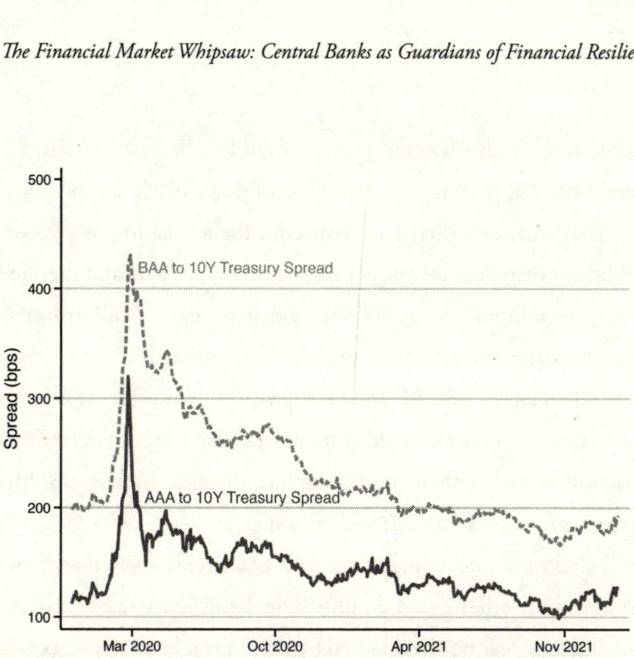

Figure 9-4: Bond spread is defined as the difference between the AAA (BAA) rated bonds interest rate minus the ten-year US Treasury interest rate. Source: FRED 2021

However, policy interventions succeeded in stabilizing markets much faster than in 2008, as highlighted in figure 9-4. Default risk has remained elevated, but the **price of risk** has come down. Figure 9-4 also shows that spreads between high-yield, relatively risky corporate bonds and the relatively safe investment-grade bonds increased substantially in March 2020. Those spreads quickly came back down from their March 2020 peaks. Intuitively, the two curves measure the price of risk. In other words, they are measures of the additional compensation that investors demand for holding corporate bonds instead of Treasury securities (given that these corporate bonds are riskier).

Monetary policy is not only about controlling the short-term risk-free rate. It also has the power to reduce the price of risk and ensure financial stability in crisis conditions, such as in March 2020. Many debt markets have **two equilibria.** The first is a "good" equilibrium by which investors perceive debt to be safe and therefore accept a low interest rate. The second is a "bad" equilibrium by which investors perceive the same debt as unsafe and, given those beliefs, demand a spread and a high-risk premium. When the interest rate is high, companies have a harder time servicing their debts, which makes them more likely to default. That is, the high interest/high risk outcome is self-fulfilling.

By eliminating endogenous (self-generated) risk, the central bank can fend off the bad equilibrium. Exogenous risk, such as a new pandemic, cannot be affected by the central bank. But a central bank that takes on financial risk has the power to reduce the price of risk.

This also prevents the *amplification* of negative shocks that results from the misallocation of risks across the economy. Markets can powerfully deal with small economic shocks, but markets, especially financial markets, are not self-stabilizing after large shocks. Targeted central bank interventions can provide resilience. They can pave the way for an economic recovery and, by providing a **backstop**, remove tail risk to enable economic agents to bounce back from a crisis.

The Fed focused on supporting credit in 2020 with the ultimate goals of limiting economic damage and positioning the economy for a rapid recovery.[206] Given the unprecedented nature of the fundamental shock, the Fed's key focus has been to avoid post-crisis scarring[207] by providing firms with insurance.[208]

Concretely, the Fed's facilities during the Covid-19 crisis

have included purchases of commercial mortgage-backed securities (backed by commercial real estate), corporate bonds, and loans to small and medium enterprises (SMEs).[209] In addition, corporate credit facilities provide medium-term funding for companies with restrictions attached, such as dividend restrictions or share buybacks.[210] Because the Fed cannot directly fund companies, a **special purpose vehicle (SPV)** was set up with the Treasury taking the equity tranches and being the first-loss absorber.[211]

In case a situation deteriorates, the central bank stands ready to step in with those new facilities to take on risk by purchasing more risky assets. Corporate bond purchases, most notably by the Fed, have been very small up to now, but the promise of the Fed's intervention (if needed) has been sufficient to stabilize markets.[212] So far, the ultimate result of the central bank's interventions has been a reduction in the price of risk.[213] As of April 2021, the Fed had wound down some of these emergency measures designed to preserve liquidity. For example, it will no longer allow banks to exclude holdings of Treasury bonds and excess deposits from the supplementary reserve ratio. This limits bank leverage and the use of borrowed funds for the banks' activities.[214]

In contrast to the reliance of US firms on corporate bonds, corporate firms in Asia and Europe have displayed much greater reliance on bank financing. By depending on corporate bonds, firms gain a direct way of accessing external capital without bank intermediation. However, interest rates are very sensitive to bond ratings. On the other hand, bank finance is provided via a financial intermediary, which has greater incentives to monitor the specific firm.

In March 2020, the big sellers of bonds and equity[215] in the

European market were institutional investors, with a smaller share coming from insurance companies.[216] National central banks, in contrast, were net acquirers of debt.[217] Also in March 2020, the EU saw a typical sell-off of foreign assets across borders. In April, the pullback effect dissipated for less vulnerable and more vulnerable countries alike. Residents of these countries experienced stabilization.[218]

The main goal of the European Central Bank's Pandemic Emergency Purchase Program (**PEPP**) has been debt market stabilization. The objective is different from the ECB's QE asset purchasing program, which is to fight deflation. This is noteworthy because, officially, the ECB's mandate is not financial stability.[219] That said, the ECB's actions can be justified by the need to ensure that the monetary transmission mechanism works.

There is a lot of evidence that PEPP has contributed to market stabilization. According to several measures, the euro area has seen significant stabilization.[220] Sovereign bond yields, for example, are an important indicator for the ECB because they are also closely reflected in bank funding and are passed on to households' cost of credit.[221]

This effective backstop by a central bank does not come without cost. **Risk-taking** is encouraged by central banks as they systematically remove tail risks, which warrants concerns about future moral hazard.[222] To mitigate those concerns, it could be possible to further regulate systemically important participants in financial markets and strengthen liquidity insurance requirements for highly leveraged entities.[223]

Summer 2020 Bond Bonanza

Once the Covid-19 economic shock stabilized, the tables turned. The following discussion centers on the US experience, but other countries around the world witnessed similar developments. During the summer of 2020, we saw an unprecedented "**bond bonanza**." Bolstered by record-low interest rates, corporate bond issuances rose massively. Firms filled up their cash buffers and some even bought back some equity. The latter action is very troubling from a financial stability perspective. As firm leverages increase, the corporate sector becomes more vulnerable to interest rate hikes, for example, which undermines the resilience of those firms.

Figure 9-5 highlights the surge in corporate bond issuances in 2020.[224] It far exceeds any of the previous peaks. The bond bonanza is partly driven by a desire to refinance debt at historically low interest rates. Replacing older high-interest bonds with new bonds allows firms to lock in low interest rates for the foreseeable future.

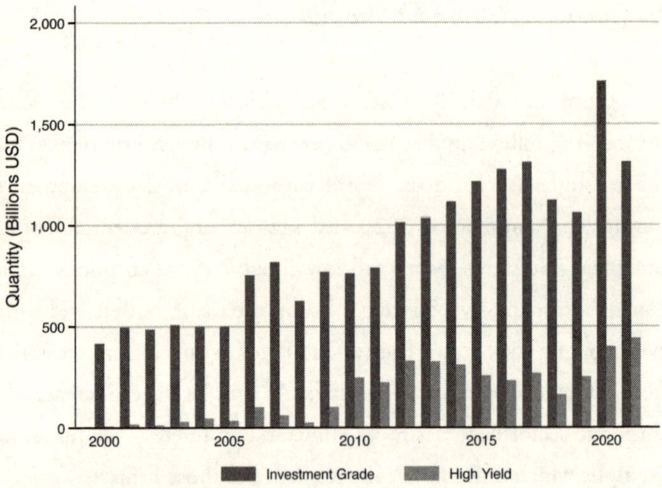

Figure 9-5: Corporate bond issuances in the US reached record highs in 2020. Source: Mergent FISD (WRDS)

While the initial market meltdown was comparable to the crisis in 2008, central banks reacted much faster in 2020. The effects are visible in the corporate bond bonanza. Rapid interventions stabilized markets within weeks, which provided support to firms that could raise funds in corporate bond markets. The markets rapidly bounced back. In terms of resilience, one might argue that 2020 served as a lesson for how 2008 should have been handled.

Bank Loans

Corporate bond market interventions do not directly affect all firms. Many small and medium enterprises rely on bank loans, particularly in Europe and Asia, but also in the US. In March

2020, when corporations began drawing down preexisting credit commitments (also known as **credit lines**), we saw a "**dash for cash**." Banks provided large amounts of funds to corporations. However, a credit crunch loomed on the horizon. With so many funds going to pre-committed credit lines, banks did not have enough margin to make new loans. This occurred at the expense of financing for new real investments.

In contrast to traditional banks, shadow banks (e.g., hedge funds), money market mutual funds, or structured investment vehicles, have always been more lightly regulated and have not been subject to stricter regulation since the 2008 financial crisis. Banks have proved reliable on servicing existing credit lines, but the shadow banking sector has been less stable during the Covid-19 crisis and has contributed less to the resilience of financial markets.

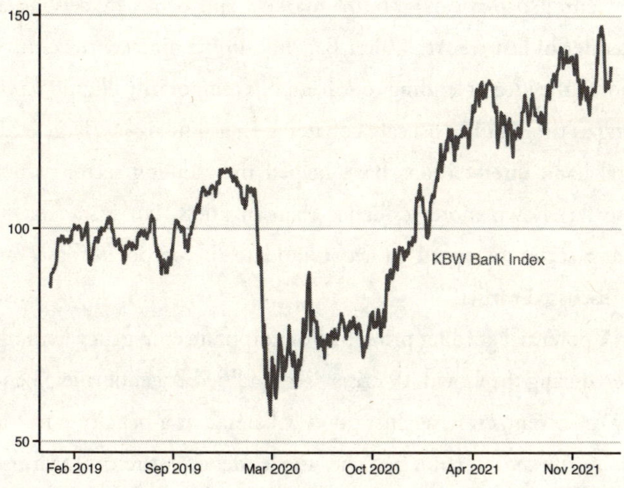

Figure 9-6: Slow recovery of the bank equity price index KBW in 2020. Source: KBW Nasdaq bank index

Banks were hit particularly hard by the Covid-19 shock. Bank equity prices dropped more than the stock market average. Figure 9-6 illustrates that banks only reached pre-crisis levels in late 2020 or early 2021, whereas the overall stock market reached those levels much earlier.

Lender of Last Resort

The main reason we care so much about the banking sector is that it intermediates capital, ideally toward productive firms that are financially constrained. How should banks be encouraged to extend loans for real investment? Part of a central bank's strategy is to allow banks to refinance their debts and use loans as collateral.

Central banks can stabilize markets and banks by serving as the **lender of last resort**. Walter Bagehot, in the nineteenth century, proposed the idea of lending to solvent but temporarily illiquid *banks* as long as they could post safe collateral. In a similar way, large-scale central bank interventions have helped the banking sector, which has so far shown more resilience than in 2008. For instance, the banking sector managed to accommodate the corporate dash-for-cash discussed earlier.

A potential guiding principle for corporate emergency lending, as seen during the Covid-19 crisis, is a modified Bagehot rule: "Lend freely to solvent *firms*, against good collateral, at a penalty rate." In this way, the central bank becomes the lender of last resort for firms, not just for banks.[225]

Venture Capitalist of Last Resort

Before delving into the principles that might govern how central banks administer direct aid to firms, I will first explore why banks do not extend more support to the corporate sector. One argument is that banks could raise equity in order to extend more loans while maintaining capital requirements. However, in practice, banks do not raise equity in recessions, in part because share prices are depressed. In fact, bank stocks in 2020 have been among the biggest stock market losers, which complicates their attempts to raise additional equity. Stockholders are also likely to oppose efforts to raise new equity because it dilutes their shareholdings. As a result, other forms of direct support for firms might be needed.

Proposals have been made for the central bank to provide direct support to firms, not just indirectly via the banking sector. However, with the danger of a long-lasting **debt overhang** problem, the challenge is to provide support to firms without amplifying that problem. Additional loans to firms do not meet that criterion because they would further burden firms with debt. Instead, interventions must involve **equity injections**, as emphasized by Jeremy Stein. The critical difference between debt and equity is that the equity claim loses value if the firm performs poorly whereas the debt claim is noncontingent.

On a microeconomic level, the key rationale for supporting firms is to preserve long-run viable businesses that have temporary liquidity shortfalls, and to do this without creating excessive debt overhang. On a macroeconomic scale, there is a view that amplification of externalities from the financial accelerator, fire sales, or aggregate demand needs to be contained.[226]

Jeremy Stein argues that policy could be guided by a "**venture capitalist of last resort principle**." In this case, funding would be provided in **stages, contingent on success**. The central bank would stabilize impaired **corporate sector balance sheets**. Given the significant uncertainty, funding should be made widely available and with low priority in bankruptcy to avoid saddling firms with large debts.[227] That is, central banks should hold junior, riskier debt, or even equity in firms.

When venturing into this type of new territory, clear guidance for central banks is required. A venture capitalist of last resort needs to decide which firms should survive with continued funding and which should not. This raises at least two more questions: What should be the venture capital stages? And at which turning points should funding be withdrawn? **Political economy** considerations would also have a bearing, because cutting off funding at later stages would be contentious. This type of policy would go far beyond the central bank's traditional policies, and it would involve significant risk. But avoiding debt overhang by taking contingent equity claims in firms would provide resilience. Such a scheme could potentially be run by the Treasury, which might be better suited for the job than the central bank.

The main lesson from this chapter is that central banks can powerfully perform various roles that help to safeguard financial market resilience. As market maker, lender, venture capitalist, and asset purchaser—all of last resort—central banks can perform a critical function in ensuring that financial markets bounce back, even after substantial disruptions like the Covid-19 crisis. However, by doing so, central banks take on significant risks, including political risks. All of that might go beyond their mandates.

CHAPTER 10

High Government Debt and Low Interest Rates

Enhancing Resilience with Fiscal Stimulus

In 2008, a comparatively smaller fundamental shock—the default of US subprime mortgages—triggered a devastating global financial crisis. Then in 2020, when the large fundamental pandemic shock occurred, some observers worried that a 30 percent reduction in US GDP during the second quarter would translate into an abysmal recession.

However, in 2020, aggressive expansionary fiscal and monetary policy averted the danger. Unemployment at the beginning of the pandemic soared in the US and then quickly recovered. In many European countries, unemployment rates did not reach euro crisis highs and GDP rebounded in the third quarter. The outlook at the time of this writing remains uncertain, but it appears that a Great

Depression scenario has been prevented.

The recovery (so far) from the recent pandemic shock highlights the power of government to add resilience to an economy, and it raises new questions about how the 2008 crisis was handled. During the 2008 financial crisis, China's fiscal policy was substantially more aggressive than in the US. Its extraordinarily large stimulus program made the Chinese economy very resilient, which also helped the global economy.

What if advanced economies had applied more aggressive policies in 2008? Could they have avoided the recession and contributed more to resilience? Or could there be an underlying difference between the 2008 recession and the 2020 crisis? For one, the 2008 shock was caused by a financial crisis and the 2020 shock was caused by a disease outbreak.

We might also hypothesize that policymakers learned from the 2008 recession. In March 2020, as financial markets were shaking, central banks could build on their 2008 experiences to craft emergency plans. As a result, policy intervention was extremely fast in 2020. Rapid government action clearly fostered resilience. By reducing the size of the economic fall and its duration, central banks attenuated the danger of long-term scarring and improved the position of economic agents to bounce back.

The Covid-19 crisis is also different from the 2011-2012 euro crisis. The pandemic crisis did not originate from national policy mistakes. In 2020, all euro area countries were "in broad compliance" with the area's fiscal framework at the onset of the Covid-19 shock. On the banking side, the single supervisory mechanism, which was implemented in 2014, enhanced banking supervision.[228]

In general, we can see that **policy** plays a critical role in preventing long-run scarring. Providing ex-post insurance can cushion a shock and pave the way for a faster recovery. Common moral hazard worries—that higher insurance also promotes excessive risk-taking—do not apply in the case of the Covid-19 crisis because the pandemic was not anyone's fault.

Up to now, most government policy in dealing with the Covid-19 shock has followed the principle of "**whatever it takes**," leading to a large increase in government debt. But that raises the question of whether it will be followed by a second "Oh God, what have we done?" moment. Resilience means having extra spending capacity in bad times, which requires the build-up of redundancies in good times. In other words, being frugal in good times is an essential part of resilience.

High Public Debt

Could today's high public debt levels cause problems down the road by reducing future economic growth? By increasing debt now are we limiting fiscal space for handling future crises? If so, that would reduce macroeconomic resilience. Or given that interest rates are low, which lowers the interest rate burden of the public debt, are we in an unusual situation?

US government debt has soared from about 60 percent of GDP to more than 100 percent of GDP over the past two decades (figure 10-1) and is projected to reach all-time highs in the coming years. Never in peace times has the US seen such a large stock of public debt. In Japan, the fiscal situation is even more striking.

The government is managing a debt-to-GDP stock exceeding 200 percent and has posted budget deficits for fifty of the last sixty years.[229] Approximately **half of Japanese government debt is held by Japan's central bank**, the Bank of Japan.[230] As we will soon discuss, the reserves issued to finance this debt must still be counted toward the government's total liabilities.

Government debt has also increased substantially in many European countries, first during the 2008 recession and then during the subsequent Eurozone crisis. Now the Covid-19 crisis has added more debt to European countries. In France, the government debt-to-GDP ratio exceeds 100 percent and in Italy it is surpassing 150 percent.

Why Are Interest Rates So Low?

Despite today's high public debt levels, which were swelling long before the pandemic, record-low real interest rates have made public debt sustainable and created fiscal space. This blessing for ministers of finance reflects broader macroeconomic trends.

Figures 10-1 plots the evolution of US government debt to GDP (shaded area) as well as interest payments to GDP (the dashed line). Since the 1990s, government interest payments in relation to GDP have come down significantly while public debt in relation to GDP has almost doubled.

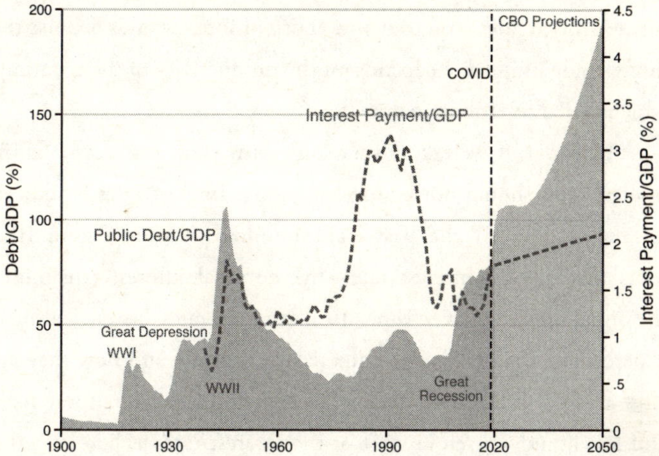

Figure 10-1: US debt ratio and interest payment relative to GDP, and post-2020 CBO projections. Source: FRED 2021 and CBO

To obtain a full picture of government debt, it is first important to understand the reasons for low interest rates. **High precautionary savings**, for which we have already seen clear evidence, have put downward pressure on the interest rate of safe assets, particularly government bonds. The market's willingness to bear risk has been low, so prices on safe assets have been rising, yields have been falling, and risky assets have seen increasing risk premia. **Demographic changes**, especially longer life expectancy, have also placed downward pressure on interest rates. Older households typically prefer lower exposure to risky assets. And, due to increased longevity, older people usually accumulate more savings for more years in retirement. The result is increased demand for safe assets, which drives down the interest rate for government bonds.

Weak growth—the **secular stagnation** hypothesis—is likely to put additional downward pressure on interest rates.[231] Low future growth rates tend to depress current interest rates because the interest rate ultimately depends on the productivity of the economy, which is tied to economic growth.

However, if we take a very long-term view, the steady fall in interest rates should not be too surprising. Interest rates have been on the decline for the past eight hundred years.[232] Figure 10-2 plots the US real interest rate—the nominal interest rate minus the inflation rate—over time. Real interest rates hovered around 5 percent at the onset of the nineteenth century, and now they are close to zero. Admittedly, earlier bond investments were more risky and less liquid; therefore, part of the interest-rate decline reflects a reduction in risk and an increase in liquidity.

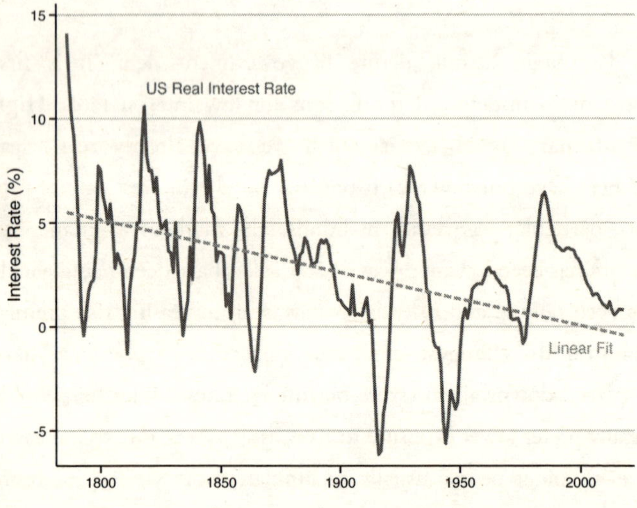

Figure 10-2. The real interest rate in US has been falling for a long time. Source: Paul Schmelzing, Bank of England Staff Working Paper 2020

Finally, **increasing inequality** might affect interest rates. Wealthy people tend to save more than poorer households. As the wealth share of the rich increases, the economy's total savings supply increases, which tends to reduce interest rates. However, a share of those savings flows toward riskier assets, so the impact on government bond yields is less clear. Arguably, the increased cash holdings and savings of corporate firms play a more important role in depressing real interest rates than the savings of households.

These forces lead to extra demand for bonds. That drives up bond prices or, equivalently, lowers their interest rate. On the other hand, the high public debt level increases the supply of bonds.

As the savings abundance leads to low interest rates, there can be a side effect: the danger of excessive build-ups in leverage and asset price bubbles in land or real estate.[233]

Safe Asset Status of Government Bonds

The steady increase in public debt levels over the past decades brings up a range of questions about debt sustainability. High debt is not necessarily a problem, as long as people are willing to hold all the bonds at low interest rates.

The popularity of government debt is partly explained by its **safe asset status**. Households and firms value government bonds because they are safe, even when bond yields are low. A safe asset can be sold without much or any discount in times of crisis when the ability to obtain funds to finance consumption or investment is particularly valued. Financial economists call these assets, which do not fluctuate much in relation to the overall stock market, "low-beta assets."

What would happen if the government lost the safe asset status of its debt? Even worse, what if investors began to worry about an outright default or an implicit default via inflation? In light of record debt levels, due in part to the Covid-19 crisis around the globe, these are the economic questions of our times.[234]

The two key characteristics of a safe asset are illustrated by the "good friend" analogy and the safe asset tautology. A safe asset is like a good friend. It is there and valuable when needed during a personal shock or an economy-wide shock. People can sell safe assets without much markdown in case of an unforeseen contingency.

Citizens who manage to avoid a personal shock are often willing to buy safe assets. This is due to their low transaction costs and because they can come in handy during a future shock. Intuitively, we think of safe assets as being continuously traded in the economy. Households that suffer a negative shock sell safe assets to weather the storm. Others worried about possible future shocks happily buy those assets. When the buyers get hit by shocks, they will again sell the asset . . . and so forth. The second characteristic of safe asset is a tautology: Safe assets are safe because they are *perceived* to be safe. This illustrates why there can be multiple equilibria. In the first equilibrium, the safe assets are perceived to be safe and hence trade at a high price. But there is a second equilibrium that arises when safe-asset status is lost.

Selling safe assets in times of need allows people to self-insure and thereby reduce their risk. In other words, besides cash flow, safe assets serve as insurance against risks. This type of benefit is called "service flow." Another type of service flow stems from the fact that government bonds are accepted as good collateral, which facilitates collateralized borrowing. To recognize this requires us to modify classic asset pricing. We need to augment the classic asset pricing equation, which only features the appropriately discounted cash flow, with a discounted stream of service flows.[235]

Moreover, the service flow is particularly valuable in times of crisis when risk is high. The increased value of service flows in economic downturns boosts the value of the safe asset and the good friend feature. The fact that a safe asset will increase in value exactly in times of crisis makes it even more desirable. In other words, people are more willing to hold it at a low interest rate because it offers other services.[236]

High Debt and Vulnerability to Interest Rate Spikes

As long as its safe asset status can be maintained, debt can be issued by the government at favorable interest rates. Citizens are willing to receive a low interest rate since they enjoy the service flow described above. The interest rate will be lower when uncertainty and, as a result, precautionary savings are high. Importantly, as long as the interest rate is below the growth rate of the economy, the government might even be able to run a **Ponzi scheme**; that is, pay off the maturing bonds with newly issued debt and then issue more for additional expenditures. Government debt is essentially a bubble. As long as GDP is growing faster than the new debt needed to pay off the interest payments, the debt-to-GDP ratio can decrease.

The government can even "**mine the bubble**." Issuing bonds at a faster rate acts like an inflation tax on bond holdings. However, this also erodes the issuing price of the bonds and, consequently, lowers the "tax base" value of the bonds. The tax revenue is the tax rate times the tax base. By increasing the tax rate beyond a certain level, by issuing too many bonds too fast, the tax base erodes so much that the overall revenue from bubble mining declines. This is in contrast to what proponents of the Modern Monetary Theory (MMT) claim. There is a limit to raising new amounts of debt, even in the favorable case when the real interest rate is below the economic growth rate.[237]

Such a bubbly Ponzi scheme debt strategy is risky because the interest rate on government bonds might not permanently stay below the growth rate of the economy. For example, when uncertainty vanishes—and with it the motives for precautionary savings—the interest rate increases.[238]

Another major concern about high public debt levels is the danger of **multiple equilibria**. There is an inherent risk that the bubble might pop. In the good equilibrium, economic agents perceive the debt to be safe and therefore demand a low interest rate. However, for the same level of public debt, there is also a bad equilibrium: The debt is perceived as unsafe and therefore investors demand high compensation for that risk. What this means for our time in history is that, after the world's initial ultra-expansionary fiscal policy, we could enter an "Oh God, what have we done?" phase during which the equilibrium pivots toward the bad equilibrium and previous fiscal expansions begin to haunt government budgets.

Thus, from the standpoint of maintaining resilience, countries must remain vigilant about the safe asset status of their government debt. Once the jump to the bad equilibrium occurs and government bonds are stripped of safe asset status, it is almost impossible to return. This would result in a fiscal policy trap. Interest rates would soar and the government would face a substantial interest burden.

Central banks will play an important role in such circumstances. Money—cash and central bank reserves—is a special form of government debt. Money provides another service flow as a medium of exchange for transactions. Nonetheless, money is ultimately a government liability, but with special characteristics. The maturity of money is infinite, meaning that it never has to be paid back. Cash does not even promise cash flows in the form of interest rates. Money is distinct from government bonds, which typically make coupon payments and repay the principal at a pre-specified date of maturity. Central bank reserves pay interest on a floating basis, which changes with the policy rate. Thus, the duration is very short (high interest rate sensitivity) and the maturity is infinite. So, when central banks conduct quantitative easing, they swap infinite-maturity money for finite-maturity government bonds. These and other monetary measures lead us to the next chapter.

Additional Implicit Government Debt

Explicit and Implicit Government Debt

It is worthwhile to make an additional point. Total debt owed by the state comprises explicit debt (mostly outstanding government bonds) and implicit debt, such as pension obligations. Implicit debt cannot be traded freely and therefore cannot be considered as a safe asset. This fact raises intricate political economy considerations when governments must decide between servicing public debt or pension obligations. The market might assume that governments will trim benefits, such as social security, and treat explicit government debt as senior. However, it's not clear how political economy considerations will play out. Pensioners form a powerful voter base, especially in aging societies.[239]

Fiscal vs. Monetary Policy Space with Low Interest Rates

In an environment with low interest rates, fiscal policy has more capacity to intervene and engineer a quick rebound, whereas monetary policy has less room to maneuver. Specifically, when the real interest rate is low, the government's interest burden is low. This opens up extra fiscal space. Governments can easily expand their spending in times of crisis and enable a quick rebound. On the other hand, in a low interest rate environment, nominal interest rates are also lower—assuming that inflation remains fixed. If the nominal interest rates are already low, then the central bank has less room to cut them further in order to stimulate the economy, especially because interest rates cannot be too negative. In short, in a low interest rate environment, the power of monetary policy to stimulate the economy to bounce back after a shock is reduced. Monetary policy considerations are the key focus of the next chapter.

CHAPTER 11

The "Inflation Whipsaw"

Resilience is about bouncing back after a shock. Monetary policy can play an important contributing role. Avoiding traps plays a crucial role in that process. The high debt levels discussed in previous chapters points to a build-up of two types of traps: a **deflation trap** and an **inflation trap**. Central banks must act within a narrow corridor. If they move outside of those parameters, they face the "risk" of getting stuck at an inflation rate that is permanently too low and thereby hurts growth, or they get trapped by a high inflation rate, possibly breaking the inflation anchor—a **tipping point**. Central banks should not focus on just one type of trap. They need to be vigilant in regard to both dangers. Resilience management therefore needs to be supplemented by trap avoidance analysis.

The bicycle analogy I used to explain the social contract's resilience also applies in the case of inflation. The bike might fall to the right, blown by the winds of deflation, or it might fall to the left, forced off course by **inflation.** As a result, resilient policy requires an element of flexibility to ride the bike between an inflationary and a deflationary trap.

The Inflation Whipsaw: A Dynamic Perspective

Figure 11-1 depicts an "inflation whipsaw." After a short period of low inflation, or even deflation, inflation spikes upward over a longer horizon and overshoots its initial level. This inflation scenario is possible in our current crisis. An inflationary trap might loom on the horizon.

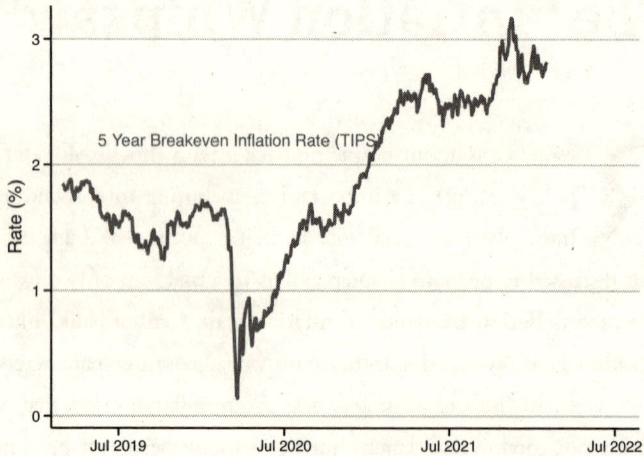

Figure 11-1: The curve depicts five-year inflation expectations for the US inferred from the interest rate break-even point between inflation index US Treasuries (TIPS) and regular US government bonds. Source: FRED 2021

During the lockdown, inflation overall fell (there are measurement challenges), for reasons I will explain soon. Therefore, the immediate concern was a long-term deflationary trap during which inflation would be suppressed and economic growth would be depressed for a long time. This has been called "Japanification," named after Japan's macroeconomic history since the 1990s. Some observers summarize it as "low growth, low interest rates, and low inflation."

Our situation today could lead to an even worse problem. We might face both traps sequentially: an inflation whipsaw. This occurs when short-run forces push toward deflation while the longer-run outlook indicates inflationary pressures. It is a very delicate balancing act to "wade in these currents." In other words, there might be a second whipsaw in addition to the financial stability whipsaw discussed in chapter 9.

Inflation Expectations

There is significant uncertainty about which type of trap we might face after the Covid-19 shock. Therefore, our inflation expectations and forecasts should reflect an increase in individual-level variance. Likewise, because people disagree more about whether we are close to an inflation trap or a deflation trap, our forecasts should include an increase in variance between individuals.

Panel A of figure 11-2 shows that **uncertainty** of inflation expectations increased substantially among professional, expert inflation forecasters. The **disagreement** among them also increased from the last quarter of 2019 to the second quarter of 2020. The light bars are more spread out. Yet, from panel A to panel B we can also observe a whipsaw pattern. Inflation expectations increased again from the second to the fourth quarter of 2020.

Figure 11-3 depicts the inflation forecasts of households in the US. Several patterns are noteworthy. First, households persistently expect inflation rates that are too high. The average household expects 3 percent inflation whereas actual inflation has been around 2 percent for the past three decades. Second, households are uncertain about inflation. The dashed lines outline the confidence bands of households. We can see that uncertainty increased substantially in early 2020 and remains elevated. The dashed lines are farther apart. But third, there is also increasing disagreement across households, as shown by the wider shaded area. Some households expect inflation whereas others are more concerned about deflation.

The pattern of rising disagreement could be consistent with worries about an inflation whipsaw in the longer run. The disagreement also suggests that some households are more worried about a deflationary trap whereas others are worried about an inflationary trap.

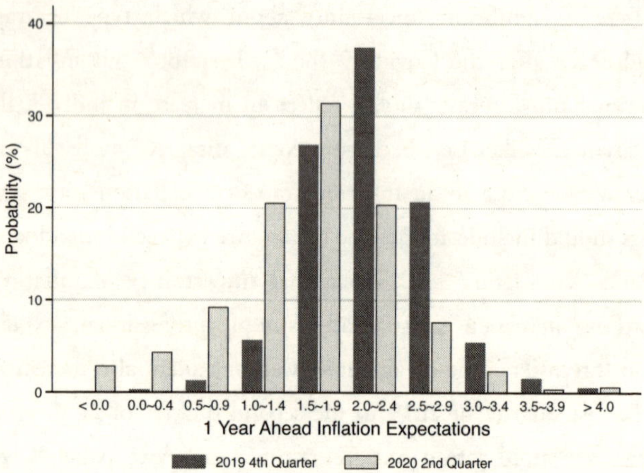

Figure 11-2 Panel A: Professional forecasters' inflation expectations (one year ahead). The chart above illustrates the shift to lower inflation at the beginning of the Covid-19 crisis and higher disagreement among professional forecasters. Source: Federal Reserve Bank of Philadelphia 2020, Survey of Professional Forecasters

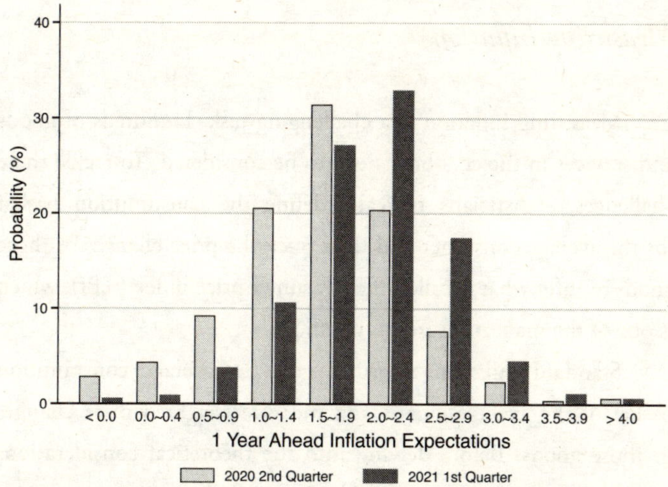

Figure 11-2 Panel B: The chart above shows the reversal to higher inflation expectations in the second half of 2020 and early 2021. Source: Federal Reserve Bank of Philadelphia 2020, Survey of Professional Forecasters

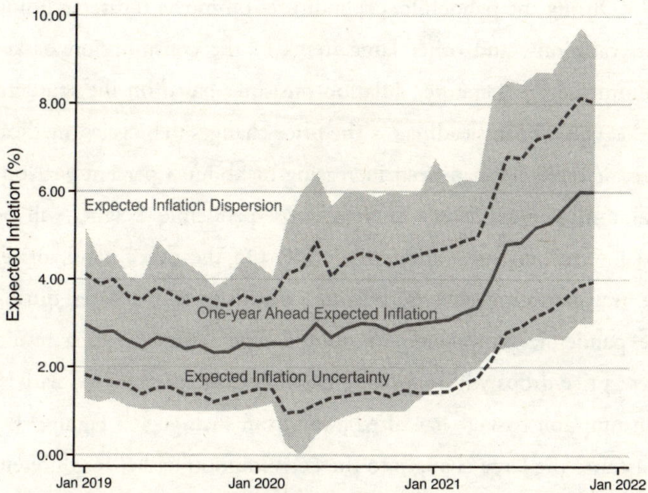

Figure 11-3: Households' inflation expectations over time. In the spring of 2020, households' inflation expectations rose, uncertainty about future inflation expectations rose, and there was increased disagreement among households about future inflation (shaded area). Source: Federal Reserve Bank of New York 2020, Household Survey [240]

Measuring Inflation

Measuring inflation is a challenging task. Hundreds of goods and services in the economy need to be considered. To tackle these challenges, statisticians typically define the consumption basket for the average consumer and then track the price changes of those goods to infer what is called the consumer price index (CPI), which is one of the main measures of inflation.

Standard inflation measures take the average consumption basket of the average citizen and measure weighted price changes in those goods. Before delving into the theoretical considerations surrounding the impact of Covid-19 on inflation, it is important to recognize that consumption baskets changed massively within weeks of when lockdowns started.

During the pandemic, expenditures on movie theaters, dining out, vacations, and other large items in the consumption basket plummeted.[241] Therefore, inflation measures based on the standard basket could be misleading.[242] The price changes to bicycles, medical care, or cable TV had been increasing by about 5 percent year-on-year until August 2020. Therefore, pre-pandemic weights will be too low to be used during this crisis. On the other hand, prices for transportation, hotels, business clothing, and airfares during the pandemic plummeted by double digit figures.[243] As a result, these price drops will be overweighted because the new "Covid-19 consumption basket" has tilted away from such goods. Figure 11-4 illustrates the large changes to the consumption basket for different product categories. Credit card spending on arts, entertainment, and recreational activities were 50 percent lower in November 2020 compared to the pre-pandemic period. On the other hand, expenditures on groceries were persistently higher than in pre-pandemic times.

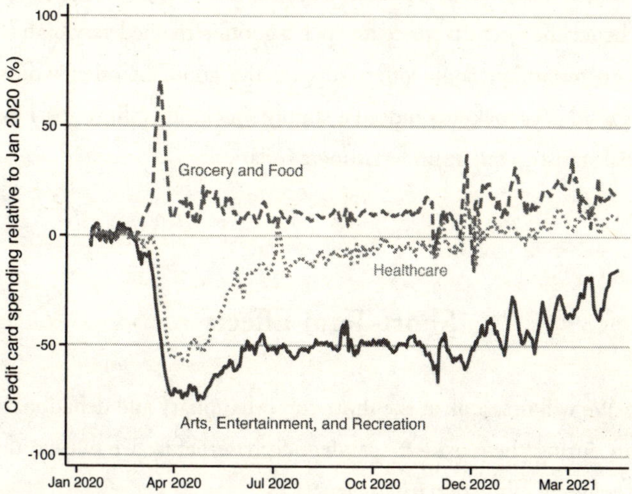

Figure 11-4: Change in consumption basket. US credit card spending relative to January 2020. Source: Opportunity Insights 2021

The evolution of rents, which account for 40 percent of the CPI consumption basket in the United States, also strongly affects measures of inflation. In Manhattan, the median rent fell from \$3500 to \$2700 in 2020.[244] The effect might only be temporary. If people flock back to the Big Apple in 2021, rents might rise and induce a substantial increase to costs of living and consumer-price based measures of inflation.

The exact definition of a "good" matters a lot for measurement purposes. It can also help to clarify whether the Covid-19 economic crisis was a demand or a supply shock. At first sight, one might think that the Covid-19 shock resulted in negative demand for restaurant visits. However, defining a good as a nice meal in a healthy restaurant environment might indicate that such a service was simply *unavailable*, especially indoors. Demand for such a good, and hence the potential price for such a good, remained very high.[245] But no restaurant could offer (supply) the good. In other words, the Covid-19 shock was indeed a supply shock. This illustrates how official statistics might underestimate inflation.

Short-Term Effects

We will first look at the short-run inflationary and deflationary forces during the Covid-19 pandemic phase before we outline the post-pandemic inflationary forces.

Forces

Short-run inflationary forces were muted until the end of 2020, for a variety of reasons.[246] First, there was some degree of **forced savings.** This occurred because many sectors had to shut down or were unable to operate normally. Forced savings particularly impacted higher-income households because wealthier individuals typically spend more in the contact-intensive sector.[247] This tended to create deflationary pressures, the same way that higher risk tends to boost savings and reduce spending.

A second factor was **misallocated capital** across sectors, which reduced supply and tended to increase inflation. Prices can rise if capital that is needed in a low-contact sector cannot be reallocated from the contact-intensive sector.

Precautionary Savings and Flight to Safety

During the Covid-19 shock, a huge increase in uncertainty at the onset of the lockdown increased the **demand for safe assets**. As a result, in March 2020 we witnessed a textbook flight-to-safety, with investors rebalancing their portfolios toward safe assets and away from risky capital. Liquid asset holdings among households surged. In addition, by April 2020, US household savings had increased by 20 percent year-on-year and checking account balances rose by 30 percent.[248] Rising demand for safe assets and money created short-run deflationary pressures as demand for consumption goods fell.

Figure 11-5 highlights the surge in savings, particularly in the spring of 2020. The strong decline in spending on leisure activities, shown in figure 11-4 above, further illustrates this effect. As museums, theaters, and opera houses remained closed, those who love the arts were forced to save the money they would have spent on those activities. The subsequent spikes in US savings in late 2020 and early 2021 are due to the US government stimulus checks given to US households.

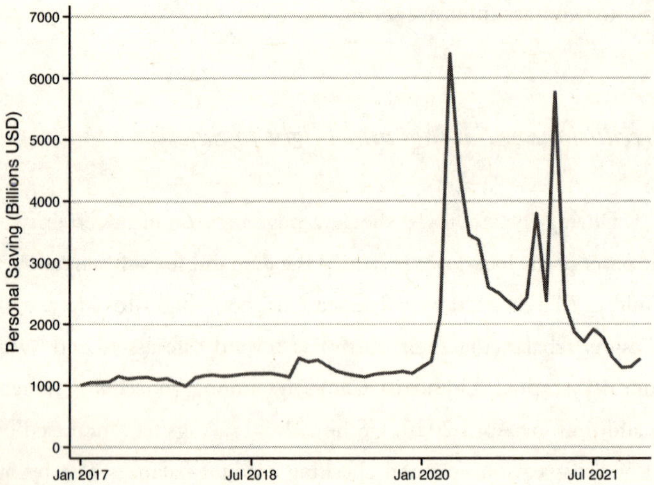

Figure 11-5: Personal savings by US households (annual rate). Source: FRED 2021

Another form of cash-holding came from firms. During the pandemic, businesses, especially large firms, drew down existing credit lines and held the liquidity in liquid short-term assets that could easily be converted to cash if needed. When firms **dash for cash**, the demand for money increases, which reduces inflation pressure.

Breaking Up Global Supply Chains and Excess Capacities

Another factor that influenced inflation and deflation forces during the pandemic was the breakup of **global supply chains**. This partially reversed the productivity gains from globalization, causing prices for some traded goods to rise.[249] On the other hand, **excess capacities** and high unemployment put further downward pressure on prices.[250] However, in the summer of 2021, the global scarcity of lumber and computer chips put significant upward price pressure on those goods.

Central Banks and Unconventional Monetary Policy

Policy with Side Effects

According to Keynesian economics, there is a tradeoff between inflation and unemployment. These theories emphasize that, in the short run (at least), lower unemployment can be achieved at the cost of inflation. This negative relationship between inflation and unemployment is called the Phillips curve. If expansionary monetary policy via low interest rates stimulates aggregate demand, more workers will have to be hired. This will require wage increases unless there is extremely high unemployment in the labor market. As long as the central bank does not raise rates, unemployment should fall—and inflation should increase. Thus, policymakers have to pick sides: Do they prefer low inflation or low unemployment?

However, during the 2000s (longer in Japan), the Phillips curve has been remarkably flat. Lower unemployment was achieved without higher inflation. This facilitated stimulus for the labor market but made it harder to affect inflation.

Many advanced economies have tasked their central banks with achieving a specific inflation target. The US Federal Reserve targets a symmetrical inflation rate of about 2 percent. When inflation is 2 percent, nominal interest rates are higher because creditors want to be compensated for inflation. As a result, there is ample room for cutting nominal interest rates before reaching a zero nominal interest rate. In August 2020, the Fed announced its new Flexible Average Inflation Target of 2 percent. Thus, if the inflation rate becomes too low for a while, then the inflation target can be raised above 2 percent in order to achieve an average inflation rate of 2 percent. In Europe, the ECB aimed (until recently) to achieve an inflation rate of just under 2 percent. In the summer of 2021, the ECB switched to a symmetrical inflation target of about 2 percent.

However, central banks in advanced economies have had trouble achieving inflation rates of 2 percent or higher since the 2008 financial crisis. Given the persistent failure to reach this stated objective, central banks have increased efforts in unconventional monetary policy. But persistent stimulus over the last decade has not affected inflation rates much.

Harvard economist Jeremy Stein points out that persistently low inflation despite large-scale expansionary monetary policy is reminiscent of a doctor who increases the dose of a medication if a first dose does not have an effect on the patient. The doctor might administer a second dose and maybe a third one, but continuously increasing the dosage can come with side effects. The side effects of monetary policy include concerns about financial stability, for example, because asset price bubbles might be building up.

Quantitative Easing with the Objective of Impacting Inflation

Traditionally, central banks set short-term interest rates. In the early twenty-first century, during the 2008 global financial crisis, they exhausted interest rate cuts and began using unconventional monetary policy measures. For example, they began to intervene with a major policy tool called quantitative easing (QE). This involves large-scale purchases of longer-maturity assets with the goal of affecting interest rates along the yield curve. The aim of lowering the long-term interest rates of safe assets, such as government bonds, is to encourage risk-taking. Theoretically, if investors earn low interest rates on safe assets they will switch to riskier investments, such as corporate bonds. That, in turn, will lower financing costs for firms.

Concretely, QE amounts to the central bank acquiring longer-term bonds in exchange for its reserves. Central bank reserves have infinite maturity and therefore are conceptually similar to consol bonds, which pay interest at regular intervals forever but never pay back the principal. Nowadays, reserves pay interest that changes with the policy rate. In other words, the reserves' maturity is infinite, but their interest sensitivity is high (i.e., their duration is low).

The Central Bank Balance Sheet

Quantitative easing affects the central bank's balance sheets. The additional securities purchased by the central bank show up on the asset side. On the liability side (below the zero line in figures 11-6 and 11-7), the amount of outstanding reserves soars.

Figure 11-6 outlines the evolution of the US Federal Reserve's balance sheets so far during the twenty-first century. Figure 11-7 shows the same information for the ECB's balance sheets. In both figures, assets are reported above zero. They largely consist of securities, but they also include gold reserves and lending claims that each central bank has acquired from monetary policy operations. The two main liabilities of these central banks, shown below the zero line, are the outstanding currency in circulation and reserves. Repurchase agreements and, in the US, the Treasury General Account (the US Treasury's account at the Fed) make up the remaining liabilities. The difference between assets and liabilities is the central bank's equity. Since balance sheets have to balance by definition, assets and liabilities plus equity must evolve symmetrically.

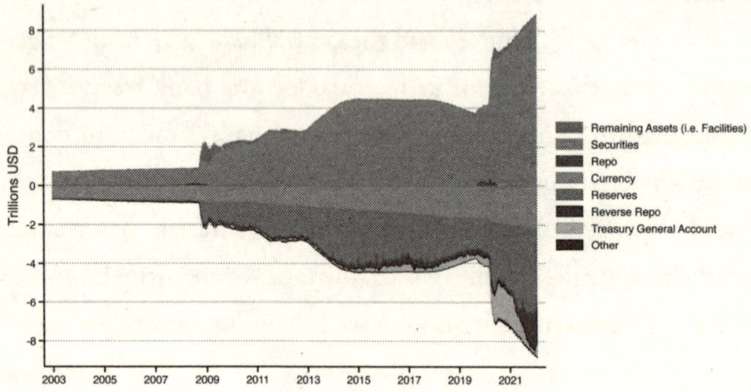

Figure 11-6: US Federal Reserve balance sheet. Assets are above the zero line, while liabilities are below the zero line. Source: FRED 2021

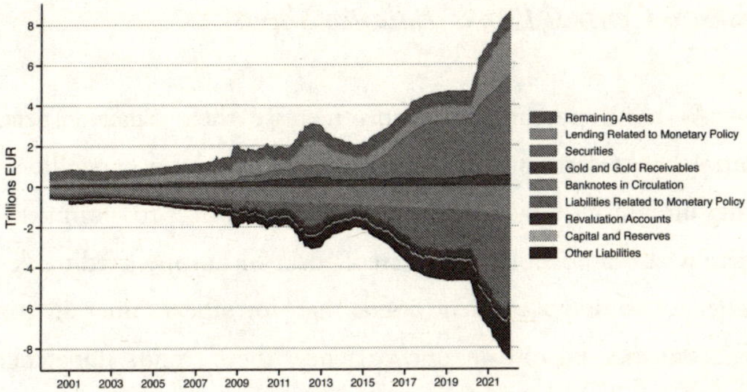

Figure 11-7: ECB balance sheet. Assets are above the zero line, while liabilities are below the zero line. Source: European Central Bank 2021

A first major consequence of the 2008 recession, the euro crisis, and the Covid-19 shock is the surge in the balance sheets of both central banks since 2008. Figure 11-6 illustrates three waves of US quantitative easing. Each time, the central bank issued large amounts of reserves to purchase government securities. The increase in purchases in March 2020 exceeds the three previous QE waves during the 2008 financial crisis. It is worth noting that the Treasury General Account has also substantially increased, owing to the large-scale Treasury interventions.

The ECB has used both QE and repurchase agreements (repos), which are a form of short-term collateralized lending. The continuous purchasing of assets (mostly government bonds but also some corporate bonds) has contributed to large balance sheet growth, especially since 2015. In addition, during the financial crisis, lending operations have fueled balance sheet growth. As one can see in figure 11-7, the pandemic emergency purchase program (PEPP) in 2020 led to another large increase in securities held by the ECB.

Risks to Central Banks' Balance Sheets

As bond purchase programs increase their balance sheets, central banks carry significant risk. One risk is the possibility of rising interest rates, which would cause bond prices to plummet.[251] There is also a possible default/credit risk. In Europe, credit risk is higher for some government bonds than for others. Since all euro area countries borrow in one currency, they cannot unilaterally devalue their currency to repay their debt in any circumstances. This issue was powerfully illustrated during the euro crisis.

Related to this, central banks must consider the dangers of government bonds losing **safe asset status**. If such a trap were to occur, macroeconomic policy would become substantially more complicated. Fiscal authorities would scramble to sustain the refinancing costs of their debt, especially in countries with limited fiscal capacity and limited ability to raise revenue via higher taxes.

Finally, we should take a more holistic perspective and recognize that a central bank is simply one branch of government. That, of course, implies the absence of institutional frictions between the government and the central bank. But it highlights the fact that QE replaces one form of liability—long-term government debt—with another type of liability: central bank reserves.

Flexible Average Inflation Targeting

In 2020, the Fed shifted from a fixed inflation target (about 2 percent) to average inflation targeting. In this new regime, the Fed no longer needed to achieve its inflation target at every moment.

Instead, if inflation happens to be lower than 2 percent for a while, the Fed can let inflation overshoot that target, as long as the overall average is around 2 percent.[252]

At first glance, this approach might seem counterintuitive. If the Fed cannot even reach a 2 percent inflation rate, it seems like it would be harder to achieve a new flexible target. However, the Federal Reserve's hope is that people will realize that interest rate hikes will be shifted into the future. The delay in interest rate increases is consistent with the Fed's expressed policy of allowing inflation to run above 2 percent for a while if necessary. That should contribute to higher inflation expectations.

Helicopter Drop

In April 2020, many US households received a $1,200 per capita check from the Treasury, followed by $600 in December 2020. In the spring of 2021, the Biden administration paid another $1,400 to many US taxpayers. Conceptually, these actions were similar to Milton Friedman's famous "helicopter drop" by which the central bank drops money onto the people with the aim of stimulating inflation. This has long been proposed as the most direct intervention to generate inflation.

At the time of this writing, the inflationary impact of these pandemic-related efforts is not totally clear. A large part of those payments was initially saved rather than spent. In a sense, households brought their new money to the banks. The banks hold excess reserves, and the Fed holds US government debt to back the stimulus checks. However, if households begin to spend the stimulus money, inflation could follow. Larry Summers and Olivier Blanchard argue that the Biden stimulus will overheat the US economy and trigger inflation down the road, a topic we will revisit.

Emerging Markets Developments

Quantitative easing has been used in many countries with various forms of implementation. Brazil has, for example, engaged in a form of "**tropical QE**" by shortening the maturity structure of its debt. Interest rates on short-term debt are usually lower than the per-annum rates on long-term debt. Therefore, Brazil's treasury can reduce its interest expenses by switching to short-term debt. Effectively, this strategy attempts to exploit the steep slope of the yield curve. Government issuance of short-term debt is different than QE. With QE, the central bank swaps long-term bonds for central bank reserves.

Tropical QE ultimately also involves the central bank. If the market becomes unwilling to refinance short-term government debt, the Brazilian central bank will eventually have to jump in and pay the bondholders with newly issued bank reserves. This can cause inflationary pressures and weaken the exchange rate. If, despite its large foreign reserve holdings, markets lose confidence in Brazil, the nation could find itself in a perilous situation.[253] The short-term gains of shortening the maturity structure come at the potential cost of not being able to roll over debt when it comes due.

Long-Term Effects

In the short term, the outlook appears at this time to be deflationary, but other long-run forces could contribute to a potential whipsaw pattern in the future. Redistribution, government commitments, pent-up demand, and margins for large firms can contribute to inflation. Moreover, the lending programs set up by governments around the world might increase inflation or at least reduce future deflation, depending on the pandemic's duration.[254]

Redistribution and government commitments should maintain the purchasing power of households. That should sustain consumption and keep firms afloat. Both of these factors will likely contribute to price increases. We will go into more detail about pent-up demand momentarily.

Economic Recovery and Flight to Consumption

As the economy recovers and risk fades, the earlier flight to safety will reverse. Households will rebalance their portfolios toward riskier assets and away from money and safe assets. Demand caused by rising consumption will put pressure on the aggregate price level, which will add another longer-run inflationary force.

Pent-Up Demand and Supply-Demand Interaction

The most salient force that might drive greater consumption is pent-up demand caused by lockdown restrictions. Many travelers had to cancel 2020 holiday plans and those people could fuel a travel boom once the pandemic is largely overcome. Other sectors—movies, theaters, restaurants, etc.—could experience similar surges in consumer demand.

A lockdown is typically a supply shock, but it can translate into a demand shock as well.[255] Suppose the production of left shoes is halted, but right shoes continue to be produced as usual. Obviously, a right shoe sold separately from a left shoe would have little value to most consumers. So, shutting down left-shoe production would spill over into the right-shoe sector. Consumers would stop buying shoes. If they save the money that would have been spent on shoes so that they can buy them later, then the post-shutdown demand for shoes might soar. This could cause a supply shock for left shoes and a demand shock for right shoes. Throughout the pandemic, we have seen this type of scenario play out among highly complementary products: expensive wine and restaurants; weddings and wedding photographers; popcorn and local movie theaters.

In economic terms, the "intertemporal elasticity of substitution" refers to how much consumers are willing to postpone consumption in exchange for a given interest rate on their savings. The "cross-sectoral elasticity of substitution" refers to the willingness of consumers to substitute goods in one sector for goods in another sector at a given point in time. These two key forces can be at work in the context of a lockdown.[256]

If cross-sectoral elasticity is very low, consumers during a lockdown will resist substituting missing products from one sector with products from other sectors. In this case, a lockdown would lead to a large drop in spending. This large drop in spending could potentially fuel pent-up demand once the lockdown is lifted because households would have more wealth after the period of forced saving.

In this way, short-term depressed demand can be a source of higher demand and inflation in the future, which precisely illustrates the inflation whipsaw mechanism. Inflation might be treacherously low and then strongly rebound.

The Biden Stimulus and the Overheating Debate

The US embarked on an aggressive fiscal expansion during the Trump presidency, in the form of a corporate tax cut followed by a massive fiscal response during the Covid-19 crisis, including the July 2020 CARES Act. This expansionary fiscal policy continued with the $1.9 trillion Biden stimulus package. At the end of July 2021, it appears that more spending, such as a large-scale infrastructure package, will follow.

The December 2020 and March 2021 stimulus bills add up to $2.8 trillion in new spending compared to an output gap estimated to be no more than $900 billion.[257] The output gap measures the difference between the hypothetical GDP of an economy in full-employment and the actual GDP. Knowing whether stimulus measures will overshoot the output gap critically depends on fiscal multipliers. If households save the entirety of their stimulus checks, the multiplier will be zero, but if they spend all of their stimulus money, the multiplier can be larger than one.[258] There is significant uncertainty about the value of the multiplier, but most estimates point to a value of well above 0.3. This is the approximate multiplier value for which $2.8 trillion in spending would close a $900 billion output gap.

In 2021, Lawrence Summers and other prominent economists therefore argued that while some stimulus has been imperative, the size and pace of the Covid-19 relief packages might be too much of a good thing because they threaten to overheat the economy and spark inflation. Warren Buffet has noticed that prices for several raw materials across the holdings of Berkshire Hathaway were soaring in the spring of 2021 with the economy running "red hot."[259]

Similarly, Paul Krugman said in 2021 that to avoid overheating the economy, the $1400 pandemic relief checks sent to households by the Biden administration would need to be "non-stimulating," which means that the money would need to be saved rather than spent.[260] The stimulus checks—financed by issuing more US Treasuries—are not stimulating if people park the money in their banks. That merely results in higher excess reserves in the Federal Reserve System, which leads the Fed, via quantitative easing, to hold more US Treasury securities. In other words, the US government simply issues more US Treasuries that are then indirectly held by households through their extra savings. As explained earlier, this self-financing mechanism explains why helicopter money was not stimulative at the height of the Covid-19 crisis. On the other hand, if people were to spend the checks, then the money would be stimulative and potentially overheat the economy. Paul Krugman nevertheless supports the large Biden stimulus in the US for political reasons—to heal a divided country.

Breaking the Inflation Anchor

How long citizens are willing to postpone consumption depends on *expected* inflation. If they expect high inflation in the future, they will prefer to consume earlier. For this reason, expectations are key. As long as expectations are anchored, consumption shifts will remain small. However, inflation expectations can change. Real danger arises when the long-term inflation anchor breaks. The inflation anchor depends on what people believe about inflation. The anchor also depends on what they believe *others* believe or *will believe* about inflation.

An overheating economy could force the Federal Reserve to act quickly to fend off inflation, either by hiking interest rates or by slowing down—or even halting—open-market asset purchases, as in the "Taper Tantrum" of 2013. Indeed, in February 2021, US interest rates on long-dated debt were temporarily on the rise, despite the Fed's very dovish actions. The large and abrupt nature of the US stimulus packages poses several risks, so it might be safer to spread out the stimulus over time in smaller steps.

In contrast, the inflation anchor could also break on the downside, when deflation cripples the economy. If everyone expects prices in the economy to fall slightly during the coming year, many people might refrain from larger purchases until those price declines materialize. Deflationary expectations can be self-fulfilling. As the population delays consumption, especially of big-ticket durable goods, the lack of demand causes prices to fall even more. The more that households expect deflation, the more they will wait to make purchases, which can accelerate deflation and generate a persistent deflationary trap.

Monetary, Fiscal, and Financial Dominance

Inflation and the Government Budget

How is inflation linked to the government budget? The monetarist Milton Friedman famously claimed that inflation was always and everywhere a monetary problem, but Thomas Sargent said that inflation is always and everywhere a fiscal phenomenon. In other words, inflation is codetermined by current and future government taxes and debt. The **fiscal theory of the price level (FTPL)**, advocated by Christopher Sims and others, emphasizes that the real value of outstanding debt—government bonds and money—must be backed by current or future primary government budget surpluses. If a government runs a persistent budget deficit and becomes unable to pay off its nominal debt with future tax revenues, inflation must rise. That, he said, was the only way for a government to pay off its "real" debt and avoid default. The government must "inflate away" its nominal debt by causing or allowing higher inflation rates. Therefore, stable prices depend on balanced government budgets in the long term. This contrasts with the views of monetarists who attribute inflation exclusively to monetary policies—not to general government debt—and who define money supply as cash, bank deposits, and reserves.

The fiscal theory of the price level has a simple implication. If the fiscal position of a country deteriorates permanently and nominal debt remains the same, the adjustment must happen via a price-level increase—higher inflation.

FTPL further posits that when governments issue debt in their own currency they can never default, simply because governments can always print money to cover the debt payments. However, countries that borrow in foreign currency face distinct challenges. Printing more money to directly pay back the debt is not an option when the debt is denominated in foreign currency. For example, in the Eurozone, if Italy issues new government debt, it cannot unilaterally print more euros to pay off that debt.

Modern Monetary Theory (MMT) goes one step further. This theory argues that as long as unemployment does not exceed the natural rate, there is no need to worry about government spending at all. For those who adhere to this theory, stagflation is not possible.

Historically, large fiscal expenditures have typically resulted in higher inflation. Figure 11-8 reports US budget deficits in the solid line and inflation rates in the darker dashed line, since the US Civil War. The correlation between high inflation and large budget deficits is striking. Moreover, the light dashed line shows the nominal interest rate measured as the weighted average of the rate on three-months commercial paper, which are short-term debt obligations by nonfinancial corporations.

In each major war—the Civil War, World War I, World War II, and the Vietnam War—deficits soared while prices substantially increased. As deficits declined again, inflation was controlled. A similar pattern can be observed in the 1970s and 1980s. The only exception to this pattern occurred during the last decade, in which large budget deficits coincided with very low inflation.

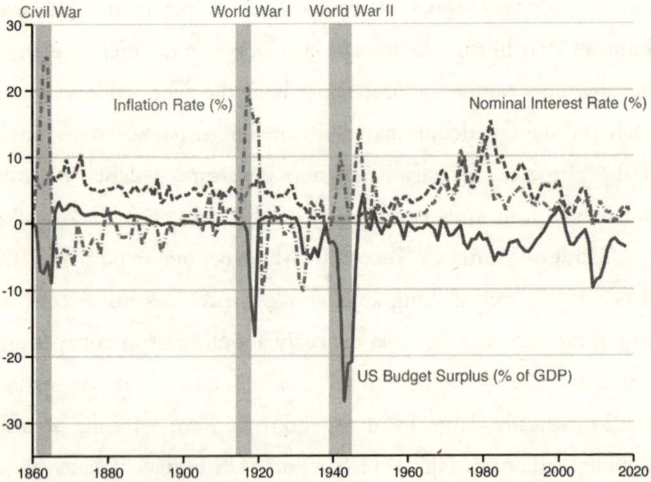

Figure 11-8: The fiscal-inflation link, especially in relation to war financing. The figure shows US wars, budget surpluses, short-term nominal interest rates, and inflation. The budget surplus data and nominal interest rate data comes from FRED 2020. The nominal interest rate is a composite of yields on nonfinancial bonds with a duration of less than three months. The inflation and GDP data come from Officer and Williamson 2021 and Johnston and Williamson 2021, respectively.

Today's high government debt levels, which in the US are in excess of 100 percent of GDP, are largely unheard of in peace times. Nevertheless, large government deficits have occurred and have been conquered before. This provides insights into how monetary and fiscal authorities have interacted in the past.

The approaches of other countries in dealing with the aftermath of war also provide insight into this question. During World War I, all countries involved in the war accumulated large budget deficits because most war expenditures were debt-financed. As a result, short-term inflation affected all war participants in the aftermath.[261]

But over the medium run, Germany's experience strongly contrasts with the Anglo-Saxon experience. The US and the UK imposed high taxes to fight inflationary pressures and to consolidate their governments' budgets. The UK even returned to the gold standard. On the other hand, Germany's fiscal consolidation plan failed, paving the way for the 1923 hyperinflation.[262] This demonstrates that **future tax policy**, and especially **expectations** about it, matter. One might argue that inflation is always and everywhere a political phenomenon because inflationary outcomes depend on whether society and its institutions are strong enough to push through anti-inflation measures.

It is important to remember that wars are also different from pandemics. For example, wars lead to a massive demand stimulus.[263]

Institutional Arrangements

Governments determine budgets and nominal interest rates. In the past, some countries aligned monetary and fiscal authorities under the roof of the ministry of finance. Such a setup, however, bears political economy problems. Prior to elections, it is tempting for politicians to lower interest rates in order to stimulate the economy, even though such action can lead to a post-election surge in inflation. This type of political business cycle is particularly damaging when inflation is already high and interest rate increases are needed.

Even if a government promises low inflation ex-ante, politicians will likely want to renege on that promise as elections approach. A consequence of this time-inconsistency problem is that central banks in many countries have been set up as independent monetary branches of government.[264] Nonetheless, there are important interactions between the central bank and the finance ministry.

When it comes to reining in inflation, the interaction between monetary and fiscal policy is crucial. To address that dynamic, we first explore how monetary and fiscal authority interact. For example, when the central bank raises the interest rate, does the government lower its spending?

Importantly, there is also a third important player to consider: the financial sector. The latter part of this chapter discusses how the possibility of a dominant financial sector, which might require fiscal and monetary policy to adjust accordingly.

The Game of Chicken

To control inflation, the central bank needs the option to step on the brakes and raise interest rates. Hiking the interest rate will increase the government's interest burden. So, for an interest rate hike to be effective, the government would need to reduce expenditures or increase taxes. For this reason, the US Treasury and finance ministries in other countries typically disdain interest rate hikes. The outcome is a conflict between the monetary authority and the finance department. Who will prevail?

In a scenario of **fiscal dominance**, the government simply ignores the central bank's interest rate policy. Imagine, for the sake of the argument, that the central bank increases interest rates to 5 percent. Then the government continues to issue more bonds to cover the higher interest rate burden. With aggregate demand being further stimulated, inflation continues to rise. The central bank might subsequently need to further increase interest rates to curb inflation, to which the government might respond with even more bond issuance. If the government is stubborn, the central bank would lose its power to conduct independent monetary policy.

In a context of **monetary dominance**, the central bank is in the driver's seat and the government is in the passenger seat. The government cuts back on expenditures or increases taxes. This stabilizes inflation.

In reality, we do not know if the monetary or the fiscal authority is in the driver's seat. The conflict resembles the game of chicken, with two race cars speeding toward each other. Who will chicken out first and deviate from the trajectory? The driver who remains stubborn will win unless both remain equally stubborn. If that happens, there will be a crash.

Forceful monetary policy is needed in the short run to accelerate an economy in a deflationary phase. It is equally important to have a monetary policy that can step on the brakes later. Only a central bank with good brakes can act aggressively. The tension is analogous to a race car driver who can take more risks if he knows that his car has strong brakes.[265] The brakes in this case are central bank independence and, as we will see later, macroprudential measures.

Financial Dominance and the Game of Chicken 2.0

As mentioned earlier, there is a third player in the game of chicken between the government's monetary authority and fiscal authority: the financial sector. If that sector is highly resilient, the government might shift losses there. For example, Spain imposed a mortgage moratorium during its Covid-19 crisis. This measure prevented banks from foreclosing on people who could not pay their mortgages on time. It therefore became less likely that mortgages would be paid back in full, which translated into potential losses for the banking system.

If the government shifts losses to a resilient financial sector, then the financial sector will have incentives to pay out dividends and repurchase shares rather than build up buffers. This weakens the financial sector's resilience. If the financial sector is already weak, then the government typically will not shift losses in that direction; rather, the government might provide the financial sector with a bailout.

Who will pay for the bailout? A game of chicken 2.0 emerges. The government might bail out the financial sector with a transparent transfer of resources. Monetary policy can also recapitalize the banking sector by changing asset prices. Lowering interest rates can increase the value of banks' assets and lower the value of liabilities on their balance sheets.

In a regime of financial dominance, **macroprudential policy** can play a critical role in avoiding these bailouts and in ensuring that the financial sector is well capitalized. Macroprudential policy aims to limit economy-wide consequences from financial sector problems. Good macroprudential policy closely watches the risks associated with the build-up of leverage. In addition, stress tests allow regulators to forbid dividend payouts and share buybacks if banks are found to have insufficient buffers.

Central banks can increase the buffers by cleverly designing other policy instruments. For example, they could focus on purchasing bonds only from those firms that conduct solid financial risk management, such as those that did not raise payouts or bolster equity buffers during the pandemic. The US does not have a countercyclical management buffer, but modifying the bond-buying program can invoke capital and liquidity buffers, and it can force banks to cut their share repurchasing activity.[266]

Very Long-Term Inflationary Forces

Charles Goodhart and Manoj Pradhan highlight how today's combination of high public debt levels and an aging population creates additional long-term inflationary pressures.[267] As the population ages, budget deficits are likely to increase as governments seek to finance, for example, larger social security expenditures or medical care for the elderly.

Generally, there are three ways of reducing the large fiscal deficits. First, economic growth could boost tax revenues and hence reduce deficits without much necessity to cut spending. However, productivity growth has been lackluster over the past two decades. Moreover, an aging population with an increasing ratio of elderly people dependent on younger people implies low labor force growth.

Second, in the absence of strong and sustained economic growth, the government could adjust taxes. The third option is to reduce spending. However, these two approaches are politically unpopular, which leaves only the least unpopular solution: higher inflation. If that occurs, central bank independence will increasingly come under threat. Conventional monetary policy frameworks require an independent central bank that can implement monetary tightening in the face of higher inflation. However, governments with large debt burdens will be reluctant to surrender to a regime of monetary dominance. Doing so would imply a surge in the government's interest burden.

Monetary Policy beyond the Taylor Rule

During the 1990s, establishing inflation targets emerged as the standard approach to monetary policy in advanced economies. The central bank could move the interest rate to achieve its inflation target in relation to how inflation and the "output gap" evolved. If inflation rose beyond the target, or if output exceeded the full capacity potential of the economy—a positive output gap—the prescribed remedy was to raise interest rates. On the other hand, in a period of low inflation or in a recession with a negative output gap, the central bank could lower interest rates. This mechanical **Taylor rule**, which is only slightly more involved in practice, provided a simple guideline for central banks—until the 2008 financial crisis.

Since then, governments have been using unconventional monetary policy measures. Now that they are commonplace, it is no longer sufficient to exclusively focus on the interest rate. Central banks have become heavily involved in influencing the price of risk and term spreads by using large-scale asset purchases. This results in the need to monitor central bank balance sheets and their growth.

To manage all of these policy instruments, a more holistic view of the economy is required. Beyond excess inflation and the output gap, the central bank should also focus on fiscal and financial risks. It also needs to monitor the risk that government's interest burden might suddenly rise. Recall that monetary policy feeds back into the government's cost of refinancing its debt. In addition, the central bank needs to consider the nonlinear feedback loops of monetary policy and its impact on the government's debt financing costs. Thus, the simple Taylor rule needs to be expanded, in terms of underlying economic inputs and outputs. An expanded view of the Taylor rule should include not only the interest rate, but also quantity measures of money and other unconventional instruments.

Redistributive Monetary Policy

Finally, it is important to stress that monetary policy has a redistributive component.[268] This is also true for traditional ways of conducting monetary policy because any movement of the interest rate affects bond prices. Borrowers benefit from interest rate cuts whereas savers lose out.

Beyond the direct effects of moving interest rates or spreads, any central bank action targeted at inflation also redistributes. (Unexpected) inflation lowers the value of nominal claims in the economy, such as savings. Likewise, unexpected inflation causes losses to lenders if the inflation is not priced into the interest rate they charge. In contrast, borrowers benefit from surprise inflation because the real value of their debt declines. Holders of real claims, for example inflation-protected bonds (TIPS), also benefit.

Redistributive monetary policy can therefore be used to stabilize sectors with impaired balance sheets. During the 2008 recession, the household and banking sectors had impaired balance sheets. Monetary policy indirectly recapitalized the banking sector and reduced the price of risk. During the Covid-19 shock, fiscal measures such as stimulus checks alleviated household balance sheets, but parts of the corporate sector in many advanced countries took a strong blow. These redistributive aspects of monetary policy lead us naturally to the next chapter, which deals with inequality and its connection to resilience.

CHAPTER 12
Inequality

Inequality in the US has been increasing for several decades. Prior to the Covid-19 pandemic, a growing share of total wealth was owned by the top 1 percent of households. They captured the bulk of the gains from technological improvements. Increasingly, new technologies gravitated toward a winner-takes-all dynamic by which only the largest firms succeeded and pocketed the largest gains. However, US median wages, have remained relatively flat over the past fifty years. In consequence, a sense of insecurity has emerged among many Americans. In recent years, the life expectancy for the average White male American has fallen.[269] In light of rapid medical progress, this is a depressing development that rarely occurs in most countries.

Although inequality has increased *within* many countries, the distribution of *global* wealth points to a reduction in inequality between nations. New technologies and outsourcing to China, East Asia, and Eastern Europe has brought millions of new workers into the workforce. The emergence of a global middle class in those countries has reduced global inequality across countries. However, the bargaining power of workers in advanced economies has declined because they have had to compete with a much larger global labor force and many new technologies.

This chapter focuses on resilience and its implications for inequality along several economic dimensions. After discussing individual resilience and heterogeneity, I will address different measures of inequality and the caveats associated with each. Building on these insights, the discussion will then center around societal inequality.

Inequality in Individual Resilience

The inequality of resilience between the rich and poor has substantial social implications. When a shock hits, wealthier households have ample buffers that enable them to weather the storm, which makes them more likely to remain wealthy in the future. Poor households are more vulnerable and thus have a harder time bouncing back. They are at risk of poverty traps in which they continually fall behind. This widens the gap between the rich and poor even more.

Another effect worsens inequality over time. Because wealthier people know they are likely to bounce back from an adverse shock, they are able to take more risks. For example, they might be more willing to invest in riskier assets, which promise greater expected returns in the long run. But poor households with less resilience cannot withstand volatility and thus might avoid risky but profitable opportunities. Sendil Mullainathan and Eldar Shafir emphasize that the poor spend a lot of energy ensuring day-to-day subsistence, which prevents them from taking risks.[270] In the long run, the ability to take risks amplifies the initial level of inequality because wealthier households usually earn higher returns on investments than poorer households.[271]

Different Forms of Inequality

To best analyze how individual resilience affects inequality, we need to distinguish between different forms of inequality. Journalists commonly report that inequality is increasing, but in practice there are different concepts of inequality. Often overlooked is the inequality of resilience. Those who are more resilient can take on riskier and more profitable opportunities, which makes them better able to generate income. The long-term outcome is greater wealth inequality.

Income Inequality

Income is a flow variable over a certain time interval, say a year. Income inequality is a measure of the dispersion of incomes across individuals. The richest Americans might have earned millions of dollars in a year, whereas many households might have had incomes below $30,000 in the same year. The impact of the Covid-19 crisis might not have had a leveling effect at the very top of the income distribution, but it might have caused some leveling below the top 1 percent. As an example of leveling, consider the many small business owners who often feature in the upper half of the income distribution. During the pandemic, many sustained substantial income losses, even after taking government subsidies into account. By contrast, other less well-off citizens were able to at least maintain their normal salary incomes.

Wealth Inequality

Evaluations of income inequality do not include the value of a family's house, financial assets, or other stock variables. Likewise, measures of wealth inequality only provide a snapshot of inequality at a point in time, say at the end of a particular year. However, wealth measures change when people save additional income, and they change when assets gain or lose value. The values of assets are hugely affected by changes in the interest rate. Take for example the holder of a bond that pays $100 in a year. An interest rate decline will not change the income from the bond, but the bond's present discounted value would rise due to the lower interest rate. This would represent a pure capital gains effect and the bondholder would become wealthier on paper, despite the unchanged income.

Measuring inequality is not a straightforward task. Some possible approaches include using tax returns or inferring wealth from estate tax payments. Once a data source has been settled on, delicate questions about how to value assets need to be tackled. One particularly large challenge is how to value people's future social security claims.[272] Payments that lie decades in the future need to be appropriately discounted and expectations about future taxes and benefits payments need to be factored in. Using a higher interest rate to discount future social security payments will reduce their present value. Over a forty-year horizon, even small changes in assumptions about interest rates can matter a lot, reminding us of the power of exponential growth.

Another challenge is to assess the value of private firms. Many people in the top 1 percent of the income distribution are entrepreneurs. They are not only Silicon Valley entrepreneurs. They are also doctors and lawyers who run successful private practices. In contrast to public firms whose market value can be inferred from the stock price, a private firm's value is much harder to gauge.

Despite these measurement challenges, most authors find that wealth inequality in the US has risen since 1980. The extent of this increase, however, is being hotly debated.[273] Outside the US, it is much less clear if wealth inequality has risen. In France, Britain, and Denmark—the countries with some of the best available data—the picture is much more mixed. Inequality, if it has increased at all, has increased less than in the US.

Many emerging economies are characterized by high inequality as well. In China, inequality has increased significantly over the past three decades. Today, China is one of the most unequal societies in the world.[274]

Resilience Inequality

Resilience inequality is a new concept. It conveys the truth that people have unequal *abilities* to bounce back after facing an adverse shock. For the rich, the Covid-19 crisis might only be a temporary shock. But poor workers without savings—the majority of Americans cannot cope with a $1000 unexpected expense—might face long-lasting consequences. In the presence of labor market scarring, a temporary and unexpected shock such as Covid-19 can morph into a permanent knockdown. In other words, poor people are typically less resilient than rich people. As explained above, resilience inequality amplifies income inequality and, given its persistence, worsens wealth inequality in the long run.

Social Mobility

Individual resilience is also linked to social mobility. Social mobility is elevated when high-income earners in one period become low-income earners in the next period and vice versa. If these changes occur all the time, resilience is high because low-income earners can escape traps and move out of the low-income bracket.

Health Inequality and Resilience

Among advanced economies, the United States was particularly ill-prepared for the healthcare crisis imposed by the Covid-19 pandemic. In contrast to Canada's and Europe's **universal health insurance**, about 10 percent of the US population did not have health insurance.[275] Thus, Americans had weak resilience against the spread of the virus. In the early phase of the Covid-19 pandemic, many avoided testing and treatment because they feared large out-of-pocket expenses. Moreover, the US population was (and still is) relatively unhealthy, making them more susceptible to the worst Covid-19 outcomes. The poor overall health of Americans is exemplified by the nation's stalled life expectancy in recent years. In contrast, life expectancy has steadily increased in other advanced economies.

Many US workers in the bottom half of the income distribution do not have access to **paid sick leave**.[276] This has been exacerbated in recent years by job growth in the **gig economy**, which offers few protections for workers.[277] During this pandemic, insufficient protections for sick workers have created the potential for negative health externalities. When sick workers are forced to work in order to maintain their incomes, they put coworkers at risk of infection. These health fissures are particularly relevant because Covid-19 has its worst effects among those suffering from preexisting conditions.[278] Improving **health insurance** coverage and **access to healthcare** can enable people to bounce back, which contributes to aggregate resilience.

Job security, especially in the US, plays a double role. Jobs obviously provide incomes for a decent living, but they are also a major source of access to health insurance. When workers lose jobs, they also lose health insurance. Bill Clinton's healthcare plans, at the beginning of his presidency in 1993, were designed to help people maintain health insurance coverage during job transitions.

Thus, inequality has strongly interfered with efforts to slow the spread of SARS-CoV-2. In the US, richer counties tend to benefit most from **social distancing** measures, perhaps because more workers can switch to work-from-home and thus minimize workplace infection risks.[279]

For the poor, this switch to home offices is often not an option. The situation is worse in developing countries. In Indian slums, social distancing is more of an ideal than a reality. The proximity of living quarters, and the necessity to work, prevents effective social distancing.[280] Additionally, poorer households are often more affected by income losses when shutdowns hit, even though part of their income losses have been absorbed by expanded "social assistance," at least in Latin American countries.[281]

Regional Inequality

Health inequality often has a regional component. Affluent neighborhoods have better hospitals and often more hospital beds per capita. Given the substantial segregation of US cities and suburbs into more affluent and poorer neighborhoods, health inequalities have large differential effects on local communities. Similarly, in Brazil, healthcare provision to poor neighborhoods is inferior compared to richer neighborhoods.[282] A lack of access to proper sanitary conditions is an additional challenge. As a result, poor neighborhoods in Brazil have been particularly affected by Covid-19.[283]

Resilience inequality during the Covid-19 crisis, and its impact on income and wealth inequality, also has a regional element. For example, the areas in Manhattan, in New York City, that experienced the greatest drop in consumer spending were affluent, such as the Upper East Side. In March 2020, spending on in-person services all but evaporated.

Figure 12-1 shows the **spending patterns of rich and poor**

households in California. Spending by the poor recovered to pre-pandemic levels within three months, partly owing to large fiscal stimulus efforts. On the other hand, spending by the rich remained depressed by about 10 percent in December 2020.

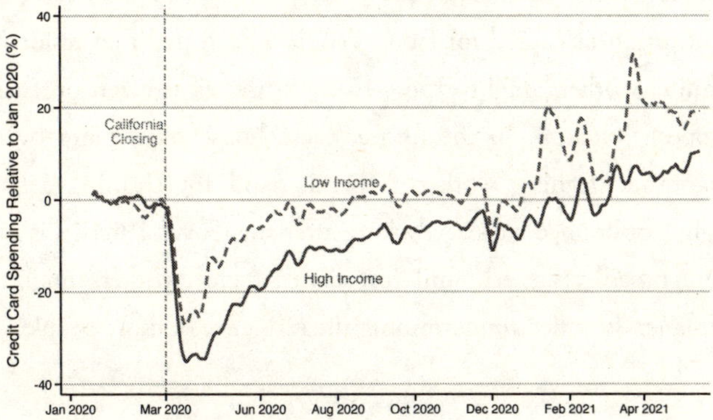

Figure 12-1: Spending of high-income individuals versus low-income individuals. Source: Opportunity Insights 2021

Spending and employment have also displayed important geographic patterns. Richer neighborhoods have experienced larger declines in low-income employment. As a result, "the poor serving the rich" have suffered the most during the Covid-19 crisis.[284] US counties with high ex-ante inequality have witnessed an increase in inequality because affluent households have been largely shielded from Covid-19, in part because they could switch to home offices. Workers in non-essential services have borne the largest burden. Combined with resilience inequality, the Covid-19 crisis might further widen the gap between affluent and poorer households. A critical question is therefore how poor households can bounce back from the crisis.

The Robot Vacuum Effect and Scarring

These disparities might be amplified by a "**robot vacuum effect**." Fear of contact-intensive services, at least before vaccines became widely available, had the potential to accelerate the substitution of capital for labor. People who feared that residential cleaning workers might expose them to the virus often purchased a robotic vacuum. In the future, these households might be less reliant on cleaning workers. The demand for cleaning services might not bounce back, even long after the Covid-19 crisis is over. More broadly, the rebound for service sector workers might be permanently stifled, undermining the resilience of those people.

Learning Inequality: Scarring Caused by Unequal Opportunity

Rather than mitigating inequalities, the Covid-19 crisis might amplify them and create permanent traps. This possibility is exemplified by the divide in online learning participation. Low-income students are doing far fewer math exercises on a commonly used app than their high-income peers.[285] Even Google searches for online learning resources are more frequent in higher income areas.[286] This trend is sobering because education is a critical input for developing resilience; it makes workers more flexible and better able to adapt.

In the Netherlands, students who took final exams during the lockdown displayed a 3 percentile points learning loss compared to those who took the final exams prior to the lockdown. Those losses were significantly larger for students with less-educated parents.[287] This type of education loss negatively affects resilience to future shocks. There can also be a stark divide between private and public school systems. Students in British private schools were twice as likely as state school pupils to receive daily online lessons.[288] At the same time, pupils from lower-income backgrounds were more likely to miss a day of school.

Some students might permanently fall into a trap. Impediments to human capital accumulation will also undermine resilience for those whose learning has suffered during the pandemic. Moreover, many American children receive their lunches at school. As a result, children living in families with food insecurity face a double burden when they shift to an online learning environment.

In developing countries, these challenges are even more acute. School can be an equalizing force, but when lockdowns force children to stay home from school, there is a significant danger that they might never return. The formation of human capital would be profoundly impaired, which is another source of long-run scarring. Marcia Lima reports that, in Brazil, the share of middle school students with a cell phone and internet access is very unevenly distributed. This is particularly the case in the North and Northeast areas of Brazil, where few students have access to the equipment needed for homeschooling.[289]

Inequality and the Resilience of the Social Contract

A society is more resilient if its social contract is broadly accepted among most of its members. A lack of fairness, equal opportunity, gender equality, and racial disparities undermine the resilience of the social contract. Therefore, politics should not unjustly favor or disadvantage certain groups in the society. Fostering resilience equally among all individuals makes society as a whole more resilient. In the remainder of this chapter, we take a closer look at the gender imbalances, racial disparities, and policy differences that have emerged during the Covid-19 crisis.

Gender Disparities

In addition to being unfair, gender disparities can inhibit women from taking more risks and hinder their ability to rebound after a shock. This can translate into long-lasting scarring in their careers and incomes.

Novel data sources reveal that women were hit much harder by the Covid-19 shock in March 2020. Men typically suffer more from recessions than women. But the Covid-19 recession has been quite different than any post-World War II recession. It has impacted the service sector disproportionately relative to manufacturing. Male employment skews toward durable goods industries, such as manufacturing, while female employment skews toward the service sector. The surge in unemployment across genders caused by the Covid-19 crisis was unique in its magnitude. In addition to facing massive job losses, women also had to carry the lion's share of extra household and childcare duties, including homeschooling, that arose during school lockdowns.[290]

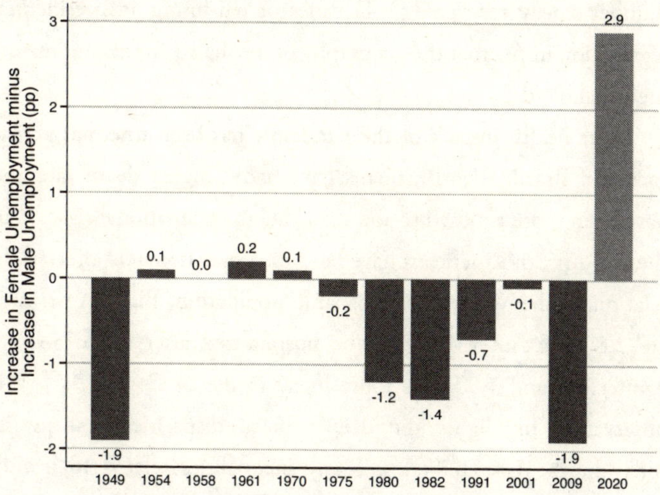

Figure 12-2: Female unemployment rate minus the rise in the men's unemployment rate from the first to the last month of each recession in the United States, according to NBER business cycle dates. The underlying series are seasonally adjusted. Source: Alon et al., 2020

Racial Disparities and Resilience

In the US, racial disparities and tensions increased during the Covid-19 crisis in 2020. African American and Hispanic workers are more likely to work in high-risk occupations, and they are more likely to live in densely populated housing. They also have less access to healthcare and a higher rate of comorbidities.[291] A similar pattern emerges when we look at how small business owners fared during the crisis. Minority, immigrant, and women entrepreneurs were hit hardest by the crisis. The number of active African American business owners dropped by 41 percent in April 2020 before that number slowly recovered.[292] Decades of red-lining and residential segregation imply that the geography of inequality in the US mirrors the racial divide.

The health impact of the pandemic has been **unequal across races**. In Brazil, Afro-Brazilians have had a higher death rate and have been more exposed to the virus due to occupational risks.[293] In the US, African Americans have been disproportionately affected. In relation to the White, non-Hispanic population, Black Americans are 2.8 times more likely to be hospitalized after a SARS-CoV-2 infection and 1.9 times more likely to die of Covid-19.[294] This observation highlights the deeper racial disparities that persist today in the United States. Many inequalities related to health, income, education, achievement, violence, and work environments particularly affect African Americans.

After the murder of George Floyd in May 2020, the racial divide in the US also turned into a **political crisis**. Lisa Cook has argued for deep changes beyond superficial "blue sky thinking" with the goal of achieving lasting structural change.[295] Among her recommendations for antiracist policies and practices, she cites the need to address the under-representation of minorities in the fields of science, technology, engineering, and math (STEM). She points to the importance of restructuring police forces.[296] And she says that the US Congress should address the glaring racial wealth gap (see figure 12-3).[297] Since the US civil rights era in the 1960s, progress on closing the racial wealth and income gaps has been painstakingly slow. Both gaps roughly stand where they were fifty years ago. The wealth ratio between White and Black men has fluctuated between four and six, meaning that the average White man has four to six times more wealth. Earnings are about twice as high for White men relative to Black men. So far, the equalization of civil rights has not been mirrored by a reduction in economic inequality.

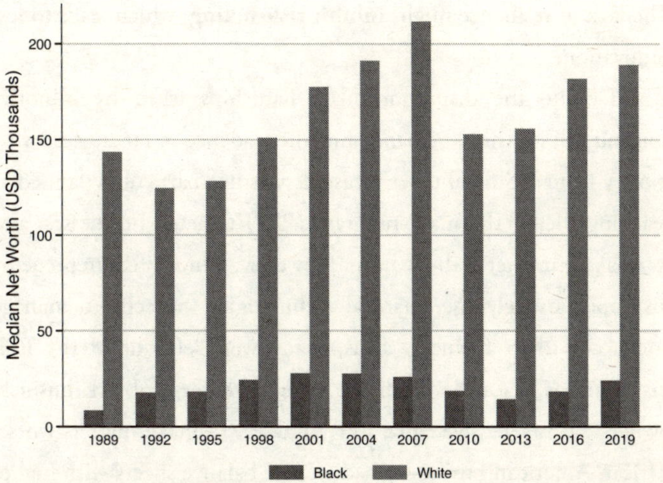

Figure 12-3: Median net worth between US Black, non-Hispanic, and White non-Hispanic people. Source: Aliprantis, Carroll, and Young 2020; and Federal Reserve Board of Governor 2020, Survey of Consumer Finances

The **racial wealth gap** spills into **entrepreneurial inequality**. More than a third of US small businesses rely at some point on a gift from family members or friends. Because of the large racial wealth gap, **African American** entrepreneurs are significantly less likely to receive this kind of support. Runway Social Finance, based in San Francisco, California, aims to address this problem. They provide funding to small businesses, including to those owned by

African Americans, under the sole condition that they have a strong business plan.[298] The general lack of business investment support for African Americans illustrates how resilience inequality can exacerbate economic inequality. If African American entrepreneurs are less resilient due to smaller buffers, a temporary recession can cause **permanent scarring effects** among minority communities. The lack of resilience might **inhibit risk-taking**, which leads to less innovation.

Despite the disproportionate hardships faced by minority communities during the pandemic, the evidence so far suggests that money from US fiscal relief measures was not particularly aimed at reaching them. The main program (PPP) targeted businesses, and it was administered by banks. However, minority entrepreneurs disproportionately use financial technologies (fintech) to manage and access their finances. Thus, many were left out of the PPP distributions. Counties with the highest shares of Black business owners did not receive equal PPP funds.[299] To make matters worse, African American businesses had weaker balance sheets with higher leverage before the Covid-19 crisis started.[300]

A common cause of these inequities is **systemic racism**.[301] Lisa Cook finds that the lack of African American engagement in the **innovation process** has resulted in the US losing 4.4 percent of GDP each year. These losses exceed the 2.7 percent annual loss caused by the discrimination of women.[302] Beyond the economic losses, the longstanding racial achievement gaps raise the question of whether we as a society can be really free if there is no equal opportunity.

Outlook and Lessons from History

In the future, the Covid-19 pandemic will probably be considered as one of those rare tragedies that had far-reaching consequences. But the long-term effects of the pandemic on inequality cannot yet be ascertained. Many tech firms and their shareholders have made large gains whereas many poor people have suffered terribly. Previous pandemics, such as the Black Death plague in the fourteenth century, have caused large changes to inequality.

In fact, Walter Scheidel observes that income and wealth inequality have only been brought down in the past by large crises, most notably wars with large-scale mobilization, "transformative revolutions," state failures, and pandemics.[303] He qualifies these as the four horsemen of leveling. Any one of these four horsemen, he says, must appear in large scale with near "apocalyptic" effects on contemporaries to have a leveling effect.

Both world wars in the twentieth century destroyed large amounts of capital. The impact was mostly felt by the wealthy, who disproportionately held the capital. The death of many males in prime working age also restricted labor supply, driving up real wages. Moreover, Scheidel argues that the world wars "also served as a uniquely powerful catalyst for equalizing policy change, providing powerful impetus to franchise extensions, unionization, and the expansion of the welfare state. The shocks of the world wars led to what is known as the 'Great Compression,' massive attenuation of inequalities in income and wealth across developed countries.[304] Mostly concentrated in the period from 1914 to 1945, it generally took several more decades to fully run its course."[305] The Russian Revolution and the meltdown of modern-day Somalia are examples of revolutions and state failures that produced long-lasting effects.

Finally, the Black Death's large redistributive effects toward labor can be attributed to the dramatic decline in the "human capital stock" as millions of people died across Europe. Consequently, the relative price of labor increased as labor became scarce relative to capital. Paradoxically, a human catastrophe can foster resilience equality.

Will the Covid-19 crisis cause a similar overturn of income distribution, or perhaps even wealth? This pandemic is different than the world wars, the fourteenth-century plague, or state failure. It features neither of the two key economic mechanisms that can drive leveling. The physical capital stock has not been destroyed and the human capital stock, at least so far, has remained mostly intact. Moreover, a significant margin of adjustment in recent decades has been the replacement of workers with robots. This trend could put more downward pressure on wages in sectors susceptible to automation.

The Covid-19 pandemic has been a major shock for us, but it might not be that significant compared to other shocks in history, and it might also be more temporary than the four horsemen emphasized by Walter Scheidel. Leveling of inequality requires massive shocks that inhibit or prevent any mean reversion. Whatever happens today, equality—not inequality—should be resilient.

PART IV

GLOBAL RESILIENCE

CHAPTER 13

Resilience Challenges of Emerging Economies

During the past ten thousand years of human history, **world population grew** to about four billion people by the mid-1970s. In the past forty-five years, global population has increased by almost another four billion people. In the 1970s, a prominent topic of discussion (often fueled by the Club of Rome) was the "limits of growth." At that time, the outlook must have seemed daunting: How to feed this rapidly growing population and how to ensure that humanity prospers?

Despite that somewhat pessimistic backdrop, humanity has been remarkably successful. Hundreds of millions of people over the past four decades have escaped from poverty and moved into the global middle class. Increasing globalization has played a key role in this success story. In the early 1990s, 1.9 billion people, or 36 percent of the world's population, still lived in extreme poverty. Today, approximately 650 million people are living in extreme poverty, even though the world's population has increased. The global economy has experienced a "big bounce" that lifted hundreds of millions out of poverty.[306]

Over the second half of the twentieth century, **global inequality has decreased** substantially. The economic rise of India, China, and the East Asian Tigers has lifted hundreds of millions of people out of poverty into the global middle class. Those countries have grown faster than advanced economies, leading to a substantial reduction in global inequality. Nevertheless, the threat of getting stuck remains.

How Poverty and Middle-Income Traps Inhibit Resilience

A common tendency is to treat all emerging and developing economies **(EMDEs)** as a monolith, but they are quite **different** in terms of institutions, stages of economic development, and development strategy. They also have to battle with many challenges that inhibit resilience.

Poverty Traps

Poverty is often defined as falling below a certain income level, the so-called absolute "poverty line," which is based on the minimum resources needed for physical well-being. A more dynamic definition of **poverty** relates to our concept of resilience. A man is poor if an adverse shock, say a crop failure, prevents him from being able to send his children to school. That makes it harder for the whole family to recover from the shock. We could make a big difference by simply offering the man the ability to bounce back after a shock, even if his income does not immediately rise.

Individual poverty traps are compounded in some of the least-developed countries (LDCs). In fact, large populations in LDCs are living at the edge of a poverty trap, or they have already crossed the tipping point. When a whole country finds itself in a poverty trap, there is a lack of aggregate resilience and the economy as a whole will not be able to climb out of the hole.

Middle-Income Traps

In the early phases of their economic development, many nations have escaped poverty traps and have made significant technological strides. By offering cheap, often unskilled labor, and by consuming little and investing extensively, many countries can achieve substantial growth rates. This lifts them out of low-income situations in which they must focus on basic survival and moves them toward middle-income status. But then these emerging markets face new challenges. As they avoid poverty traps, gain a substantial middle class, and find some fiscal space to fight the economic consequences of shocks (like a pandemic), they might fall into the disputed **middle-income trap**.

Organizing an economy that is catching up is different than running an economy at the technological frontier. Catching up can often be achieved with investment-based development. By investing a large share of GDP, at the expense of higher consumption, the capital stock is rapidly built up and countries grow. The US has consumed about 67.5 percent of GDP per capita over the last decade.[307] This figure is between 50 and 55 percent in China.[308]

In the investment-driven phase, nations face sizeable, fixed costs to set up new industries and infant-industry protections. These protections might include placing some limits on competition so as to incentivize the development of new industries and startups.

However, as economies get closer to the technological frontier, development strategies must move toward an innovation-based strategy. During the catch-up phase, countries need to deploy large amounts of capital. But economies at the technological frontier grow through innovation. So middle-income countries need to pivot to a different growth model as they mature. In the innovation-based phase, the largest remaining gains come from the efficient allocation of people who manage economic activity.[309] To sustain technological growth, the most skilled managers need to manage the most important innovative activities. However, in this phase, limited competition can lead to the suboptimal allocation of skilled managers to those critical activities. If the nations do not correct the misallocation of managerial talent, and if they fail to build up human capital, they risk falling into the middle-income trap where growth substantially slows after the initial growth spurt from low- to middle-income status. The goal of catching up to advanced economies might be delayed or never be achieved at all. To prevent such an outcome, more competition, more investment in human capital, and more effort to develop frontier innovative sectors are required.

Fostering the development of human capital by expanding and deepening the education sector enhances workers' skills. It also provides resilience—if more workers can easily be reallocated to different tasks in the face of shocks. In contrast, neglecting critical areas for advanced development makes economies vulnerable. One shock can destroy resilience or push countries into a trap.

Export-Driven and Import-Substitution Development

Countries pursue various growth models. The most successful approach to development is the **export-driven growth model,** which has been employed by most Asian countries. It has worked phenomenally well, lifting hundreds of millions of people out of poverty in China, South Korea, India, Hong Kong, Singapore, and Taiwan. Expanding economic and financial globalization has further amplified those gains. However, this export-driven model is coming under threat. If developed countries turn inward, then the developing countries that rely on trade and foreign direct investment (FDI) will pay the highest price.[310] Impeding the development of emerging markets could lead to a global form of economic scarring. So far, the pandemic has not caused developed nations to re-shore production. As of the spring of 2021, the global emphasis has been centered around diversifying supply chains across multiple suppliers in different countries.

On the other hand, Brazil's **import substitution industrialization (ISI) development model** tries to replace imports with local production by using import tariffs to shield domestic firms from foreign competition. The state-led ISI model, which Brazil adopted in the 1950s, has been stagnating since the 1980s.

Brazil's closed economy has failed to catch up with advanced economies over the past decades, and it has experienced excessive state involvement in economic policy and high inequality.[311] Amid spiraling debt, slow growth, social tensions, and a shaky Brazilian democracy, risks run high.[312] Brazil's suboptimal development model and high budget deficits prior to the Covid-19 crisis have placed limits on the nation's fiscal space—and impaired the economy's ability to rebound from the pandemic. Moreover, when the Covid-19 crisis hit, Brazil, in contrast to other Western economies, was just coming out of a recession.[313]

Health Resilience

As is true in advanced economies, resilience in EMDEs also involves health resilience. In EMDEs it is more difficult to bounce back from health shocks, such as the pandemic. The health tradeoffs in these nations are different, lockdowns are less effective, and population density is often higher. On the other hand, EMDEs typically have younger populations, which was a positive factor during the first waves of the pandemic because young people are usually less vulnerable to the serious impacts of Covid-19.

Visible versus Invisible Health

The initial reaction to a shock like a pandemic can adversely affect the overall health of a population. This was illustrated by the tradeoff between visible and invisible deaths in emerging markets.

As nations focused energy and resources on public health responses to Covid-19, negative side effects emerged in other areas of public health. Immunizations against other diseases were often held back. More than one million Indian children missed crucial immunizations during the lockdown and riskier at-home births increased. A major worry for health experts in India has been tuberculosis. Deficiencies in tuberculosis care during the Covid-19 pandemic could lead to more than six million additional cases in India, leading to 1.4 million deaths by 2025.[314] Hence, there has been a tradeoff between fighting Covid-19 and the struggle to contain other infectious diseases. Low Covid-19 deaths might mask many invisible deaths due to delayed immunizations or the postponement of other health procedures.

On the other hand, taking the Covid-19 crisis too lightly has had dire consequences, as illustrated by India's second wave in the spring of 2021. Daily confirmed cases reached more than four hundred thousand by early May 2021. The true number of cases was estimated to be five to thirty times larger.[315] Large crowds at religious festivals and political rallies contributed to the disaster. When cases began picking up in the state of Maharashtra, which is ruled by an opposition party, the central government arguably did not provide much help. A failed health-care system fueled the crisis as the pandemic rapidly spiraled out of control. Lack of oxygen and overwhelmed hospitals forced many people to die on the streets while waiting to be admitted to hospitals. Some doctors were attacked by the relatives of those whom they could not treat or save.[316] Some people even contemplated moving from Delhi, the heavily hit capital, to the South of India. In the midst of this tragedy, local support networks of citizens sprang into action. These social networks enhanced resilience, which illustrates how strong communities can be an additional support to help people cope with a severe crisis.

Almost all EMDEs were hit by Covid-19, including Argentina, Rwanda, and Nigeria. Brazil and South Africa suffered from contagious variants of the virus.[317] India's Delta and double variants of the virus spread to other countries, which was devastating to India and the world. The threat of additional mutations, and thus of renewed outbreaks, remains.

Less-Effective Policy Measures in EMDEs

Shocks of all types can be severe in EMDEs, but government responses are often more muted due to limited policy space. For example, Covid-19 lockdowns in EMDEs have been more expensive and difficult to implement because large numbers of workers live hand-to-mouth. If the basic, always-urgent questions of subsistence are left unattended, more deaths might occur than those caused by Covid-19.[318] In these contexts, extensive social distancing and business restrictions are less-feasible tools for ensuring livelihoods and survival.[319]

Notwithstanding their unique challenges, emerging markets have imposed stringent lockdowns. A **lockdown** can be an instrumental tool to **signal** the seriousness of the health crisis to the population. Despite their crucial signaling role, lockdowns in EMDEs have been unsustainable because few jobs can be done at home in such countries.[320] Many emerging economies have had to reopen before the virus was contained, leading to substantial economic damage and sometimes disappointing health results.[321] **Poor living conditions** can weaken adherence to social distancing. Evidence from cellphone data in Brazil demonstrates that residents of *favelas,* low-income informal settlements, **do not socially distance** as much as residents from other areas. Crowded living quarters and the close proximity of dwellings also challenge the imposition of public health measures.[322]

Resilience through Fiscal Policy Space

Good policies provide supports that can speed up a post-shock recovery. These policies are costly and therefore depend on a country's fiscal capacity. First, the capacity to redistribute losses and insure citizens requires taxing power, which is more limited among EMDEs. Second, building up buffers in good times prior to a crisis provides extra resilience. Third, the ability to borrow depends on credibly anchored tax plans, international tax competition, and the danger of losing safe asset status.

One striking feature of the Covid-19 crisis is that emerging markets have significantly more fiscal space than in previous crises. This is the result of low interest rates in the US, which contribute to sustained capital flows into emerging markets. Nevertheless, EMDEs still have substantially less fiscal space than advanced economies and they are more vulnerable to reversals of capital flows.

Capacity to Redistribute and to Improve EMDEs' Taxing Power

Fiscal policy relies heavily on a government's taxing power. It is interwoven with a country's development model, its informal economy, and its institutional framework. A country with taxing power can redistribute and compensate populations within a society who suffer the most from a shock. This ensures that those most affected by a shock can bounce back, which is the precondition for social resilience.

The extent of government responses to the Covid-19 pandemic has been quite diverse.[323] Advanced economies spent, on average, about 20 percent of GDP on direct fiscal support and government **guarantees** in 2020. (The breakdown was about equal between the two.) For emerging economies, such as Brazil, Bulgaria, and India, all fiscal measures and guarantees have accounted for only about 6 percent of GDP. In comparison, the low-income developing countries (LIDCs), the relatively poorest countries on the planet (e.g., Myanmar, Ethiopia, or Senegal), only had 2 percent of fiscal relief.[324] As a result, those countries near the bottom of the global development ladder are at risk of substantial scarring, which could impair their ability to catch up in the future. **Less ex-ante fiscal space implies lower resilience** in cases of large shocks like a pandemic.

During the pandemic, even *within* each group of countries, there has been large heterogeneity in the implementation of fiscal measures. Turkey, for example, almost exclusively relied on **loans and guarantees** but had relatively little direct fiscal spending (13 percent vs. 1 percent of GDP). Chile strongly prioritized **direct**

fiscal measures (8 percent vs. 2 percent of GDP).[325] Guarantees are cheaper for the government because they do not entail direct fiscal expenditure, but they worsen firms' debt overhang problems.

How should countries decide on whom to tax in order to finance these support programs? Labor, capital, or both? A traditional option, going back to Ramsey, is to tax the less-mobile factor because that approach is less distortionary. Many workers face challenges to migration, but capital is internationally mobile. Thus, capital taxation is supposedly ineffective because capital can simply relocate to another country. This is especially true in today's knowledge economy, in which large technology firms can easily reallocate activity to countries with advantageous tax rates. This argument makes the case for high taxes on labor and relatively low taxes on capital. One proposal to achieve higher taxes on capital, despite capital's mobility, would be a tax on global income, similar to the current system for US citizens. Basically, US citizens' income on capital and labor is taxed by the US regardless of where they live in the world. This system could be extended to corporations as well.[326]

To achieve this aim, an agreement among major countries about how to tax the rich, and how to tax and share capital, would be needed. In the spring of 2021, the Biden administration supported an international initiative for the global taxation of corporate profits. This reanimated a view that the OECD in Paris had long been advocating.

Beyond shifting profits abroad, firms can also avoid taxes by shifting profits into the informal sector. This is a significant problem in EMDEs. In Brazil, conservative estimates show that 40 percent of the economy is informal.[327] The vastness of the informal sector in many EMDEs creates opportunities for tax evasion and complicates tax collection efforts. After all, higher taxes on the formal sector might incentivize firms to shift economic activity into the informal sector. **New digital tools** can facilitate tax collection. Electronic payments are easier to monitor and automating tax collection can lead to efficient solutions without demanding much human capacity to enforce tax laws.

Movements of **commodity prices** also affect the fiscal space of emerging markets and developing countries. Commodity prices wobbled sharply when the Covid-19 shock hit. Oil prices plummeted. For some countries that heavily rely on oil imports, such as India, the decline in oil prices was a boon. Countries that export oil and other commodities took a big hit.

Remittances from migrant workers provide another buffer and source of income for many EMDEs. Some countries, such as Kyrgyzstan, Nepal, and Honduras, usually receive remittances of 20 percent of their GDP or more.[328] A decline of these flows in crisis times has vast consequences for local economies.

Countercyclical Policies, Buffers, and Borrowing Capacity

The Covid-19 crisis has taught us that resilience requires credible fiscal buffers. Countercyclical fiscal policy can powerfully enhance resilience. In boom times, governments can reduce deficits and even generate surpluses as tax revenues accrue aplenty. Being more frugal in good times ensures extra funds to finance a post-shock rebound, enabling governments to borrow at large scale without hitting their borrowing limits. This provides fiscal resilience.

Some emerging economies failed to build up buffers prior to the Covid-19 pandemic. This has made it more difficult for them to provide relief. Brazil, for example, already had been operating with sizable budget deficits since 2014, which has limited the nation's resilience during the pandemic.[329]

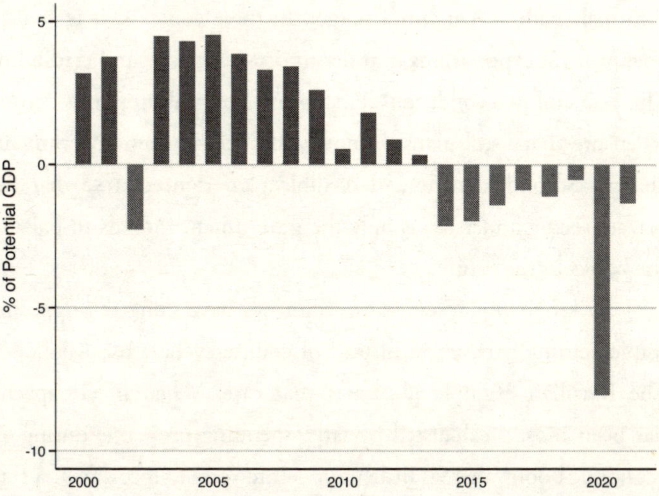

Figure 13-1: Brazil's primary budget surplus/deficit as a percentage share of GDP. Source: International Monetary Fund

These preexisting problems in many emerging markets explain the lack of government relief programs.[330] Public and private debt overhang has acted as a resilience killer. Governments with debt overhang and insufficient fiscal capacity have not been able to provide the fiscal support needed for their economies to bounce back. The debt of private firms has induced them to cut back on investment. This has further contributed to economic scarring and has delayed the recovery. As a result, the fall in economic growth could be quite prolonged. Moreover, even more debt is piling up in the private sector because firms have needed to raise new debt to stay afloat. As private debt becomes public debt during crises, the debt risks pile up.

In general, the borrowing capacity of emerging economies is more limited because institutions are weaker and the untaxed informal shadow economy is larger. In these contexts, it is vital to anchor fiscal expectations in order to provide clarity and credibility. This relies on two conditions. First, broad political support is needed to ensure that fiscal plans do not swing wildly when governments change. Second, a clear and credible plan is needed so that the private sector understands how the government intends to balance the books in the future.

Strikingly, many emerging countries have done the opposite, implementing procyclical instead of countercyclical fiscal policy.[331] The Brazilian example illustrates that case. When fiscal capacity has been mostly exhausted by large spending programs during an economic boom, there is little room left to react to recessions. A trap opens up. In other words, if policies are insufficiently expansionary during downturns, then the risks of a prolonged downturn and permanent long-term scarring will increase. Additionally, countercyclical policy, unlike procyclical policy, can lead to a spike in the borrowing interest rate during crises. In such a scenario, financial markets put pressure on domestic fiscal policies. This often results in austerity measures that are needed to maintain borrowing capacity at moderate interest rates.

Policy Space and the IMF's Special Drawing Rights

A critical question is whether international organizations can support emerging and developing countries that have limited national fiscal power. If international support is feasible, it would foster global resilience.

One potential measure is to provide immediate relief through a general allocation of **special drawing rights (SDRs)** offered by the IMF.[332] This idea was advocated by Treasury Secretary Janet Yellen in late February 2021.[333] SDRs give their holders the right to draw on the foreign currency reserves of stronger IMF members. An allocation of new SDRs would boost the foreign exchange reserves of EMDCs, and the SDRs could be converted to US dollars or other hard currencies to finance imports, for example.

The value of each SDR reflects a basket of international currencies, with weights determined by the IMF. Currently, the basket consists of US dollars, euros, Chinese renminbi, Japanese yen, and the British pound. A SDR fulfils the three functions of money, although with many limitations.

First, it is a reliable and stable unit of account defined as a basket of main currencies. Second, it is a stable store of value. Indeed, a SDR is a valuable reserve asset for central banks. As a basket of currencies, it enjoys diversification benefits that provide more stability than each individual currency. Third, SDRs are a medium of exchange and an albeit limited instrument for payments. The SDR department is a closed system that has no interactions with any other monetary and financial systems. SDRs can only be transferred between participants within the department, which include governments, central banks, and international institutions. SDRs can only serve to settle payments between those official entities. That is, private agents do not have access to SDRs and therefore cannot use them to make private transactions. Furthermore, even settlements between participants in the SDR department are conditional. Any party paid with an SDR must agree, beyond certain limits, to receive them as payment.

After new SDRs are allocated, IMF member countries can approach the IMF to swap them into hard currencies—in order to enhance fiscal space. Hard currencies are provided by a group of countries with strong reserve positions and that have volunteered to accept the SDRs of other member countries upon request. These countries provide the requested currencies (mostly US dollars or euros) out of their own foreign reserves, or they simply "print" the currency, if they are the issuer. The country that receives the hard currency can then spend it with no strings attached. Thus, SDRs immediately provide additional foreign exchange reserves to a country in need. These reserves can be sold to widen fiscal space or they can be used to make payments to other countries' central banks.[334] Indebted IMF member countries could pay off maturing outstanding debt, say to the Chinese government.

Another advantage of this fiscal measure is that it does not affect the political economy of debtor countries. While many IMF programs come with strings attached, such as the obligation to carry out reforms, SDRs do not carry such conditions. SDRs can benefit all countries, even those that do not attempt reforms.[335]

Ultimately, SDRs are a hybrid of monetary and fiscal policy. While the transaction seems monetary in nature, it has a clear fiscal component and represents an agreement for future official aid.

What is the advantage of SDRs over direct aid from a development bank? One major advantage is international coordination. The use of the SDR currency basket brings many countries into the same boat. The second "advantage" is related to a political argument. SDRs allow advanced economies to provide aid without including it in their national budgets, which bypasses political conflict and prolonged parliamentary negotiations. It also diminishes the risk of negative domestic press coverage of leaders who allocate domestic resources to international aid.

However, some have argued against the increasing use of SDRs. Critics point out that SDRs are not essentially designed for fiscal relief but rather to provide international liquidity.[336] The purpose of SDRs, they say, should be to bridge short-term emergencies. They also argue that the size of implicit fiscal transfers via SDRs is small compared to the actual relief that EMDEs need.

Debt Restructuring

Writing off large amounts of debt in times of crisis gives countries more breathing room and a chance to rebound. Debt restructuring can be an important element of resilience. However, debt restructuring needs to be done efficiently and rapidly. Currently, restructuring can take up to six years. These inefficiencies in debt restructuring render the whole process impractical. A prolonged process requires countries in need to worry about bridge financing for the duration of the restructuring process. Large fiscal deficits during the Covid-19 crisis have further strained government budgets; thus, the burden of public debt might grow substantially after the crisis.

Unsustainable Debt

The Covid-19 crisis has reduced tax revenues simultaneously with increased government spending. Naturally, fiscal budgets have come under pressure. This can lead rating agencies to downgrade the quality of a country's debt. This happened to Colombia's debt in May 2021.[337] There was an outright partial default on Zambia's debt in November 2020.[338] Countries like Ghana and Angola, which had been spending 50 percent of their government budget just to meet interest payments, also came under pressure.[339] In all cases, the dire fiscal situation that has emerged during the pandemic risks increasing the cost of raising new debt, making debt potentially unsustainable.

Some economists distinguish between "the good, the bad, and the ugly" debt problems.[340] When large, publicly funded, growth-enhancing investment programs cause debt to accumulate, it is called "good" debt. After all, the debt used for investment increases the country's capital stock, raising potential GDP along the way. "Bad debt" has been defined as wasted spending that culminates in debt overhang and potential long-run scarring. Finally, "ugly" debt finances corruption and is often diverted to private accounts in offshore havens.

Debt is also more burdensome if it is not denominated in the domestic currency. In the 1980s and 1990s, the major cause of currency crises was called the "original sin": **foreign currency**

borrowing by the sovereign. By devaluing the domestic currency, suddenly the value of the US-dollar debt went through the roof. Thankfully, EMDEs in recent decades have largely overcome the original sin.[341] However, private debt is often still denominated in foreign currencies and so foreign exchange risk remains.

Proactive Policies and Procrastination

When debt problems emerge, countries face two choices: act proactively or procrastinate.[342] Sound policies, good debt management, an IMF program, and voluntary debt restructuring can all contribute to making fiscal burdens manageable and to mitigating the risks of high debt.

Procrastination is substantially more common than proactive policies to mitigate public debt burdens. The tendency of countries to delay the restructuring process amplifies the problems.[343] Procrastination occurs for at least two reasons. First, debt restructuring might impair a country's ability to borrow in sovereign debt markets in the moment of need. IMF bridge financing should incentivize governments to start the renegotiation process sooner and to include creditors in the process of debt reconstruction. Second, necessary fiscal adjustments can be very unpopular with domestic voters. Announcing severe cuts to the government budget is never enjoyable. It can therefore be politically opportunistic to delay solutions needed to address the fiscal emergency.

The Holdout Problem, Collective Action Clauses, and the Paris Club

Another challenge is the **hold-out problem**. Solving a major fiscal crisis requires coordination among the many creditors, but no lender wants to be the first to make concessions. Doing so would indirectly benefit other lenders, for a simple reason. If some creditors renounce a portion of their claims, which is called "taking a haircut," the chances that other creditors will be repaid in full improves.

In the 1980s, sovereign debt was often held only by a few major US and European banks. The Paris Club, a group of officials who represented major debt-holding countries, could therefore facilitate debt negotiations. Since then, hedge funds and many other institutional investors have entered the market for sovereign debt. As a result, negotiations involving all creditors have become impossible to coordinate. For example, when Argentina defaulted in 2002, hedge fund Elliott Management and some other creditors holding a total of 7 percent of the defaulted debt refused to take a 70 percent haircut. Instead, Elliott pursued Argentina in court for more than a decade. The ultimate outcome was a court settlement in which Argentina agreed to repay the debt. This did not occur without many twists and turns, including the seizure of an Argentinian ship in Ghana.[344]

At the moment, there is no unified approach for handling the bankruptcy of a country. To formalize the overall process and to move away from a case-by-case approach, proposals were developed in 2002 by the IMF's Anne Krueger for a sovereign debt restructuring mechanism (SDRM).[345] The underlying idea of an SDRM is to create a quasi-bankruptcy law for countries, similar to bankruptcy law for firms that provides uniform guidelines for processing cases of corporate insolvency. However, these proposals have not yet led to tangible international agreements. Instead, one opted for **collective action clauses (CACs)**, a contractual arrangement that prevents a small minority of bondholders from blocking an agreement between the majority of bondholders. A settlement for debt restructuring becomes legally binding for all creditors if the majority agrees. However, CACs are not included in old debt contracts. New debt instruments, such as oil-backed loans that are collateralized by natural resources, are also often outside the scope of CACs.

Another challenge for debt restructuring is the fuzzy distinction between **private and public lenders**. The Chinese Development Bank tries to maintain its status as a private lender; thus, it is not affected by any public sector concessions and debt reductions.

Resolving the holdup problem is even more complicated because, typically, neither the total amount of debt nor the identity of the lenders is **public knowledge**. There are no statistics on loans provided to governments by various sources, so creditors cannot know the exact extent of a government's commitment to other creditors. Recent research by the Peterson Institute of International Economics discovered that explicit clauses forbid many Chinese debtors from disclosing their debt. Moreover, borrowers have agreed to keep their loans from China away from collective debt restructuring. In some cases, they grant China indirect influence over domestic and foreign policies.[346] China, as a large creditor of EMDEs, will have a critical role in debt restructuring processes.

Reprofiling

A special version of debt restructuring is called "reprofiling." Instead of taking an explicit write-down of debt, only the maturity of the debt is lengthened. Reprofiling is useful if the level of debt is sustainable, but the country will face a temporary rollover risk.

Debt rollover risk can lead to a run on the debt. When debt comes due, governments often need to refinance part or all of it. In technical terms, they roll over their debt. If investor A, whose debt is due this week, expects investor B not to roll over a country's debt next week, she will likely also not roll over her debt. If she did decide to roll over her debt, she would risk losing full repayment if investor B does not provide an extension of funding. It is easy to imagine how this could lead to a chain of aborted rollovers, culminating in a run on the debt followed by government bankruptcy. A second equilibria occurs if investor A *expects* all subsequent investors to roll over their debt. In this case, investor A would typically prefer to roll over his debt.

To alleviate these pure liquidity problems, forced rollovers can provide a solution. They are sometimes called **debt reprofiling**. In this case, the debt is not forgiven; it is only delayed. No investor has to take a loss, but the country immediately benefits from a longer debt maturity structure.

Debt Service Suspension Initiative (DSSI) and the New Common Framework

One concrete example of reprofiling was the G20's debt

service suspension initiative (DSSI) in April 2020, which aimed at low-income countries' sovereign debt. Under this plan, developing countries that accepted the initiative did not have to service government-to-government debt payments until June 30, 2021.[347] The plan provided immediate fiscal relief, at least on debt owed to other governments or their policy banks.[348] A key political advantage of the DSSI is that it brought China, as one of the G20 members, into the boat with other nations on debt restructuring processes.

DSSI only amounted to reprofiling of debt owed to *public* creditors. Private debt was not included. Therefore, private creditors under the plan are paid back in time whereas public creditors are moved down the queue. The new **common framework** developed by the World Bank and the IMF aims to more broadly generalize the DSSI structure. The framework would apply a coordinated approach to debt restructuring for seventy-three low-income countries that are eligible for the DSSI. Beyond the traditional member countries of the Paris Club, mostly from North America and Europe, the new common framework would also include India, China, Saudi-Arabia, and Turkey. If an eligible debtor country initiates the new common framework, the restructuring burden would be equally shared among all participating creditors. **Comparable treatment** is another major element of the common framework. Private creditors are not to be treated more favorably than public ones. This could help to bring privately held debt into the debt restructuring process.[349] Ultimately, a new debt restructuring process can only be successful if the mechanism includes carrots and sticks for creditors—to ensure that other creditors participate.

New Debt

Many worry that debt restructuring invites "bad" or "ugly" debt because it alleviates the preexisting debt burden. Once debt has been restructured, governments can recover some fiscal capacity and might engage in further spending. Without the right incentives, the new debt might be poorly allocated. In such a scenario, debt restructuring provides a short-term solution but no added future resilience. New ugly debt might even put the country in a worse position than its original situation.

CHAPTER 14

New Global World Order

With the Covid-19 pandemic, humanity confronted a **common global enemy.**[350] Yet, despite many proposals, no solid *global* initiatives to fight the disease have occurred. With global coordination of, for example, travel restrictions and efficient testing, we could have fostered more resilience. Instead, the pandemic revealed preexisting international tensions.

The US during the Trump presidency was notably absent in assuming global leadership of the pandemic response. China's **face mask diplomacy**, by which China tried to combine face mask shipments with diplomatic goals in March 2020, ultimately backfired. In late 2020 and early 2021, **vaccine diplomacy** began to emerge, with the same intention of improving China's image abroad.[351] The US initially pursued a "US first" approach and did not deliver any US-produced vaccines abroad. In contrast, the EU exported about 40 percent of the vaccines it produced.[352] India also exported a lot of vaccines before temporarily halting shipments abroad during its second Covid-19 wave in the spring of 2021.[353]

China exported vaccines to several emerging market economies.

These strategic rivalries mirror the larger changes brought on by the **emergence of China** and **globalization**. As the world became more interdependent over the last forty years, gains from trade were maximized. Countries specialized in their comparative advantages in industry and commerce, and the volume of global trade grew substantially. That trend was fueled more by China's acceptance of capitalism in the late 1970s and the fall of the Iron Curtain in Eastern Europe in 1989.

But **economic integration** has also **undermined resilience**. Some firms have relied on suppliers in other parts of the world, often without any diversification in their supply chains. When Covid-19 emerged in spring of 2020, many countries began to regret their dependence on imported face masks and personal protective equipment. That dependence forced them to scramble to secure adequate stocks of these goods.

This chapter explores the various dimensions of globalization. We start by discussing geopolitics and **how Covid-19 has reshaped the global order**. Building on that discussion we will zoom in on **global finance** and **trade,** and their connections to resilience.

Geopolitics and Global Order

Geopolitics, by its traditional definition, describes how geographic factors, such as natural defenses, shape international politics. The modern definition of geopolitics, however, often deals with zero-sum games among nations: One country's gain is considered to be another country's loss. But there is a natural tension between these zero-sum scenarios and opportunities for international policy coordination to benefit all parties involved. Covid-19 vaccines are a prime example. Countries that produce vaccines, or those that have excess vaccine capacity, have the prospect of gaining international influence. By distributing vaccine doses abroad, these countries can hope for immediate political benefits, and they accumulate political goodwill for the future.

Geopolitics is embedded in the global order, which can be understood by looking at two dimensions. The first dimension is whether arrangements are multilateral via international institutions or bilateral on a country-by-country basis. The second dimension relates to the distinction between an institution-based order and an outcome-based order.

Multilateral or Bilateral? Outcome-Based or Institution-Based?

The global order can inherently be **multilateral** or **bilateral**. A multilateral global order, often accompanied by international institutions, is characterized by broad agreements among many countries. In addition, there are regional multilateral agreements, such as the EU and the Association of Southeast Asian Nations (ASEAN). The alternative is a bilateral global order in which pairs of countries negotiate agreements. This approach tends to favor the more powerful countries because they have superior bargaining power in each bilateral negotiation.

The global order after World War II has been mostly

characterized by rules and international institutions.[354] Multilateral institutions—the United Nations, the World Trade Organization (WTO), the International Monetary Fund (IMF), the World Bank, and the World Health Organization (WHO)—have played a key role in shaping the global order and providing a forum for the international community to address political, economic, and social challenges.

The **rule-based global order, or institution-based global order,** promotes predictability in an increasingly complex world. Additionally, it limits adverse feedback loops, such as trade or currency wars. However, a rules-based approach is less flexible, making it harder to adapt to unexpected shocks. Due to the world's unpredictability, rule-based recommendations can be misguided and undermine resilience when the global economic structure is subject to unexpected but permanent changes. A rule-based order also tends to restrict large powers because they must comply with the same rules as everyone else.

An **outcome-based** international **order** places much less weight on institutions, which provides flexibility in the wake of unexpected shocks like the Covid-19 pandemic. However, this approach can be much less stable. Without global rules to govern trade or the international monetary system, the risk of currency and trade wars increases. The outcome-based approach need not limit the power of the largest nations, which are the ones that would most likely shape the rules of an institution-based order. Importantly, rules are established before the nature of a shock is known.

International arrangements can fall into various categories across these two dimensions. The Paris Climate Accord is both outcome-based (centered around 2-degree global warming) and multilateral.[355] On the other hand, the European monetary policy established by the ECB is multilateral and also rule-based.

The "Cry" for a Multilateral Approach and Vaccine Development

An obvious area for international cooperation, which was particularly relevant during the early days of Covid-19, was international financing of **vaccine development**. Initially, when countries did not know how well their vaccine trials would fare, it was attractive to hedge against negative outcomes by joining a global funding and distribution pool. If one nation developed a successful vaccine, it would be distributed among all members. By one calculation, each country would only need to contribute about 0.15 percent of GDP.[356]

With the successful development of several vaccines by December 2020, these plans lost relevance. However, the potential for international cooperation remains. Perilous situations continue to threaten international **vaccine distribution,** and the lack of international leadership by the US and other developed countries have been obvious.[357] One international approach by the WHO is **COVAX**. With financing from donor countries, the World Bank, and private foundations, such as the Bill and Melinda Gates foundation, COVAX aims to secure vaccine access for poor countries. By December 2020, it had secured up to two billion doses that will be shared among the 190 participating countries.[358] Additionally, countries that purchased many more vaccine doses than they need for their own populations are starting to contribute excess vaccine doses to COVAX, or to distribute doses to countries that lack vaccine commitments.[359] Countries that secured excess vaccine doses often use them to pursue geopolitical objectives.

US-China Relations

The **great power struggle** between the US and China, which is illustrated by the Trump administration's trade war and the struggle for technological standard setting (e.g., the Huawei 5G and TikTok controversies), is likely to result in a prolonged drag on efforts to strengthen global resilience.[360] China's 2025 program to drive toward self-sufficiency illustrates China's rise and ambitions.

Technology competition also affects the hearts and minds of young people, as well as data privacy. Digital relations between open and authoritarian societies are inherently asymmetrical. While China excludes many US technology companies from its domestic market, China can influence young people in the US and other Western societies with its own apps, such as TikTok. As a result, there are one-way digital borders. The questions are whether these technologies will proliferate in the future, and whether the West will tolerate one-way borders or demand two-way borders. More questions abound: What are the economic consequences if we splinter the internet? And who owns the data?

Technological competition will not remain confined to China and the US. Instead, the prospect of digital borders will loom much larger. When tensions between **China and India** mounted in May 2020, because of **border clashes** in the Himalayas, opportunities opened for Silicon Valley to enter the large Indian market, which is so far mostly dominated by Chinese tech companies.[361]

In May 2020, Larry Summers compared the relationship between the US and China to two shipwrecked people surviving in one lifeboat. Even if the relationship is antagonistic, it will likely take both parties to row the lifeboat.[362] China has the ambition to project its power abroad, such as through its Belt and Road Initiative. China seeks to increase its influence over countries by building roads, bridges, and ports to create a new "silk road" with infrastructure that reaches from the Pacific shores in Shanghai to the Atlantic and North Sea shores in Europe. Infrastructure projects in Sri Lanka, Pakistan, and Djibouti have already been financed.[363] Some worry that the loans provided to countries to finance these projects will create future financial dependence. Hidden public debt exacerbates asymmetric information problems if debt restructuring becomes necessary.

Likewise, Australia, Japan, India, and the US—the so-called quad—are all deeply concerned about China's expansion in the Indo-Pacific region, causing tensions to heat up recently.[364]

The Regional Comprehensive Economic Partnership (RCEP), which was signed in November 2020 by China and fourteen other countries, showcases China's growing influence in South Asia. This agreement replaces the Trans-Pacific Partnership, to which the US agreed in 2016 during the Obama presidency, but then abandoned during the early days of the Trump administration.[365] A looming worry is that China could establish a similar but less-ambitious free trade agreement to further marginalize the US. For now, RCEP is the largest free trade agreement in the world, "covering nearly a third of the global economy."[366]

The new Biden administration in 2021 abandoned Trump's

bilateral "America first" approach. The US is now pursuing a multilateral approach and building alliances with foreign partner countries. One of the new administration's first measures was to strengthen "the quad" by developing a plan to distribute Covid-19 vaccines to countries in Asia. This effort is part of a broader strategy to counter China's influence.[367] India's vaccine production capacity plays an important component in this initiative. Because the US did not export vaccines before its own population was vaccinated, the world relied heavily on Indian supplies. One reason India promised to export vaccines was to elevate its international influence in relation to Chinese counterparts.[368] The Indian government probably regrets that decision now. During its second Covid-19 wave in April and May 2021, India's population suffered with the highest daily Covid-19 death toll in the world.

Frictions between the US and China became apparent in March 2021 during a confrontational meeting in Anchorage, Alaska between US Secretary of State Antony Blinken, US National Security Advisor Jake Sullivan, and their Chinese counterparts, Director Yang and State Councilor Wang. The US officials argued in favor of a rule-driven global order. Chinese officials asserted that there were two distinct forms of "democracy" in the world while stressing the importance of "the United States to change its own image and to stop advancing its own democracy in the rest of the world," and that "the Western world does not represent the global public opinion." In light of these statements, it is questionable whether we will see one global world order. We might instead see the continued polarization of the world into **two blocs of countries with two competing systems**, one close to China and one close to the US.[369]

Europe's Role

In this conflict between two blocs, Europe's role is pivotal. China obtained a strong foothold in Europe with its investments in Eastern EU members during the euro crisis. For example, the Piraeus Port in Greece, Europe's seventh largest port, was purchased by the Chinese shipping firm Cosco. During the Covid-19 crisis, China's foreign policy became much less diplomatic and more outspoken. Tensions rose because of China's so-called **face mask diplomacy**, which involved China's attempt to portray itself as more helpful to Italy than other European countries.

When Covid-19 first emerged in Wuhan, China, European firms shipped medical equipment to China in January and February 2020 without much fanfare. Later, in the early days of the European Covid-19 crisis in March 2020, China—one of the world's main providers of critical medical equipment—shipped thousands of face masks, testing kits, and ventilators around the world.[370] Pushes for extensive media coverage and attempts to drive a wedge between some European Union countries prompted a severe backlash and infuriated European diplomats.[371] Later in 2020, China even claimed that the virus originated in Europe.

On the other hand, the West also tries to promote democratic values and human rights in China. Its longstanding approach toward China is best illustrated by the German dictum *Wandel durch Handel,* which means "change through trade." However, despite deepening economic ties, China has not moved toward democracy.[372] Foreign policy hawks are therefore calling for a firmer stance on China, but China's strong economic ties around the world render any kind of decoupling almost infeasible—in stark contrast to the Cold War.

In addition, many think that China's treatment of foreign investors is very restrictive. While Chinese state-owned enterprises—meaning the state (at least indirectly)—acquire technology abroad, China heavily regulates foreign ownership of its own companies. Recent events underline the tensions. When a Chinese firm took over the German robot manufacturer, Kuka, in 2016, many German foreign policy strategists became alarmed. Laws for foreign ownership of German companies were swiftly tightened over fears of a sellout of German knowhow.[373]

In late 2020, when Germany held the EU presidency, the EU drafted the China-EU comprehensive agreement (CAI). The agreement is designed to strengthen economic ties and to facilitate European investments in China by removing, for instance, the requirement to form joint ventures with Chinese companies when entering the Chinese market.[374] Whether this agreement will be ratified is not yet clear.

A key question regarding international relations is whether Europe will strengthen its transatlantic relationship with the US now that the Trump administration is over, or whether Europe will attempt a rapprochement with China. The US and Europe could form an influential counterpart to China, notably if they cooperate and set common standards among themselves. That process has slowed down since the failure of the Transatlantic Trade and Investment Partnership (TTIP).

In May 2021, India and the EU relaunched trade deal negotiations to counterbalance China's influence.[375] Importantly, India had already decided not to join the RCEP agreement between China and its major neighbors in the Asia-Pacific region.

Global Finance

International relations between governments and the private sector rely on a stable and resilient global currency. In the nineteenth and early twentieth centuries, the British pound took on that role. After WWII the US dollar emerged as the dominant global currency.

Role of the US Dollar

The dollar plays three key roles in the modern economy: as a global **unit of account**, a medium of exchange, and a store of value. The dollar is likely to remain the dominant international currency, but the US dollar could become fragile if foreigners become wary about holding US debt. Some cracks appeared when the US Treasury market choked in March 2020, for example, a topic we discussed earlier in the book.

The US dollar also serves as the unit of account in some countries. Ecuador, which does not have a domestic currency, is a case of a fully dollarized economy. In many EMDEs with less dollarization, firms tend to borrow in US dollars, exposing them to US monetary policy. Many commodities, including oil, are also invoiced in dollars.

Moreover, the US dollar serves as a **medium of exchange** for international trade, with the exception of the Eurozone and its neighbors.[376]

Finally, the US dollar serves as a **store of value** for the private sector; that is, many loan contracts are written in US dollars. In the public sector, most central banks hold US dollars as a **reserve**

currency. In addition, there are large offshore markets for US dollars where they are traded outside US jurisdiction.

For the US, the global safe asset status of US government liabilities implies that the Fed can act **like a hedge fund**. It can issue low-interest liabilities and reinvest the funds in riskier outlays, such as foreign direct investments (FDI) that offer far greater return.

Flight to Global Safety and Loss of Local Safe Asset Status

Many countries hold dollar reserves in order to defend the local safe asset status of their domestic government bonds. In response, citizens hold these local government bonds for precautionary reasons, as a safety buffer to help them face an adverse shock. If they face a crisis, they can sell the bonds in local currency. However, it must be credible that the local bond will maintain its value, otherwise citizens would rush directly to US Treasuries as a safe asset. That type of switch is more likely when the US interest rate is high. Put differently, if the US Federal Reserve cuts the interest rate, the local bond can more easily maintain its local safe asset status because its returns will exceed returns from US Treasuries. In contrast, if the US interest rate is higher and a shock like Covid-19 hits the world economy, flight to global safe assets can follow.

A run on US dollar assets would devalue the local currency and increase the real value of dollar-denominated debt. With many emerging economies carrying public and private debt burdens in dollars, a depreciation might backfire and undermine resilience rather than support the recovery. On the positive side, **devaluing**

the exchange rate can help to boost economic recoveries in dollar-dependent economies. A weaker exchange rate generates extra demand from abroad for the exports of EMDEs because those exports become relatively cheaper, which should lead to a faster short-term rise in GDP. On the other hand, a devaluation of the local currency will raise the import costs of commodities. This strains household budgets in countries that rely on these imports.

During the pandemic, the flight-to-safety period in March and April 2020 was unprecedented and threatened the resilience of the global financial system. **Capital outflows** from EMDEs were at record levels at the onset of the Covid-19 crisis compared to other notable periods, such as the 2008 global financial crisis (GFC), or the 2013 "Taper Tantrum." When the Federal Reserve announced in 2013 that it would apply the brakes on its quantitative easing programs, it sent shivers through the global financial sector, as evidenced by rising interest rates and financial stress in EMDEs. In March 2020, when everyone wanted to hold reserves, even ten-year US Treasuries were not good enough. The outflows stabilized only after the Fed intervened, most notably with swap lines to provide dollar liquidity to EMDEs. By using swap lines, the Fed effectively loaned US dollars to foreign central banks. In a sense, the Fed acted as a global lender of last resort.

Later in 2020, after the initial flight to safety had subsided, we observed historically large inflows to emerging markets.[377] As interest rates in developed economies remained close to zero, investors sought higher yields and $17 billion flowed back to EMDEs within the first three weeks of 2021.[378] The Fed's policy stabilized and ultimately re-reversed capital flows. Such policies contributed greatly to the resilience of EMDEs and international capital markets.

Global Financial Cycle

The dollar dependence of emerging markets subjects them to the **global financial cycle**. Consider a cycle that starts with a risk-off phase during which investors are reluctant to take on risk. The price of risk is high. At some point, global investors might switch to a phase of perceived low risk during which EMDEs can cheaply borrow from abroad. They are tempted to create their own local and bubbly safe asset. (Recall that issuing a safe asset at a low interest rate reduces the government's interest burden.) During that phase, domestic citizens and firms often hold domestic bonds as safe assets to hedge their idiosyncratic risk. In addition, they might borrow at the low US interest rate in US dollars. The relatively cheap US-dollar borrowing rate boosts economic growth, making the local safe asset bubble sustainable. However, when fear of a possible risk-off phase kicks in, the bubble becomes wobbly. A sudden stop might occur, at which point domestic citizens might shift their savings to US Treasuries as a precaution—instead of borrowing in dollars and instead of holding their own country's domestic bonds for precautionary reasons. Economic growth collapses, which further undermines the sustainability of the bubble.[379]

Spillovers from US Monetary Policy

Beyond the risk-on, risk-off cycle, US interest rate policy can also drive the global financial cycle. High US interest rates correspond to the risk-off phase whereas low US interest rates correlate with risk-off phases. Therefore, US monetary policy has

large spillover effects for EMDEs. When US interest rates fall, more capital flows to emerging markets thereby causing sizeable output effects. However, these effects reverse when US monetary policy tightens, which threatens resilience. Because many emerging markets rely so heavily on US monetary policy, they are forced to adjust to US developments and cannot only respond to domestic economic conditions.

Global Lender of Last Resort via Swap Lines: Resilience in Case of a Global US Dollar Shortage

The global dominance of the US dollar is best demonstrated by the large size of **offshore US dollar markets**. Collectively, they are often referred to as the "Eurodollar market." Eurodollars have actually nothing to do with euros per se. They are US dollar deposits outside the US, which therefore circumvent US regulation. Historically, the Eurodollar market emerged in the 1950s. Stringent banking regulation, including caps on deposit rates, limited how much US companies could earn on their domestic deposits, for example. As a consequence, these companies started to place their deposits abroad. Today, the Eurodollar market is the largest offshore funding market for US dollars. Many European banks, for example, use cheap short-term dollar funding from the Eurodollar market to finance dollar loans. Because this occurs outside the US regulatory eye, it boosts international trade and is financially attractive—as long as dollar deposits are cheaply available.[380] There are also tax advantages.

Typically, banking involves maturity and liquidity

transformations. Banks invest in long-term illiquid assets and issue short-term liquid dollar deposits. But the business of non-US banks engaging in dollar lending critically relies on the availability of cheap dollar funding, which can dry up in times of crisis. If dollar funding dries up and creates illiquidity problems, the typical policy solution is to use the central bank as lender of last resort. For example, the ECB provides euro funding as a last resort to European banks that might have a funding shortage.

If European banks need dollar funding, however, they cannot ask the US central bank to step in as lender of last resort because the Fed does not lend against collateral to non-US banks. In that sense, the offshore dollar is riskier than the onshore dollar. US banks *can* rely on the Fed as lender of last resort.

Absent other arrangements, the ECB can only supply euros to European banks. This is where the **swaps** come in, as illustrated in figure 14-1. Extending the Fed's dollar supply to foreign central banks ensures that foreign banks and firms need not worry about being cut off from dollar funding. They can obtain US dollars from their local central bank after it enters the swap line.

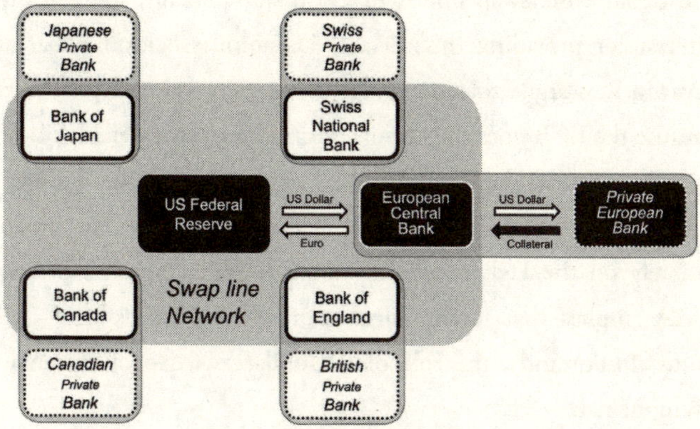

Figure 14-1: Sketch of the Fed's dollar swap lines.

On March 19, 2020, the Fed revived its swap arrangements with major central banks. Previously, those arrangements had been firmly established during the 2008 global financial crisis. The typical arrangement is a weeklong loan with a fixed exchange rate. The Fed gives dollars to the ECB while the ECB provides euros in return to the Fed. The Fed determines the interest rate. It might be, for example, a 0.5 percent spread on top of the overnight indexed swap rate (OIS). Subsequently, the ECB lends dollars to a European bank at the same interest rate against some collateral that is assessed by the ECB. De facto, the Fed lends to the European bank through the ECB.

It is worth noting that these central bank swap lines are completely **risk-free for the Fed**. If a bank in Germany needs US dollar funds, it does not directly borrow from the Fed but rather from the European Central Bank. And so the risk sits with the European Central Bank. Likewise, the Fed bears no exchange rate risk because the swap line is in US dollars. Finally, the Fed earns interest for providing this service. Economists Saleem Bahaj and Ricardo Reis argue that the swap lines are a good deal for the Fed because the ECB does the monitoring and bears the default risk.[381]

As a result, the Fed effectively acts as an indirect **lender of last resort** in the offshore Eurodollar market. Foreign central banks can rely on the Fed to provide dollar funding in times of crisis, which implies that foreign firms can rely on a supply of dollar funds. Importantly, the role of the dollar as a global currency is strengthened.

Other central banks entertain similar swap lines for their respective currencies. The ECB grants swap lines and repos to other European markets. By 2015, the People's Bank of China had established one hundred agreements related to yuan swap lines, with the intention of strengthening the international role of the yuan.

Moreover, foreign investors seeking to obtain liquidity can use US Treasuries for repo transactions at the Fed. In such a transaction, the investor deposits a US Treasury with the Fed in exchange for dollar funds. The maturity of a repo is often only a week or two. Once maturity is reached, the investor returns the US dollars to the Fed and the Fed returns the Treasury security.

Global Safe Assets (GloSBies)

Notice that the central banks of EMDEs are typically not included in the Fed's swap line arrangements. Therefore, a sudden erosion of **local safe-asset status** accompanied with a sudden stop and outflow of credit would be very costly for EMDEs. Active intervention, such as the Fed acting as indirect lender of last resort through swap lines, is one way to reduce the likelihood of sudden stops.

A superior alternative would be a resilient global financial architecture that is self-stabilizing and does not need active policy intervention. The central problem is typically not the shortage of safe assets per se, but the fact that safe assets are not symmetrically supplied around the globe. Only a few advanced economies, such as the US, Germany, and Japan, can supply safe assets globally. When a flight-to-safety episode occurs, it always involves international capital flows. In those cases, a potential solution to address the global safe asset shortage would be to create a truly global safe asset: a so-called GloSBies.[382]

There are two steps in the process of creating global safe assets from and for EMDEs. In a first step, a fraction of sovereign bonds from various countries are **pooled** together. To create a safe asset from emerging market government bonds, one may think of pooling Chinese, Indian, Brazilian, Southeast Asian, African, and Russian bonds. Subsequently, they are divided into separate **tranches**. For simplicity, let us assume there are only two tranches, labeled as senior bond and junior bond. If any of the pooled bonds default, the junior bondholders would absorb the losses. Only when there has been full default on the junior bond will the senior bondholders possibly lose money.

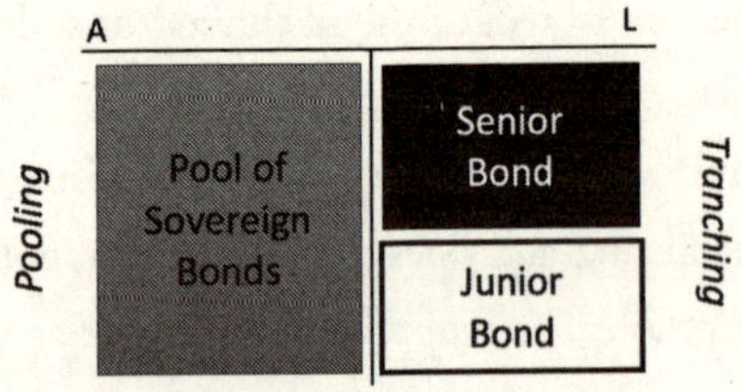

Figure 14-2: Balance sheet of a special purpose vehicle that pools sovereign bonds and divides them in tranches, specifically a senior bond (GloSBies) and a junior bond.

A simple example illustrates how the senior bond has become safer than any of the individual government bonds that were included in the pool. Suppose Brazil defaults on all of its government bonds. If you held such bonds, you would potentially take a large loss. In contrast, if you hold the senior tranche of the global safe asset, the losses caused by Brazil's default would be absorbed by the junior bondholders first. If all countries except Brazil repay in full, the owners of senior GloSBies would not suffer any losses. As a result, the senior bond is safe. It can gain safe asset status and thereby yield a lower interest rate. This would in turn increase fiscal space for EMDEs and contribute to resilience.

Should a flight-to-safety episode occur, investors can flee from the junior to the senior bond, such as US Treasuries or German Bunds. In other words, cross-border international capital flows are rechanneled to capital flows from junior to senior bonds.

The GloSBies structure is analogous to the Sovereign Bond Backed Securities (SBBS), also called the European Safe Bonds (ESBies), which were proposed for the euro area.[383] During the euro crisis, peripheral countries in the euro area suffered from flight-to-safety capital outflows. The aim of the ESBies was to rechannel these flows. Because there is no exchange-rate risk within the euro area, the ESBies junior bond did not flow to the senior bond but the global GloSBies junior bond had to absorb currency risk.

New Digital Forms of Money: Digital Currency Areas

Traditionally, the US dollar is used in the US (and by some trade partners), the Euro in Europe, and so forth. But now we increasingly conduct financial transactions digitally. The traditional roles of currency areas are changing. In the future, people might have thirty-seven digital currencies in their digital wallets and the ability to exchange one for the other within milliseconds. Currently, there is a plethora of digital currencies, such as Bitcoin, Ethereum, and Facebook's soon-to-be-launched Diem (formerly Libra). Chinese payment providers Alipay and WeChat Pay are competing in the same area. Could a new digital currency establish itself as an additional global currency, or even take a share of the dollar? Do all these digital currencies make the global monetary system less resilient?

Some Chinese restaurants in the US, for example, already accept renminbi paid with a digital device for payments. Only in January 2021 did the US government outlaw the use of Alipay and WeChat Pay in the US. With increasing digitization, the nature of money and currency areas may change. Traditionally, money has three roles: a unit of account, a store of value, and a medium of exchange. All three roles are bundled together. The increasing prevalence of digital currencies could break up or enlarge the bundle.[384] With the widespread availability of easily exchangeable digital currencies, individuals could use different currencies for each function of money. For example, a high-interest rate currency would be a great store of value, but if it is rarely accepted on other platforms, it would be a poor medium of exchange. Likewise, a digital currency that serves as a widely available medium of exchange might not offer attractive interest rates. Other new digital currencies might offer better privacy protections.

These developments might reshape our notions of currency areas. **Digital currency areas** might emerge. While traditional currency areas are defined by geographic boundaries, digital currency areas are defined by a digital network of transnational users. Therefore, digital currencies could also be integrated with other financial and nonfinancial services.

A side effect of these new forms of currency areas might be "digital dollarization." If that occurs, it would have similar monetary policy implications as conventional dollarization, which refers to a situation in which people start using primarily the US dollar instead of the domestic national currency. In a dollarized economy debt contracts are written in dollars and transactions occur in dollars. Therefore, domestic monetary policy is far less powerful because it can only affect the short-term interest rate of the national currency. Analogously, digital dollarization occurs when people use a new digital currency and therefore "import" its monetary policy and inflation.

In Southeast Asia, Alipay and WeChat Pay are increasingly used outside of China, and digital forms of the renminbi have reached beyond China. If these developments continue, Chinese monetary policy could affect those countries that use the digital renminbi. In addition, the People's Bank of China has been gradually developing its electronic renminbi for about eight years, and a large-scale launch is planned for 2022. It will certainly compete with private digital currencies and payments providers.[385] In such a world, national monetary policy, especially in smaller EMDEs, will be less powerful. The resilience function of monetary policy for these countries will be compromised.

Global Trade

The resilience of global trade faces distinct challenges. After the Covid-19 crisis, the outlook is uncertain. Even before the pandemic, the growth of trade had slowed compared to the hyper-globalization period of the late 1990s. The question we now face is how to make supply chains more resilient to temporary disruptions.

Explosion of Trade

The emergence of EMDEs coincided with a rapid increase in global trade volumes, starting in the late 1990s and lasting until the 2008 global financial crisis. From 2000 to 2008, the merchandise trade volume increased by 50 percent (figure 14-3). Global value chains emerged to fully exploit the gains from trade and specialization. Some countries produced raw materials while others processed those raw materials into intermediate goods. Other participants along the global value chain produced the final good.[386] This growth occurred in part because hyper-specialization facilitates the optimal use of comparative advantages. However, hyper-specialization potentially undermines global resilience. Much of this explosion in trade was beneficial for emerging markets, but shadows began to appear, such as rising inequality.

Slowbalization

How will the Covid-19 crisis affect the broader picture of international trade? Will it accelerate some pre-pandemic trends in the same way that it sped up home office and telemedicine trends?

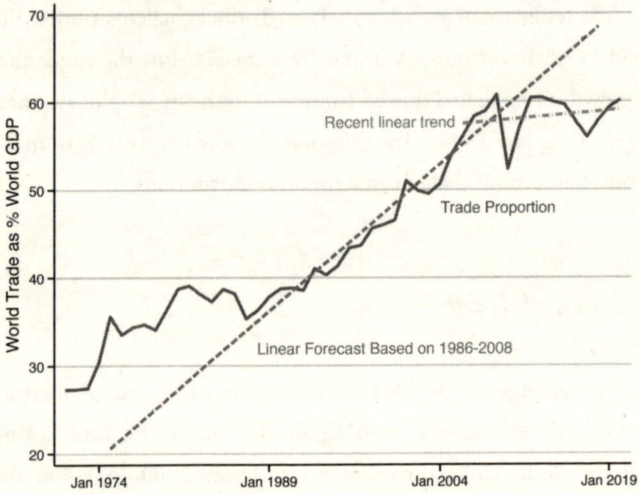

Figure 14-3: Slowbalization: World trade as a fraction of global GDP. Trade explosion from the 1980s stabilized in the mid-2000s. Source: CPB Netherlands Bureau for Economic Policy Analysis 2021

As shown in Figure 14-3, a slowdown in globalization preceded the Covid-19 crisis. In fact, that slowdown started at about the same time as the 2008 global financial crisis. Some economists have argued that the rapid globalization of the 1990s could not have maintained its pace in any scenario.[387] That being true, some flattening in the growth of international trade volumes was expected. With that history in mind, we can evaluate how the Covid-19 crisis impacted global trade. Clearly it suffered in the first months of the crisis, but the **bounce back** in the fall of 2020 was strong. At the time of this writing, there are no signs that the Covid-19 crisis will lead to a reduction in merchandise trade.[388]

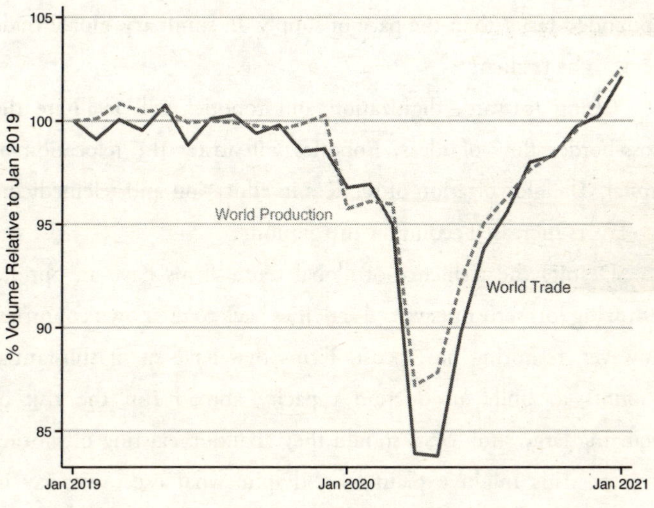

Figure 14-4: World trade and world industrial production relative to January 2019, and the strong rebound in second half of 2020. Source: CPB Netherlands Bureau for Economic Policy Analysis 2021

On the other hand, disruptions to supply chains and a shortage of workers to unload containers have severely disrupted the global shipping container business, which is the bedrock of cross-continent international trade. As Covid-19 sickened many workers, the work of unloading containers at US ports, for example, slowed down. Soon, those containers went missing in China, hindering the transport of manufactured goods to the US. That culminated in shortages of semiconductors, which are critical inputs for the production of phones and cars.[389] As a side effect, container prices surged substantially. In line with the terminology presented earlier in this book, this was a trade whipsaw. Global demand might have been insufficient in March and April 2020, but it subsequently rebounded faster than the pace of supply. In summary, global trade seems to be resilient.

Going forward, digitization and robotics will facilitate the cross-border flow of ideas. Robotics will foster the relocation of capital. The globalization of services in education and telemedicine also favors increased economic integration.

Despite the resilience of global trade, firms have an option: **reshoring** formerly outsourced activities back to their own countries. However, reshoring has a cost. Firms that have spent substantial amounts to build production capacity abroad run the risk of incurring large sunk costs should they abandon existing offshoring projects. This might explain why, despite what executives say in surveys, very little reshoring has actually happened so far.[390] The absence of reshoring also supports the view that a large reduction in trade is unlikely.

Cost Minimization versus Resilience

The Covid-19 crisis exposed weaknesses along the network of global value chains. Prior to the pandemic, **cost minimization** was the main objective when designing international supply chains. Thus, supplier choice was dictated by costs. However, such a myopic focus on costs can leave firms vulnerable. If suppliers, even the most cost-effective ones, have to shut down because of an idiosyncratic shock, then a labor strike or natural disaster would cause the firm at the other end of the supply chain to experience a moment of truth. The pandemic has precisely highlighted these supply chain risks, not only in the goods-producing sectors but also in the service sector. As an example, many service-sector companies have outsourced large amounts of back-office capabilities to emerging markets, notably India. As India's second Covid-19 wave swept through the country in the spring of 2021, several American financial firms had to reallocate activities to other offshore hubs.[391]

The key question is whether we will see the aforementioned reshoring of economic activity, which had been outsourced to EMDEs, or whether countries will diversify their suppliers. Having two suppliers is usually preferred by downstream firms in order to mitigate suppliers' bargaining power. Perhaps firms will move toward having three suppliers on three different continents, which is called multi-sourcing. This could occur without harming the economies of EMDEs as a whole.

A critical change to global supply chains should occur. When firms choose suppliers, the first-order consideration should be to build resilience and not focus only on cost minimization.[392] In other words, a "**just-in-(worst)-case**" perspective should replace the prevailing "**just-in-time**" dogma.[393] As a result, firms might use two or three suppliers from different parts of the world to hedge against country-specific shocks. That said, supply chain diversification can hedge against country-specific risks (uncorrelated shocks), but it is much less helpful when there is an aggregate worldwide shock, such as a pandemic.[394]

This shift toward less global and less vulnerable supply chains is likely to slow economic growth in the short-run.[395] It could lead to shortages during the adjustment process.[396] However, in the longer-run, it will likely produce more promising results than the export-driven development strategy of the past.

Deglobalization

Some commentators have questioned the concept of "slowbalization" and have predicted a decline in globalization. They acknowledge that the trade of goods has stabilized at an elevated level, but they argue that, from a broader perspective, globalization is receding. The definition of globalization, they say, should include "flows in investment, **services**, human capital, ideas, management practices, networks, infrastructure, and norms."[397] Based on that broader perspective, trade, foreign investment, immigration, and open borders might recede while protectionism and immigration restrictions surge.[398] As an example, a drop in immigration would immediately affect many American universities whose financing is heavily reliant on tuition from foreign students.[399] In short, even if the trade of goods only experiences slowbalization, we might witness **deglobalization in other areas**.

Political Forces and Technology

Key opposing forces are determining the future of globalization. Technological progress is pushing toward more globalization and political pressures are pushing toward deglobalization.

The effects of China's economic opening in the early 1990s, the so-called "**China shock**," were expected to be cushioned by well-functioning labor markets in advanced economies. In practice, workers in America's industrial heartland and in the former European industrial and mining powerhouses had to compete with workers in Eastern European countries and other emerging markets. Many local labor markets in advanced economies suffered severely and persistently. Wages fell and employment rates remained depressed relative to less-affected local labor markets.[400] Over the years, these developments have fueled political backlash against international trade, as exemplified by the recent US-China trade war.

Adam Posen and others have emphasized the role of **technology** in these changes. Since the advent of the computer, many innovations have been more favorable to highly educated workers. In the presence of increasingly skill-biased technological change, rising inequality would have been inevitable, even in the absence of increased globalization.

Many modern technologies incorporate **winner-takes-all dynamics**, often due to the network effects of internet businesses. Google, for instance, started with a successful search algorithm. Once people started using the engine, Google could improve its algorithm with freely obtained user data. The natural equilibrium that has emerged is one dominant internet search engine, which makes it very hard for competitors to accumulate the same amount of internal information. Thus, technological changes have driven market power, rents for successful companies, and well-paying jobs for (some of) their employees. Lagging firms are left behind.

Principles for Trade Agreements

In light of these changes, what principles can we use to design future trade agreements that produce a fairer and more resilient world? Most people agree that cross-border policy externalities are good reasons to establish global rules. But that alone is insufficient. Most policies have externalities, including those that are inherently national issues, such as education.[401]

As we think about how trade agreements can be designed to promote fairness and resilience, we can start by looking at traditional trade agreements in the past. Until the 1990s, trade agreements focused on two principles: **national treatment of foreign goods** and **no discrimination**. Once foreign goods had crossed the border they were to be treated as domestic goods and all foreign goods were to be treated in the same manner. The latter was the key component.

Then the **traditional framework** for global trade started shifting, as exemplified by the EU single market in 1993. The elimination of any border treatment within the single market created a **need for policy harmonization** across member countries. As a result of increasing interference in domestic politics, the backlash against trade started to form. Next, in the late 1990s during the era of hyper-globalization, trade agreements became increasingly used for what one might call **deep integration.**[402] This involved the insertion of rules that effectively extended the regulatory reach of domestic rulebooks and circumvented domestic preferences. For example, the EU has placed strong emphasis on animal welfare standards, human rights, and climate change in its latest trade deals, such as with Mercosur. In its overhaul of NAFTA, the US included a clause that pushed Mexico to raise wages in the automobile sector.[403] Another example is the failure of a US-Europe free trade agreement, partly driven by debates about chlorine chickens, or *chlorhühnchen* in German. Consumer fears about those chickens have contributed to a powerful anti-trade agreement narrative.

In the wake of these new types of trade agreements, we need to revisit the old economic mantra that free trade is beneficial. There is an active debate among economists about the merits and potential drawbacks of deep integration. **Conventional trade liberalization** has typically only pulled **producer lobbies and labor unions** into the fray of public debate.[404] But deep integration also involves environmental and social interest groups. Moreover, changes to standards or regulations could partly undo the effects of tariff reductions, making the welfare and resilience consequences of deep integration much more difficult to assess.[405]

The Future of Trade

How will the future of trade be shaped? And in which areas do we need **global rules**? Economists typically argue that we need interventions when there are market failures, for example because of externalities. Some believe that only a narrow range of externalities, such as **beggar-thy-neighbor policies** and **global public goods** (e.g., global health or knowledge) require worldwide coordination.

Beggar-thy-neighbor policies are those that create overall losses, and that are primarily enacted with the intention of harming the other country. In that sense, economic externalities stemming from malign intent are different from externalities that are just side effects. The former should be subject to globally coordinated measures and the latter should not.

A second argument for international coordination is the provision of public goods on a global level. Public health is a key example. Investment in public health is often undersupplied because of the positive externalities associated with its provision. For example, an early warning system for possible outbreaks of contagious diseases has many public benefits.

The case for global rules is therefore relatively limited. In many areas of international economics, even in the absence of global rules, "virtue is its own reward."[406] In other words, policies that are globally desirable are also in the interest of each individual country. Each country has incentives to supply a low level of these public goods. But once we focus on those beggar-thy-neighbor policies and global public goods, it appears that globalization since the 1990s has been distorted. This is exemplified by the lack of global rules on tax havens.[407] There is also a lack of global regulation on anticompetitive behavior, climate change, and the current public health crisis.[408]

Globally unified rules have another disadvantage. In the end, the imposition of common rules must also be traded off against discoveries from **idiosyncratic policy experimentation**.[409] If there is uncertainty about how to optimally regulate the digital sector, for example, then testing various sets of rules in different countries can provide insights about the optimal scope of regulation.

Defining Global Standards

At the same time, many technologies benefit immensely from network effects and common standards across countries. Defining global standards can be achieved via free trade agreements, but more is required. The China Standards 2035 plan defines China's ambitions. 5G technology, the "internet of things," and artificial intelligence have been identified as areas where China wants to influence the process of setting global standards.[410] Chinese policymakers commonly think that third-tier companies make products, second-tier companies design technology, and first-tier companies set standards. This again illustrates the rivalry with China, which has been one of the overarching themes of this chapter.

CHAPTER 15

Climate Change and Resilience

We all know that climate change is one of the largest challenges of our times. But we rarely consider the potential impact of man-made climate change on humanity's resilience.

In the beginning of the book, I established that a society's sustainability consists of two factors. First, sustainability requires the *absence* of an adverse, slow-moving, long-run force that threatens life on our planet. Second, sustainability requires resilience, which is the ability to withstand adverse shocks and then rebound. Climate change impacts both of these factors.

Now we have an opportunity to build on what we have learned about resilience from the Covid-19 crisis to address climate change.

Less Consumption versus More Innovation

Two wide-reaching approaches have been put forward to tackle the climate change challenge. They are polar opposites. First, some argue that we need to revert the pace of economic growth to a sustainable level. The goal is to reduce our use of limited resources to an amount that is naturally replenishable year-by-year. The second idea is to pursue breakthrough innovations that allow us to adjust economic activity toward carbon neutrality without slowing the pace of economic growth.

In the early days of the Covid-19 crisis, carbon emissions fell globally. But despite widespread lockdowns and a dramatic drop in economic activity, mobility, and consumption, the pandemic only left a small dent in global emissions. The reduction in pollution was tiny compared to what is required to achieve carbon neutrality over the next decades. Estimates point to a rather small 7 percent reduction in global emissions in the spring of 2020.[411] This suggests that cutting back on consumption will hardly be enough to impact climate change. The required changes to lifestyles are too large and they are politically impossible to implement. The yellow vests protests in France were a vivid reminder of political difficulties.

The alternative is innovation that can place us on a sustainable path. Innovation can be focused on mitigation, adaptation, and amelioration.[412]

Mitigation innovations aim at reducing the impact of climate change by lowering CO2 emissions. Electric cars are an example. By not using fossil fuels, they lead to lower emissions, which should reduce the impact of climate change. In terms of the environment, this seems to be the most attractive approach.

Adaptation innovations enable us to better adapt to the unavoidable consequences of climate change. These innovations include, for example, high-tech dikes to protect areas below sea-level from inundation. Migration is another form of adaptation. Because the impact of climate change varies substantially by region, migration can provide additional resilience. People who live close to shores or in floodplains will likely be inundated. They can gain resilience by moving to less exposed locations. The benefits of liberalizing migration on a global scale are estimated to be significant.[413] However, these calculations typically ignore the likelihood that large-scale migrations can threaten social contracts, in which case the implicit cultural understanding that underpins the social contract gets lost.

Amelioration innovations include ideas like geoengineering. The most prominent approaches involve solar radiation management accomplished by spreading aerosols in the stratosphere to reflect sunlight, or greenhouse gas removal technologies, or reforestation and ocean fertilization efforts.

Flexibility is critical in relation to these questions. We do not yet know which approach will work best. Resilience is achieved with diversification, by innovating along all three dimensions. Conceptually, the problem is similar to the development of Covid-19 vaccines, which I discussed earlier. By remaining flexible, we can reoptimize in the face of future information and shocks.

Innovations, Externalities, Traps, and Network Effects

Given the large threat posed by climate change and a broad

consensus about the need for action, why have efforts to act on climate change been so slow? One reason is the intense need for international cooperation. A small country, say Belgium, can change many domestic policies, but even if that nation becomes fully carbon neutral tomorrow, the impact on the world's climate would be miniscule. Global efforts by all countries are needed. Even for larger countries like the UK, CO2 emissions only account for 1.1 percent of the world's pollution.[414]

This problem is known as the "free-rider problem" in economics, and it does not only apply to countries. The same free-rider problem arises among individuals. If 80 percent of wood ovens need to be shut down in a country, each person who has such an oven hopes that his neighbors will shut down their ovens rather than shutting down his own. At the heart of the free-rider problem is an externality. When others protect the environment, everyone benefits—even those who do not participate in the protection efforts.

Moreover, environmental problems are plagued with the **feedback externalities** described earlier. Suppose, worldwide, everyone used a bit more air conditioning to be a bit more comfortable. Air conditioning is a major source of electricity consumption, much of which is covered by nonrenewable energies. So, more air conditioning causes more electricity consumption, which causes more CO2 emissions. Overall, this results in higher temperatures, which collectively become an externality for everyone. As temperatures increase, it is likely that the use of air conditioning will increase more and lead to an adverse feedback loop that propels us closer to climate tipping point.

Double Externalities in Environmental Innovation

Due to a **double externality,** R&D spending in environmental innovation is too low. First, consider the environmental externality. New innovations to protect the climate have externalities on the output side. Some people who benefit from these innovations do not directly contribute to developing them. They receive a positive externality.

Second, there is a classical innovation externality, a theme we discussed in the innovation chapter. Some of the knowledge generated during the innovation process spills over to other inventors, which is another positive externality that is not internalized by the inventor.

These two externalities result in a double externality that holds back climate innovation. There is too little investment in climate innovation because of the R&D externality, and too little mitigation and adaptation. If instead innovators internalize all the benefits from their inventions, they will invest more.

Chicken and Egg Problem Reloaded

The chicken-and-egg problem, also called the QWERTY problem, resurfaces. Network effects hinder the adoption of climate-friendly technologies. Take the network of electric charging stations as an example. There are relatively few stations, so many car owners are reluctant to switch to an electric car for fear of not finding enough charging stations. Because there are few electric car owners, there are more gas stations than electric charging stations.[415]

These network effects are driven by a feedback loop, which originate from strategic complementarities. If some electric charging stations are set up in a local area, it will raise incentives for people in that area to acquire an electric car, which will drive more demand for electric charging stations. That, in turn, will make electric cars even more attractive. As can be seen, there are multiple possible equilibria. If most stations are gas stations, then most people will buy combustion engine cars. If most stations have electric chargers, then more people will buy electric cars. Being stuck in the "wrong" equilibrium with too many gas stations is like a trap. It becomes more complicated to adopt climate-friendly technologies, which hinders resilience. If we are close to a climate change tipping point, being stuck in such a trap is precarious. A small shock might push us beyond the brink into an adverse feedback loop.

Setting up a large network comes with substantial sunk costs. It requires large upfront investments by suppliers and end-product vendors. If they are uncertain whether electricity or hydrogen will power the car of the future, firms will avoid sunk costs. No one will want to bet on the wrong strategy. By waiting and delaying for a time, they can realize real option values. But if they "wait and see" for too long, they will lose precious time to engage in climate change mitigation efforts. Mavericks, such as Elon Musk and his company Tesla, might be needed to bet on electric cars in order to convince others to follow. As an alternative to mavericks, the government can set standards that guide industries toward the adoption of new networks. Either way, traps can be resolved in order to foster resilience.

Climate Clubs

As a solution to the international free-rider problem, Nobel laureate Bill Nordhaus proposed the idea of climate clubs. Countries that form and participate in a climate club would agree on ambitious emissions targets. The distinct element of a club, in comparison to other initiatives, is that nonmembers would be penalized.[416] For example, the club could impose a penalty tariff on goods produced by nonmember countries. This would be similar to the border adjustment taxes discussed in the European Union. As a result, there would be incentives for nonmembers to join the club, as well as incentives for insiders to remain in the club. This approach would address the free-rider problem.[417] But tariffs and border adjustment taxes can also be abusive, especially to emerging economies, when they are disguised as protectionist measures.

Resilience and Proximity to Tipping Points

As mentioned above, a situation can be unsustainable for two reasons. The first is being close to a tipping point so that even a small shock causes an adverse feedback loop. The second is being on a slow-moving downward trend toward a tipping point. Either of these situations calls for a reversal and more resilience.

In the context of climate change, one of the most urgent questions is how to ramp-up and sustain antipollution strategies. Should we immediately make huge efforts or slowly phase-in climate friendly technologies? Several considerations are critical here. Resilience matters. If we have weak resilience to adverse climate shocks, then rapid action will be needed to avoid negative feedback loops. The duration of shocks also matters. If we expect future climate shocks to be long lasting, then we will need to avoid those shocks. Otherwise, bouncing back from permanent changes will be significantly more complicated.

From an accounting perspective, the discount factor on future costs and revenues is a critical input to our collective decision-making. If we discount the importance of future welfare, we will discourage immediate and costly actions to mitigate climate change. Moreover, interest rates have generally fallen in recent decades due to population aging, the savings glut, the low economic growth rate, and precautionary savings. As a result, discount rates are low, which suggests the timeliness of taking early action on climate change.

Tipping Points and Irreversibility

Throughout the book I have emphasized how traps and tipping points can kill resilience. They are particularly damaging when they are irreversible, which is akin to a permanent trap. In relation to the climate, many tipping points, such as the slowing speed of the gulf stream, cannot be predicted with perfect certainty. Instead, the stochastic (probabilistic) aspect of tipping points means that society must stay sufficiently far away from them to avoid them.

On the other hand, externalities risk causing delays that shove the climate toward tipping points, thereby reducing resilience. "Cheap-riding" drives this process. To better understand this concept, suppose the entire society had to fish out of one pond to survive. For fear that others will deplete the pond, everyone will fish frequently and early. But cheap-riding moves the entire group closer to the tipping point, that moment when there are not enough fish left to sustain the population. Over-fishing the oceans perfectly illustrates these mechanisms. The same is true for CO2 pollution, if climate-saving innovations are delayed and "technological redundancies" are not built up. Contingencies that can be rapidly deployed can be highly valuable in these situations.

Not all innovations are equally desirable. It might be useful to have geoengineering technologies available in case the climate rapidly worsens, but geoengineering techniques might produce unexpected side effects that lead us into a new trap. Thus, as we research such technologies, it is critical to learn about the risks and side effects far in advance.

Green Paradox

Phasing in various climate goals, such as CO2 emissions targets, bears several considerations. German economist Hans-Werner Sinn argues that a slow ramp-up of emissions targets creates strong incentives for the owners of carbon-emitting resources, such as oil and gas firms, to accelerate their usage of these resources.[418] Paradoxically, stricter future emissions targets could cause more short-term CO2 emissions and thus accelerate climate change.

Quickly ramping up emissions targets could lead to another paradoxical effect. If we immediately and aggressively cut back on emissions to stay away from tipping points, then we will also leave more fossil fuels in the ground. They will be less scarce in the future and therefore cheaper. That outcome would lower incentives to reduce future emissions. In sum, aggressive emissions targets in the present might lead to higher emissions in the future.[419]

There is a fine line that governments need to navigate when determining the optimal ramping up schedule of climate policies.

Ex-ante and Ex-post Resilience: Planning Security versus Flexibility

Coordination and Flexibility

Coordination of ramp-up strategies is critical for planning security. Suppose a steel mill is considering a shift from coal to hydrogen power.[420] Because these long-term investments are risky, companies need to be reasonably certain that environmental policies will remain stable over the planning horizon. Otherwise, the risk of a costly energy transition being a sunk cost might outweigh the benefits.

A carbon tax with clear projections will add certainty about the future price of carbon. In contrast, policy measures that target the quantity of emissions give less price certainty. An example of an emission-quantity policy is government issuance of a fixed number of tradable pollution permits. In that case, the price path would be unclear, which creates risk for firms related to the costs of emitting.[421] Some economists, such as Jacques Delpla, have argued that a government agency could step in to additionally stabilize the price by buying or selling permits on the margin.

In terms of planning certainty, it is important to reduce risks (including price risks) that are associated with implementing environment-friendly technologies. Doing so lowers the risk premia associated with such investments, which in turn should bring down the cost of adopting environmentally friendly technologies.

Locking in a fixed transition path can create some planning certainty, but it also reduces the flexibility needed to bolster resilience. If tipping points become apparent, we need the option to double down our efforts to avoid those tipping points and to achieve resilience. Reoptimizing the optimal climate policy over time is a key ingredient of a successful climate policy.

Time-Inconsistency Problem

By gradually reoptimizing, we might encounter time inconsistency problems. Initially, regulators need to promise a clear path for the long-term price of CO2, so as to help firms make plans and to minimize the transition costs for carbon-intensive industries. But regulators might want to adjust those rules in the future when new information becomes available. This flexibility allows for resilience, but it also undermines the credibility of the initial carbon price promise.

From this emerges a tradeoff between ex-post and ex-ante resilience. Ex-ante resilience requires binding certain rules that incentivize the forceful uptake of CO2 carbon measures. But ex-post, we want to retain resilience by having the option to reoptimize later. This is a lesson from the Covid-19 pandemic. Public health officials continue to need flexibility to adjust health policies in relation to the contingencies of the pandemic.

Conclusion and Outlook

For all that humanity has achieved and will achieve in the future, we will unavoidably face numerous shocks. Some shocks can be predicted and understood in advance. Others will be "unknown unknowns." Because we cannot avoid shocks as the world evolves, it is crucial for societies to be resilient—to be able to bounce back. Resilience, if we stay focused on it, can act as a reliable compass that guides individuals and societies forward through the unknown.

In addition to pandemics, other recent developments could lead to unanticipated shocks. Each of these developments is speculative, so take this discussion with a grain of salt. They offer great potential and also significant risks. They might lead us closer to dangerous tipping points, but at this stage we cannot be sure where those tipping points are or what they might entail. A big question is: How should we maintain resilience?

Cyberattacks could paralyze critical infrastructure, create chaos, and cause death. Do we need laws that ensure resilience by enforcing requirements to build redundant backup data facilities?

Such redundancies could be critical to counteract ransomware cyberattacks. The threat is very real. On May 8, 2021, a ransomware attack forced the US to shut down the Colonial Pipeline, which supplies almost half of the East Coast's fuel.[422]

Artificial intelligence (AI) will take over many decisions, possibly helping us to make some difficult choices but potentially limiting our freedom to decide. More importantly, AI might challenge the supremacy of the human mind when we cross singularity. Singularity occurs when technological progress becomes uncontrollable, perhaps due to a highly advanced form of artificial intelligence.

Perhaps we humans can keep up with AI by **merging our brains with computer power**. Instead of holding a smartphone, we could see chips placed directly in the brain. Such a brain chip could enable one individual to communicate directly to another person through each person's brain chip. This would simply be a continuation of technology in the nineteenth and twentieth centuries that used machines to extend our muscle power. The next natural step is new technologies that extend brain power. Companies like Synchron and Elon Musk's Neuralink work on chip implants for the brain.

Similarly, brain doping can boost cognitive capacity. In a competitive environment, written exams are often required to gain admission to top universities. Taking performance-enhancing medications might provide students with an edge over their peers, similar to doping in professional sports. Of course, these developments would not be without risks and unpredictable externalities. Many new ethical questions will emerge.

For example, if someone has a brain chip, is he or the chip

responsible for his actions? What if the brain chip can be hacked? Would a digital backup of a person's individuality and a reboot button provide resilience? How do we protect **privacy** and **individual personality**?

We are also entering a new world of **genetic and bioengineering.**[423] Right now, a shortage of organs for transplants leads to the deaths of many people. In the future, we will be able to create new organs in the lab or even in a tube. This will eliminate terrible suffering from patients who must wait years before an organ donor emerges. These advances could also enable us to replace weak (or old) parts of the body with "perfect" new and possibly more powerful organs. It might eventually be possible to create superhumans who each specialize in various abilities. However, these developments might cause unpredictable dangers. We need ethical safety buffers that preserve our ability to recover if something goes wrong. Importantly, these developments are unstoppable at the global level because some countries—possibly those with lower standards—will move ahead regardless of ethical concerns. Thus, to develop a resilient way of moving forward, remaining in the status-quo is not an option.

Then there is the question of genetically designed **weapons**, which might pose greater nonproliferation challenges than our current atomic, biological, and chemical (ABC) weapons. Atomic weapons, for example, cannot be engineered by a solitary individual. However, Oxford philosopher Nick Bostrom worries that individuals in the future might be able to destroy civilization with DIY biohacking tools. There will be no bounce back if such a threat materializes.[424]

The Covid-19 crisis seems almost benign compared to the

challenges associated with these developments. Nevertheless, **pandemics** might become more common in the future as the world's population grows.

Furthermore, shocks often **do not occur alone.** One crisis can fuel others. If we are battling a shock and another one hits us from a different angle, we could be knocked out. One risk can create more risks. For example, **climate change** might lead to more mosquitos, which in turn might facilitate the spread of more illnesses and pandemics.

These developments will occur in one form or other. Nothing and no one can perfectly protect us from their associated shocks. For this reason, it is crucial to make sure that possible shocks do not knock us out. We need to retain the ability to get back up after taking heavy blows. We need safety buffers, redundancies, and protected areas that we can fall back on.

The "we" should be broadly interpreted. It refers to each individual, to each layer of society, to institutions, and to the entire global society. **Individual resilience** is important for each person and family. There are many psychology books that offer suggestions for how individuals can become more resilient when facing possibly life-altering challenges.

Equally important is **societal resilience**. The glue that holds society together is its social contract. There are two rationales for the social contract. The first reason is to limit externalities that individuals might impose on each other, including those that destroy resilience. The second reason is to provide at least partial insurance against shocks.

The social contract's successful implementation relies on the interplay of the government, markets, and social norms. The

Covid-19 crisis has revealed substantial fractures in our societies and major deficiencies in our social contracts and their implementations. Unfairness, inequality, and racial disparity strain the social contract and undermine its resilience. Critically, a resilient social contract must leave space for mavericks and dissenters. They are the ones who might create unexpected solutions to unexpected shocks. Trust in scientific and rational reasoning, and a culture of open communication to advance and react to shocks, will strengthen the resilience of a society. This occurred when scientific breakthroughs developed vaccines in response to the Covid-19 shock.

The social contract also encompasses **institutions**. Many of them govern and impact the interactions of millions of people. They are important for balancing ex-ante and ex-post resilience, as discussed in this book. Importantly, these institutions should be resilient on their own, in part because they provide the soil in which individuals and families can sink roots. Institutions need to remain flexible enough to adapt to the new challenges of our times.

Finally, the Covid-19 crisis has made it blatantly clear that we do not live only in our local neighborhoods (be it physical or virtual). We also live in a **global society**. Therefore, our global order needs to adjust so that all humans and nature can rebound from shocks. For example, a global pandemic early-warning system could facilitate rapid containment of the next pandemic. Resilience is an important part of sustainability. To tackle climate change effectively, we need to stay far away from climate tipping points, which could propel society into adverse feedback loops. Innovation can provide us with sustained economic growth while reducing our carbon footprint.

Two solutions are illusory: We cannot bury our heads in the

sand like an ostrich, and we cannot stay locked in the status quo. Resilience requires flexible responses, extra buffers, and open minds to come up with solutions that allow us to rebound after setbacks. More thoughts, innovation, and flexible adaptation are needed as the future unfolds. All of our minds are needed to build a resilient society.

Endnotes

Introduction

1 The fable has many versions and, like so many insights, traces its roots back to the ancient Greek. See La Fontaine: https://www.oxfordlieder.co.uk/song/4871 or https://en.wikipedia.org/wiki/The_Oak_and_the_Reed.

2 Previous work, by the OECD for example, had a narrower focus on making the macroeconomy and macroeconomic institutions more resilient. My concept of resilience nonetheless shares similarities with this narrower focus. The idea of resilience is similar to an impulse response function, which I will develop further in chapter 2. See: https://www.oecd.org/dac/Resilience%20Systems%20Analysis%20FINAL.pdf.

3 Ramanan Laxminarayan, *Markus' Academy,* Princeton University Webinar, March 30, 2020. https://www.youtube.com/watch?v=z1yHjM7szBk&list=PLPKR-Xs1slgSWqOqaXid_9sQXsPsjV_72&index=31.

Chapter 1

4 Christina Farr and Michelle Gao, "How Taiwan Beat the Coronavirus," CNBC, July 15, 2020, https://www.cnbc.com/2020/07/15/how-taiwan-beat-the-coronavirus.html.

5 The concept of stability is similar to resilience as it also focuses on bouncing back. However, the stability concept refers to smaller day-to-day shocks, whereas resilience also encompasses shocks that break through the "robustness barrier."

6 Rueben Westmaas, "World Famous Chicago Skyscraper Sways in Wind," Discovery, August 1, 2019, https://www.discovery.com/exploration/World-Famous-Chicago-Skyscraper-Sway-Wind.

7 In statistics, resistance is a close cousin to robustness. The former refers to the fact that individual outlier data have only a small impact on the analysis. The latter (robustness) refers to being immune to mis-specified probability distributions.

8 Joe Miller, "Inside the Hunt for a Covid-19 Vaccine: How BioNTech Made the Breakthrough," *Financial Times,* November 13, 2020, https://www.ft.com/content/c4ca8496-a215-44b1-a7eb-f88568fc9de9.

9 Downside risks are often measured by the "value at risk," the worst outcome within the 99 percent confidence interval.

10 Of course, financial intermediaries take the limited liability into account and might adjust credit quantity or price of credit.

11 If we interpret figure 1-3 to represent financial returns, the Sharpe ratio of the straight line would be infinite since the volatility is zero.

Chapter 2

12 To get a feel for exponential growth, suppose, you are attending a football game in an open-air arena and it slowly starts to rain. A typical raindrop has a volume of about .05 milliliters. If one raindrop falls into the stadium each second (very mild rain) this adds up to 1,576 liters in a year. The floor might be slightly wet, at most. Assume now that the rain slowly gains in intensity and the number of raindrops per second increases by a factor of 1.03 per second. At the beginning of the game, there is one raindrop, the next second there are 1.03, then 1.032= 1.0609 and so on. After ten minutes, the field will be somewhat wet. One might say, "Oh, the players might have to deal with slippery conditions today." Three minutes later, the water is already standing at 10 centimeters (about 4 inches). We might slowly get concerned and ponder whether we should leave the arena. But we better leave immediately. Because only three minutes later, sixteen minutes after the first raindrop, the entire stadium will be under water. In the last second, after sixteen minutes of rain, 105 million liters of water will be flowing into the stadium.

13 Ramanan Laxminarayan, *Markus' Academy,* Princeton University Webinar, March 30, 2020. https://www.youtube.com/watch?v=z1yHjM7szBk&list=PLPKR-Xs1slgSWqOqaXid_9sQXsPsjV_72&index=31.

14 Another example of the global dimension of feedback loops is Christopher Clark's interpretation of the series of events that culminated in the eruption of World War I in his book *The Sleepwalkers.* After the killing of Archduke Ferdinand in Sarajevo in 1914, little steps toward escalation brought all European nations closer to a tipping point. Once the first nations mobilized, a tipping point was crossed. More nations mobilized and war became inevitable.

15 Peter Beaumont, "Tanzania's President Shrugs Off Covid-19 Risk After Sending Fruit for Tests," *The Guardian,* May 19, 2020, https://www.theguardian.com/global-development/2020/may/19/tanzanias-president-shrugs-off-covid-19-risk-after-sending-fruit-for-tests.

16 Jake Adelstein and Nathaly-Kyoko Stucky, "Japan's Finance Minister Commits Suicide on World Suicide Prevention Day," *The Atlantic.* September 10, 2012, https://www.theatlantic.com/international/archive/2012/09/japans-finance-minister-commits-suicide-world-suicide-prevention-day/323787/.

17 République Française, "Non-Respect de l'Obligation de Port du Masque: Quelles sont les Règles?" October 21, 2020, https://www.service-public.fr/particuliers/vosdroits/F35351.

18 Michael Spence, *Markus' Academy,* Princeton University Webinar, July 6, 2020, https://www.youtube.com/watch?v=92-vc238_nI&list=PLPKR-Xs1slgSWqOqaXid_9sQXsPsjV_72&index=6.

19 In the economics profession, the idea to impose a tax on an externality is called a Pigouvian tax after English economist Arthur Pigou.

20 Raghuram Rajan, "Raghuram Rajan on Covid-19: Is It Time to Decentralise Power?" Coronanomics, July 22, 2020, https://www.youtube.com/watch?v=VU9d5IyudYs.

21 Michaela Wiegel, "Wie Frankreich die Akzeptanz der Corona-Maßnahmen Verspielt," *Frankfurter Allgemeine,* September 24, 2020, https://www.faz.net/aktuell/politik/ausland/wie-frankreich-die-akzeptanz-der-corona-massnahmen-verspielt-16969296.html.

22 Ursula Nonnemacher, "Brandenburger Kreise Haben bis zur 200er-Inzidenz Freie Hand," RBB, March 15, 2021, https://www.rbb24.de/studiocottbus/panorama/coronavirus/beitraege_neu/2021/03/elbe-elster-corona-inzidenz-massnahmen-eingriff-land-brandenburg.html.

23 This logic can easily be illustrated with face mask production. What follows is a simple adaptation of Milton Friedman's famous pencil example. Not a single person in the world knows how to manufacture a face mask completely from scratch. A face mask requires processed plastic, a polypropylene made from oil that originates in Texas or in the Arab Gulf countries. A metal is needed for the nose clip, perhaps iron or steel. The face mask needs a package, which requires cardboard made from paper pulp. Overall, a complex process is at work. After the Covid-19 outbreak, the computational task of collecting all the information within the required time so as to rapidly ramp up face mask production seemed

daunting or impossible. It was certainly not practical. This example of face mask production illustrates what Hayek argued: The economy is so complex that not a single model can capture all the interactions involved. Yet, informative price signals are critical for economies evolving at the global innovation frontier to ensure an optimal allocation of resources. A famous saying is that switching off the price signals is like cutting the phone wires when people still used landlines.

24 Moncef Slaoui and Matthew Hepburn, "Developing Safe and Effective Covid Vaccines—Operation Warp Speed's Strategy and Approach," *New England Journal of Medicine* 383, no. 18 (2020): 1701-1703. https://www.nejm.org/doi/full/10.1056/NEJMp2027405.

25 Riley Griffin and Drew Armstrong, "Pfizer Vaccine's Funding Came from Berlin, not Washington," Bloomberg, September 11, 2020, https://www.bloomberg.com/news/articles/2020-11-09/pfizer-vaccine-s-funding-came-from-berlin-not-washington.

Part II

26 Latika Bourke, "International Borders Might Not Open Even if Whole Country Is Vaccinated," *The Sydney Morning Herald,* April 13, 2021, https://www.smh.com.au/politics/federal/international-borders-might-not-open-even-if-whole-country-is-vaccinated-greg-hunt-20210413-p57ixi.html.

Chapter 3

27 Ramanan Laxminarayan, *Markus' Academy,* Princeton University Webinar, March 30, 2020. https://www.youtube.com/watch?v=z1yHjM7szBk&list=PLPKR-Xs1slgSWqOqaXid_9sQXsPsjV_72&index=31.

28 John Cochrane, *Markus' Academy,* Princeton University Webinar, May 18, 2020, https://www.youtube.com/watch?v=H6sSvqD9Xsw&list=PLPKR-Xs1slgSWqOqaXid_9sQXsPsjV_72&index=18.

29 Raj Chetty, John N. Friedman, Nathaniel Hendren, and Michael Stepner, "The Economic Impacts of COVID-19: Evidence from a New Public Database Built Using Private Sector Data," Opportunity Insights. November 5, 2020, https://opportunityinsights.org/wp-content/uploads/2020/05/tracker_paper.pdf.

30 Raj Chetty, *Markus' Academy,* Princeton University Webinar, June 2017, 2020, https://www.youtube.com/watch?v=ip5pz7gOSwI&list=PLPKR-Xs1slgSWqOqaXid_9sQXsPsjV_72&index=11.

31 Chetty, *Markus' Academy,* 2020.

32 Chetty, *Markus' Academy,* 2020.

33 NBER, *NBER Digest,* August 8, 2020, https://www.nber.org/digest-2020-08.

34 Lawrence Summers, *Markus' Academy,* Princeton University Webinar, May 22, 2020, https://www.youtube.com/watch?v=cZmRtQCR2ns&list=PLPKR-Xs1slgSWqOqaXid_9sQXsPsjV_72&index=17.

35 Economically speaking, an externality is an action by individual i that affects another agent's j utility: \partial u^i(a^i, a^-i) / \partial a^-i. Strategic complementarities instead depend on the cross-derivative: how does the externality that agent j imposes on i affect i's actions: \partial\frac{partial u^i(a^i, a^-i) / \partial a^i}{\partial a^-i}}.

36 Peter DeMarzo, Dimitri Vayanos, and Jeffrey Zwiebel, "Persuasion Bias, Social Influence, and Unidimensional Opinions," *Quarterly Journal of Economics* 118, no. 3 (2003): 909-968.

37 Like a crier in front of a mountain wall hears his own words amplified by echo. ("Schreier vor dem Berg.")

38 Zeckhauser (2020) makes the same point regarding climate change policies.

39 Rajan (2020) and Cochrane (2020) make the same point, but not just for India.

40 Franklin Delano Roosevelt, "'Only Thing We Have to Fear Is Fear Itself': FDR's First Inaugural Address," History Matters, 1933, historymatters.gmu/edu/d/5057.

41 Markus Brunnermeier and Jonathan Parker, "Optimal Expectations," *American Economic Review* 95, no. 4 (2005): 1092-1118.

42 Veronika Arnold, "Ansturm auf Skigebiete trotz Lockdown: Nächster Wintersport-Ort nun abgeriegelt – 'Wurden überrannt,'" Merkur, January 5, 2021, https://www.merkur.de/welt/coronavirus-skigebiete-lockdown-oberhof-deutschland-ansturm-nrw-willingen-eifel-winterberg-90157267.html.

43 For more details on this hypothesis, consult: Bengt Holmstrom, "The Seasonality of Covid-19." Princeton Bendheim Center for Finance (Webinar), October 22, 2020, https://www.youtube.com/watch?v=z95U8FU9gMQ.

44 Google, Google Covid Case Tracker, South Dakota, 2021, https://www.google.com/search?q=covid+cases+in+south+dakota&oq=covid+cases+in+south+dakota&aqs=chrome..69i57j0l2j0i395l7.4013j1j7&sourceid=chrome&ie=UTF-8.

45 Saxony Government, "Infektionsfälle in Sachsen," March 18, 2021, https://www.coronavirus.sachsen.de/infektionsfaelle-in-sachsen-4151.html.

46 Mitteldeutscher Rundfunk, "Verschwörungstheorien in Sachsen: Ein wilder," Legenden-Mix, April 27, 2020, https://www.mdr.de/nachrichten/sachsen/corona-verschwoerungstherorien-populismus-100.html.

Chapter 4

47 Lawrence Summers, *Markus' Academy,* Princeton University Webinar, May 22, 2020, https://www.youtube.com/watch?v=cZmRtQCR2ns&list=PLPKR-Xs1slgSWqOqaXid_9sQXsPsjV_72&index=17.

48 Paul Romer, *Markus' Academy,* Princeton University Webinar, April 3, 2020, https://www.youtube.com/watch?v=q9z0eu4piHw&list=PLPKR-Xs1slgSWqOqaXid_9sQXsPsjV_72&index=30.

49 Romer, *Markus' Academy,* April 3, 2020.

50 Daron Acemoglu, Victor Chernozukhov, Ivan Werning, and Michael Whinston, "Optimal Targeted Lockdowns," MIT Economics Department, May 2020, economics.mit.edu/files/19698.

51 Daron Acemoglu, *Markus' Academy,* Princeton University Webinar, May 8, 2020, https://www.youtube.com/watch?v=NqtS8MZBuZ0&list=PLPKR-Xs1slgSWqOqaXid_9sQXsPsjV_72&index=20.

52 Econreporter, "US Needs Large-Scale Covid Testing Urgently: Nobel Winning Economist Paul Romer," June 28, 2020, https://en.econreporter.com/2020/06/its-intellectual-failure-nobel-economics-winner-paul-romer-on-why-us-needs-large-scale-COVID-testing-urgently/.

53 Paul Romer, *Markus' Academy,* April 3, 2020.

54 Suppose 1 percent of the population is Covid-19 positive, and that 10 percent of tests come back positive. (Typically, this is the case in countries that are in the middle of a Covid-19 wave.) Then consider that test results are accurate with 95 percent probability. This implies that 5 percent of the people who are infected will get a negative test result. The interested reader might be reminded of Bayes's rule from high school math. A random person that receives a negative test result is negative only with 99.94 percent probability. Thus, a small number of people with a negative result will still carry the virus. Although the marginal information gain represents only a 0.994 percent lower chance of having Covid, people might misperceive that chance to be much higher.

55 Monica de Bolle, *Markus' Academy,* Princeton University Webinar, February 25, 2021. https://www.youtube.com/watch?v=Ptsg_EjCXxw.

56 BBC, "Coronavirus: Under Surveillance and Confined at Home in Taiwan," March 24, 2020, https://www.bbc.co.uk/news/technology-52017993.

57 Welt, "Das ist Drostens Plan für den Herbst," August 5, 2020, https://www.welt.de/politik/deutschland/article212941080/Christian-Drosten-Buerger-sollen-Kontakt-Tagebuch-fuehren.html.

58 Daron Acemoglu, *Markus' Academy,* May 8, 2020.

59 Ramanan Laxminarayan, *Markus' Academy,* Princeton University Webinar, March 30, 2020. https://www.youtube.com/watch?v=z1yHjM7szBk&list=PLPKR-Xs1slgSWqOqaXid_9sQXsPsjV_72&index=31.

Chapter 5

60 ui (u-i)

61 Moses Shayo, "A Model of Social Identity with an Application to Political Economy: Nation, Class, and Redistribution," *American Political Science Review* (2009): 147-174; Gene Grossman and Elhanan Helpman, "Identity Politics and Trade Policy," Princeton University, July 2019, https://www.princeton.edu/~grossman/SocialIdentityJuly2019..pdf.

62 David McGuire, James EA Cunningham, Kae Reynolds, and Gerri Matthews-Smith, "Beating the Virus: An Examination of the Crisis Communication Approach Taken by New Zealand Prime Minister Jacinda Ardern During the Covid-19 Pandemic," *Human Resource Development International* 23, no. 4 (2020): 361-379.

63 Harold James, *Markus' Academy,* Princeton University Webinar, April 24, 2020, https://www.youtube.com/watch?v=PVIm4BdBmTI.

64 Harold James, Markus' Academy, April 24, 2020, "Morale is a crucial part in fighting any war."

65 Jean Tirole, "Allons-Nous Enfin Apprendre Notre Leçon?" LinkedIn, April 14, 2020, https://www.linkedin.com/pulse/allons-nous-enfin-apprendre-notre-le%C3%A7on-jean-tirole/.

66 Esther Duflo points out that receiving a message from a trusted source is more important than the content of the message. See: Esther Duflo, *Markus' Academy,* Princeton University Webinar, February 11, 2021, https://www.youtube.com/watch?v=15PMtvJBI-s.

67 Tim Harford, "Statistics, Lies, and the Virus: Tim Harford's Five Lessons from a Pandemic" (Blog), September 17, 2020, https://timharford.com/2020/09/statistics-lies-and-the-virus-five-lessons-from-a-pandemic/.

68 See my introductory remarks to Angus Deaton's webinar from April 2020.

69 Angus Deaton, *Markus' Academy.* Princeton University Webinar, April 13, 2020, 21:20, https://www.youtube.com/watch?v=2uzASRQz4gM.

70 Angus Deaton, *Markus' Academy,* April 13, 2020, 31:09, 31:51, and 32:02.

71 Abhijit Banerjee, Marcella Alsam, Emily Breza, Arun Chandrasekhar, Abhijit Chowdhury, Esther Dufo, Paul Goldsmith Pinkham, and Benjamin Olken, "Messages on Covid-19 Prevention Increased Symptoms Reporting and Adherence to Preventative Behaviors Among 25 Million Recipients with Similar Effects on Non-Recipient Members of Their Communities," *NBER Working Papers,* no. 27496 (July 2020), https://www.nber.org/system/files/working_papers/w27496/w27496.pdf.

72 Andreas Kluth, "Like a Virus, QAnon Spreads from the U.S. to Germany," Bloomberg, September 21, 2020, https://www.bloomberg.com/opinion/articles/2020-09-22/like-a-virus-qanon-spreads-from-the-u-s-to-europe-germany?sref=ATN0rNv3.

73 David Brooks, *Munk Dialogues.* Peter and Melanie Munk Charitable Foundation, July 22, 2020, 18:50, https://www.youtube.com/watch?v=W0dbDFJR3A4&feature=youtu.be].

74 Tyler Cowen, *Markus' Academy,* Princeton University Webinar, April 10, 2020, https://www.youtube.com/watch?v=FPsPmkp6sdM&list=PLPKR-Xs1slgSWqOqaXid_9sQXsPsjV_72&index=28.

Chapter 6

75 For example, up to 20 percent of Covid-19 patients still had chest pains two months after the infection. See: Columbia University Irving Medical Center, "Long Haul Covid: Columbia Physicians Review What's Known," March 22, 2021, https://www.cuimc.columbia.edu/news/long-haul-covid-columbia-physicians-review-whats-known.

76 Naomi Kresge, "Pfizer-BioNTech Covid Vaccine Blocks Most Spread in Israel Study," Bloomberg, March 11, 2021, https://www.bloomberg.com/news/articles/2021-03-11/pfizer-biontech-covid-vaccine-blocks-most-spread-in-israel-study.

77 This number is from Michael Kremer's webinar. Others estimate it to be $2 or $3. See: *The Economist,* "'The Covid-19 Pandemic Will Be Over by the End of 2021,' says Bill Gates," August 18, 2020, https://www.economist.com/international/2020/08/18/the-covid-19-pandemic-will-be-over-by-the-end-of-2021-says-bill-gates.

78 Michael Kremer, *Markus' Academy,* Princeton University Webinar, May 1, 2020, 19:00 and 21:46, https://www.youtube.com/watch?v=C8W8JQLTECc.

79 Michael Peel and Joe Miller, "EU Hits Back as Blame Game Over Vaccine Procurement Intensifies," *Financial Times,* January 7, 2021. https://www.ft.com/content/c1575e05-70e5-4e5f-b58c-cde5c99aba5f.

80 Lawrence Summers, *Markus' Academy,* Princeton University Webinar, May 22, 2020, 05:50 https://www.youtube.com/watch?v=cZmRtQCR2ns&list=PLPKR-Xs1slgSWqOqaXid_9sQXsPsjV_72&index=17.

81 Michael Kremer, *Markus' Academy,* Princeton University Webinar, May 1, 2020, 26:39, 27:55, and 28:30, https://www.youtube.com/watch?v=C8W8JQLTECc.

82 Michael Kremer, *Markus' Academy,* 2020, 3:30, 4:25, 4:56, and 8:15.

83 Michael Kremer, *Markus' Academy,* 2020, 20:27.

84 Michael Kremer, *Markus' Academy,* 2020, 37:15, 37:40, 40:00, and 41:05.

85 Michael Kremer, *Markus' Academy,* 2020, 47:20.

86 Ralph Sina and Dominik Lauck, "Warum Israel Genug Impfstoff Hat," Tagesschau, January 23, 2021, https://www.tagesschau.de/ausland/impfstoff-israel-biontech-101.html.

87 Christoph Gurk, "Lateinamerika wird zum Testfeld für die Pharmaindustrie," Süddeutsche Zeitung, August 3, 2020, https://www.sueddeutsche.de/politik/coronavirus-impfstoff-lateinamerika-pharmaindustrie-1.4986326.

88 Bill Gates, "How the Pandemic Will Shape the Near Future," TED, July 6, 2020, 27:00, https://www.youtube.com/watch?v=jmQWOPDqxWA.

89 This paper makes a related point conditional on vaccine effectiveness: Laura Matrajt, Julia Eaton, Tiffany Leung, and Elizabeth Brown, "Vaccine Optimization for Covid-19: Who to Vaccinate First?" Science Advances, 2021.

90 Christian Siedenbiedel, "In der Krise Horten die Menschen Bargeld," *Frankfurter Allgemeine,* September 24, 2020, https://www.faz.net/aktuell/finanzen/meine-finanzen/sparen-und-geld-anlegen/ezb-wirtschaftsbericht-in-der-krise-wird-bargeld-gehortet-16969517.html.

91 For a rigorous theoretical analysis of these ideas, though without specific application to Covid-19, see: Vianney Perchet, Philippe Rigollet, Sylvain Chassang, and Erik Snowberg, "Batched Bandit Problems," *Annals of Statistics* 44, no. 2 (2016): 660-681, https://arxiv.org/abs/1505.00369.

92 Sam Ball, "'I Won't Take the Risk': France Leads the World in Covid-19 Vaccine Scepticism," France24, November 20, 2020, https://www.france24.com/en/france/20201120-i-won-t-take-the-risk-france-leads-the-world-in-covid-19-vaccine-scepticism.

93 *The Guardian,* "Joe Biden Receives Coronavirus Vaccine," video, December 21, 2020, https://www.theguardian.com/us-news/video/2020/dec/21/joe-biden-receives-coronavirus-vaccine-video.

94 Abdelraouf Arnaout, "Netanyahu to Be First Israeli to Take Covid-19 Vaccine," *Anadolu Agency,* December 9, 2020, https://www.aa.com.tr/en/middle-east/netanyahu-to-be-first-israeli-to-take-covid-19-vaccine/2070779.

95 Tobias Heimbach, "Biden, Netanjahu & Co.: Spitzenpolitiker weltweit lassen sich öffentlich impfen – wann kommt Merkel an die Reihe?" Business Insider, December 23, 2020, https://www.businessinsider.de/politik/deutschland/corona-impfung-joe-biden-wurde-geimpft-merkel/.

96 David Walsh, "Do We Need Coronavirus 'Vaccine Passports' to Get Europe Moving Again? Euronews Asks the Experts," Euronews, December 11, 2020, https://www.euronews.com/2020/12/11/do-we-need-coronavirus-vaccine-passports-to-get-the-world-moving-again-euronews-asks-the-e.

97 BBC, "Covid: EU Plans Rollout of Travel Certificate before Summer," March 18, 2020, https://www.bbc.co.uk/news/world-europe-56427830.

98 Bill Birtles, "China Embraces Coronavirus Vaccine Passports for Overseas Travel, but Other Countries Foresee Concerns," ABC News, March 17, 2021, https://www.abc.net.au/news/2021-03-17/china-embraces-vaccine-passports-while-the-west-mulls-ethics/13252588.

99 *The Economist*, "How Well Will Vaccines Work?" February 11, 2021, https://www.economist.com/leaders/2021/02/13/how-well-will-vaccines-work.

Part III

100 Paul Krugman, *Markus' Academy*, Princeton University Webinar, May 16, 2020, 31:05 and 31:58, https://www.youtube.com/watch?v=h1ZiTIou0_8&list=PLl591lvzxc3xwUuEkOVl1PNngFm9cZnH&index=17.

101 Paul Krugman, *Markus' Academy*, May 16, 2020, 46:30.

102 Paul Krugman, *Markus' Academy*, May 16, 2020, 34:23.

103 Paul Krugman, *Markus' Academy*, May 16, 2020, 35:18, 39:20, and 40:15.

104 Jerome Powell also stressed the differences between the 2020 Covid-19 recession and the 2008 great recession. See: Jerome Powell, *Markus' Academy*, Princeton University Webinar, January 14, 2021, https://www.youtube.com/watch?v=TEC3supZwvM.

105 Paul Krugman, *Markus' Academy*, May 16, 2020, 46:30 and 46:50.

106 The figure is based on work by Takatoshi Ito.

107 Olivier Coibion, Yuriy Goridnichenko, and Michael Weber, "How Did US Consumers Use Their Stimulus Payments?" *NBER Working Papers*, no. 27693 (August 2020), https://www.nber.org/papers/w27693.

108 For an overview and a six-minute video that explains the concept, see: Daniel Rosenberg, "How Digital Coupons Fuel China's Economic Recovery," Luohan Academy, May 27, 2020, https://www.luohanacademy.com/insights/e0d638c3f840e3be.

Chapter 7

109 Jared Spataro, "2 Years of Digital Transformation in 2 Months," Microsoft, April 30, 2020, https://www.microsoft.com/en-us/microsoft-365/blog/2020/04/30/2-years-digital-transformation-2-months/.

110 Harold James, *Markus' Academy,* Princeton University Webinar, April 24, 2020, 1:03:05, https://www.youtube.com/watch?v=PVIm4BdBmTI.

111 Tyler Cowen, *Markus' Academy,* Princeton University Webinar, April 10, 2020, https://www.youtube.com/watch?v=FPsPmkp6sdM&list=PLPKR-Xs1slgSWqOqaXid_9sQXsPsjV_72&index=28.

112 Stan Leibowitz and Stephen E. Margolis, "The Fable of Keys," *Journal of Law and Economics* 33, no. 1 (1990): 1-25.

113 Nick Bloom, *Markus' Academy,* Princeton University Webinar, December 3, 2020, 10:55, https://www.youtube.com/watch?v=N8_rvy-hqUs.

114 Adam Green, "Covid-19 Pandemic Accelerates Digital Health Reforms," *Financial Times,* May 17, 2020, https://www.ft.com/content/31c927c6-684a-11ea-a6ac-9122541af204.

115 Eric Schmidt, *Markus' Academy,* Princeton University Webinar, July 27, 2020, 23:30, https://www.youtube.com/watch?v=726B0y1D5ZM&t=31s.

116 Eric Schmidt, *Markus' Academy,* July 27, 2020, 58:10.

117 Devon Carter, "Can mRNA Vaccines Be Used in Cancer Care?" MD Anderson Cancer Center, January 25, 2021, https://www.mdanderson.org/cancerwise/can-mrna-vaccines-like-those-used-for-covid-19-be-used-in-cancer-care.h00-159457689.html.

118 Erika Solomon, "BioNTech Seeks to Develop a More Effective Malaria Vaccine," *Financial Times,* July 26, 2021, https://www.ft.com/content/e112b318-aced-482b-be4f-ec76f39cdc3f.

119 Eric Schmidt, *Markus' Academy,* July 27, 2020, 43:02.

120 Eric Schmidt, *Markus' Academy,* July 27, 2020, 43:02.

121 Jose Maria Barrero, Nick Bloom, and Steven J Davis, "COVID-19 Is also a Reallocation Shock," Brookings Institute, June 25, 2020, https://www.brookings.edu/wp-content/uploads/2020/06/Barrero-et-al-conference-draft.pdf.

122 Sometimes "travel" in the form of walking to another building.

123 Nick Bloom, *Markus' Academy,* December 3, 2020, 15:10 and 38:55.

124 Nick Bloom, James Liang, John Roberts, and Zhichun Jenny Ying, "Does Working from Home Work? Evidence from a Chinese Experiment," *Quarterly Journal of Economics* 130, no. 1 (2015): 165-218.

125 *The Guardian,* "Big Brother Isn't Just Watching: Workplace Surveillance Can Track Your Every Move," November 6, 2017, https://www.theguardian.com/world/2017/nov/06/workplace-surveillance-big-brother-technology.

126 Jonathan Dingel and Brent Neiman, "How Many Jobs Can be Done at Home?" Becker Friedman Institute for Economics Working Paper, June 19, 2020, https://bfi.uchicago.edu/wp-content/uploads/BFI_White-Paper_Dingel_Neiman_3.2020.pdf.

127 This paragraph largely draws on analysis by McKinsey: Susan Lund, Anu Madgavkar, James Manyika, and Sven Smit, "What's Next for Remote Work: An Analysis of 2000 Tasks, 800 Jobs, and Nine Countries," McKinsey Global Institute, November 23, 2020, https://www.mckinsey.com/featured-insights/future-of-work/whats-next-for-remote-work-an-analysis-of-2000-tasks-800-jobs-and-nine-countries?sid=blankform&sid=cd37a5db-95fb-4455-8ed2-f6b0596b8bcb#.

128 Jose Maria Barrero, Nick Bloom, and Stephen Davis, "Why Working from Home Will Stick," Stanford Working Paper, April 2021, https://nbloom.people.stanford.edu/sites/g/files/sbiybj4746/f/why_wfh_will_stick_21_april_2021.pdf.

129 Susan Lund et al., "What's Next for Remote Work," 2020.

130 Nick Bloom, *Markus' Academy,* December 3, 2020, 52:50.

131 Nick Bloom, *Markus' Academy,* December 3, 2020, 50:00 and 52:50.

132 Lawrence Summers, *Markus' Academy,* Princeton University Webinar, May 22, 2020, 54:48, https://www.youtube.com/watch?v=cZmRtQCR2ns&list=PLPKR-Xs1slgSWqOqaXid_9sQXsPsjV_72&index=17.

133 Elizabeth Schulze, "Robert Shiller Warns that Urban Home Prices Could Decline," CNBC, July 13, 2020, https://www.cnbc.com/2020/07/13/robert-shiller-warns-that-urban-home-prices-could-decline.html.

134 Antonia Cundy, "The Home Buyers Making Their Tuscan Dream a Reality," *Financial Times,* August 19, 2020, https://www.ft.com/content/2a127c83-08ba-4ad7-8a1b-19dcaee5c6ae.

135 Nick Bloom, *Markus' Academy,* December 3, 2020, 51:20.

136 Laura Lombrana, "An Urban Planner's Trick to Making Bikeable Cities," Bloomberg, August 5, 2020, https://www.bloomberg.com/news/articles/2020-08-05/an-urban-planner-s-trick-to-making-bike-able-cities?sref=ATN0rNv3.

137 Tyler Cowen, *Markus' Academy,* April 10, 2020, 13:10.

138 Christian Siedenbiedel, "In der Krise Horten die Menschen Bargeld," *Frankfurter Allgemeine,* September 24, 2020, https://www.faz.net/aktuell/finanzen/meine-finanzen/sparen-und-geld-anlegen/ezb-wirtschaftsbericht-in-der-krise-wird-bargeld-gehortet-16969517.html.

139 Eric Schmidt, *Markus' Academy,* July 27, 2020, 51:55.

140 Nana Yaa Boakye-Adjei, "Covid-19: Boon and Bane for Digital Payments and Financial Inclusion," Bank for International Settlements, Financial Stability Institute, July 2020, https://www.bis.org/fsi/fsibriefs9.pdf.

141 Markus Brunnermeier, Harold James, and Jean-Pierre Landau, "The Digitalization of Money," Princeton University Working Paper, 2019.

142 See presentation at the European Banking Authority and: Markus Brunnermeier, "Money in the Digital Age," Speech delivered at the EBA Research Workshop, November 25, 2020, https://www.youtube.com/watch?v=QdlSzTnOlkg.

143 Saritha Rai, "Apple Alum Builds App to Help Millions in Indian Slums Find Jobs," Bloomberg, August 13, 2020, https://www.bloomberg.com/news/articles/2020-08-14/apna-job-app-aims-to-connect-india-s-workers-with-employees?sref=ATN0rNv3.

144 *The Economist,* "When Will Office Workers Return?" February 20, 2021, https://www.economist.com/business/2021/02/20/when-will-office-workers-return.

145 Chris Arkenberg, "Will Gaming Keep Growing When the Lockdowns End?" Deloitte, July 8, 2020, https://www2.deloitte.com/be/en/pages/technology-media-and-telecommunications/articles/video-game-industry-trends.html.

146 Bijan Stephen, "The Lockdown Live-Streaming Numbers Are Out, and They're Huge," The Verge, May 13, 2020, https://www.theverge.com/2020/5/13/21257227/coronavirus-streamelements-arsenalgg-twitch-youtube-livestream-numbers.

147 Mark Aguiar, Mark Blis, Kofi Kerwin, and Erik Hurst, "Leisure Luxuries and the Labor Supply of Young Men," *Journal of Political Economy,* (2021): 337-382.

Chapter 8

148 Jeremy Stein, *Markus' Academy,* Princeton University Webinar, May 11, 2020, 26:10 and 27:12, https://www.youtube.com/watch?v=0iNQNzAUDiw.

149 AIDS, which emerged in the 1960s, falls on the margin between what the WHO considers a pandemic and an epidemic. At its peak, about 3.3 million people contracted HIV per year in the 1990s, compared to more than 80 million tested Covid infections in 2020 alone.

150 For the economic mechanism and two applications to the Great Recession and to Covid, see: Julian Kozlowski, Venky Venkateswaran, and Laura Veldkamp, "Scarring Body and Mind: The Long-Term Belief-Scarring Effects of Covid-19," *NBER Working Papers,* no. 27439 (June 2020). https://www.nber.org/papers/w27439.

151 Solveig Godeluck, "Cette Épargne des Ménages qui Menace de Nuire à la Reprise," LesEchos, July 29, 2020, https://www.lesechos.fr/economie-france/social/Covid-cette-epargne-des-menages-qui-menace-de-nuire-a-la-reprise-1227200.

152 Michael Spence, *Markus' Academy,* Princeton University Webinar, July 6, 2020, 20:00 and 30:13, https://www.youtube.com/watch?v=92-vc238_nI&list=PLPKR-Xs1slgSWqOqaXid_9sQXsPsjV_72&index=6.

153 Ulrike Malmendier and Stefan Nagel, "Depression Babies: Do Macroeconomic Experiences Affect Risk Taking?" *The Quarterly Journal of Economics* 126, no. 1 (2011): 373-416.

154 Nicola Gennaiolo, Andei Shleifer, and Robert Vishny, "Neglected Risks: The Psychology of Financial Crises," *American Economic Review* 105, no. 5 (2015): 310-14.

155 Jose Maria Barrero, Nick Bloom, and Steven J Davis, "COVID-19 Is also a Reallocation Shock," Brookings Institute, June 25, 2020, https://www.brookings.edu/wp-content/uploads/2020/06/Barrero-et-al-conference-draft.pdf.

156 *The Renaissance: The Age of Michelangelo and Leonardo da Vinci,* Documentary film by DW, April 28, 2019, 22:00 to 26:00, https://www.youtube.com/watch?v=BmHTQsxxkPk.

157 Robert Hall and Marianna Kudlyak, "The Inexorable Recoveries of US Unemployment," *NBER Working Papers,* no. 28111 (November 2020), https://sites.google.com/site/mariannakudlyak/home/inexorable_recoveries.

158 Paul Krugman, *Markus' Academy,* Princeton University Webinar, May 16, 2020, 1:03:04, https://www.youtube.com/watch?v=h1ZiTIou0_8&list=PLlI591lvzxc3xwUuEkOVl1PNngFm9cZnH&index=17.

159 Veronica Guerrieri, *Markus' Academy,* Princeton University Webinar, June 19, 2020, 1:14:15, https://www.youtube.com/watch?v=x2npgxzuTVg.

160 Erik Hurst, *Markus' Academy,* Princeton University Webinar, March 20, 2021, 52:15, https://www.youtube.com/watch?v=VG7KS5sLABY.

161 Joseph Stiglitz, *Markus' Academy,* Princeton University Webinar, April 27, 2020, 30:08, https://www.youtube.com/watch?v=_6SoT97wo3g.

162 Joseph Stiglitz, *Markus' Academy,* April 27, 2020, 34:22 and 35.00.

163 Raj Chetty, *Markus' Academy,* Princeton University Webinar, June 2017, 2020, 1:00:41 and 1:01:27, https://www.youtube.com/watch?v=ip5pz7gOSwI&list=PLPKR-Xs1slgSWqOqaXid_9sQXsPsjV_72&index=11.

164 Philip Oreopoulos, Till Von Wachter, and Andrew Heisz, "The Short- and Long-Term Career Effects of Graduating in a Recession," *American Economic Journal: Applied Economics* 4, no. 1 (2012): 1-29.

165 Jonathan Heathcote, Fabrizio Perri, and Giovannia Violante, "The Rise of US Earnings Inequality: Does the Cycle Drive the Trend?" Princeton University, May 31, 2020, http://violante.mycpanel.princeton.edu/Journals/Draft_05-31-20_JH.pdf.

166 Olivier Blanchard and Lawrence Summers, "Hysteresis in Unemployment," *European Economic Review,* (1987): 288-295.

167 Olivier Blanchard, "Should We Reject the Natural Rate Hypothesis," *Journal of Economic Perspectives* 32, no. 1 (2018): 97-120.

168 Viral Acharya and Sascha Steffen, "The Risk of Being a Fallen Angel and the Corporate Dash for Cash in the Midst of COVID," *NBER Working Papers,* no. 2760127601 (July 2020), https://www.nber.org/papers/w27601.

169 Ramanan Laxminarayan, *Markus' Academy,* Princeton University Webinar, March 30, 2020, 41:45 and 51:00, https://www.youtube.com/watch?v=z1yHjM7szBk&list=PLPKR-Xs1slgSWqOqaXid_9sQXsPsjV_72&index=31.

170 John C. Haltiwanger, "John Haltiwanger Describes How New Business Applications Surged during the Pandemic," NBER, July 12, 2021, https://www.nber.org/affiliated-scholars/researchspotlight/john-haltiwanger-describes-how-new-business-applications-surged-during-pandemic.

171 Reuters, "Germany to Extend Insolvency Moratorium for Virus-Hit Companies," August 25, 2020, https://www.reuters.com/article/healthcoronavirus-germany-bankruptcy-idUSL8N2FR36J.

172 The persistence of zombie firms in Japan, after the banking crises of the early 1990s, diverted resources away from economically healthier firms thereby creating long-lasting negative effects on productivity growth. See: Ricardo Caballero, Takeo Hoshi, and Anil Kashyap, "Zombie Lending and Depressed Restructuring in Japan," *American Economic Review* 98, no. 5 (2008): 1943-77.

173 Robin Greenwood, Benjamin Iverson, and David Thesmar, "Sizing Up Corporate Restructuring in the Covid Crisis," Brookings, September 23, 2020, https://www.brookings.edu/bpea-articles/sizing-up-corporate-restructuring-in-the-covid-crisis/.

174 Tyler Cowen, *Markus' Academy,* Princeton University Webinar, April 10, 2020, 36:08, https://www.youtube.com/watch?v=FPsPmkp6sdM&list=PLPKR-Xs1slgSWqOqaXid_9sQXsPsjV_72&index=28.

175 Arvind Krishnamurthy, *Markus' Academy,* Princeton University Webinar, June 29, 2020, 41:00, https://www.youtube.com/watch?v=voVh9BY3Lp4.

176 Arvind Krishnamurthy, *Markus' Academy,* June 29, 2020, 28:40.

177 Arvind Krishnamurthy, *Markus' Academy,* June 29, 2020, 52.18.

178 Joseph Stiglitz called for a super Chapter 11. See: Joseph Stiglitz, *Markus' Academy,* April 27, 2020, 49:11.

179 Robin Greenwood et al., "Sizing Up Corporate Restructuring in the Covid Crisis."

180 Mark Fehr, "Zombiefirmen könnten Insolvenzwelle auslösen," Frankfurter Allgemeine, April 29, 2021, https://www.faz.net/aktuell/wirtschaft/unternehmen/zombiefirmen-koennten-insolvenzwelle-ausloesen-17312952.html.

Chapter 9

181 Nikou Asgari, Joe Rennison, Philip Stafford, and Hudson Lockett, "Companies Raise $400bn Over Three Weeks in Blistering Start to 2021," *Financial Times.* January 26, 2021, https://www.ft.com/content/45770ddb-29e0-41c2-a97a-60ce13810ff2?shareType=nongift.

182 Adam Samson, "Bitcoin's Revival: Boom or Bubble?" *Financial Times,* November 18, 2020, https://www.ft.com/content/a47090ee-fdf5-4cfa-9d17-47c56afad8c3.

183 Paul Samuelson (1966), quoted in: John C. Bluedorn et al., "Do Asset Price Drops Foreshadow Recessions?" (2013), p. 4.

184 Gita Gopinath, *Markus' Academy,* Princeton University Webinar, May 29, 2020, 42:15, https://www.youtube.com/watch?v=GjUBIxR5W78.

185 Gavyn Davies, "The Anatomy of a Very Brief Bear Market," *Financial Times,* August 2, 2020, https://www.ft.com/content/cd8e2299-161b-4f17-adad-ac6d8a730049.

186 Ming Jeong Lee and Toshiro Hasegawa, "BOJ Becomes Biggest Japan Stock Owner with ¥45.1 Trillion Hoard," *The Japan Times,* December 7, 2020, https://www.japantimes.co.jp/news/2020/12/07/business/boj-japan-biggest-stock-owner/.

187 LE News, "The Swiss National Bank Owns More A-Class Facebook Shares than Zuckerberg," April 4, 2018, https://lenews.ch/2018/04/04/the-swiss-national-bank-owns-more-a-class-facebook-shares-than-zuckerberg/.

188 Niels Gormsen and Ralph Koijen, "Coronavirus: Impact on Stock Prices and Growth Expectations," *NBER Working Papers,* no. 27387 (June 2020), https://www.nber.org/papers/w27387.

189 Robert Shiller, *Markus' Academy,* Princeton University Webinar, July 10, 2020, 50:16, https://www.youtube.com/watch?v=ak5xX8PEGAI.

190 Eric Platt, David Carnevali, and Michael Mackenzie, "Wall Street IPO Bonanza Stirs Uneasy Memories of 90s Dotcom Mania," *Financial Times,* December 11, 2020, https://www.ft.com/content/cfdab1d0-ee5a-4e4a-a37b-20acfc0628e3?shareType=nongift.

191 Edward Helmore, "How GameStop Found Itself at the Center of a Groundbreaking Battle between Wall Street and Small Investors," *The Guardian,* January 27, 2021, https://www.theguardian.com/business/2021/jan/27/gamestop-stock-market-retail-wall-street.

192 Lasse Pedersen, *Markus' Academy,* Princeton University Webinar, February 19, 2021, https://www.youtube.com/watch?v=ADnRm5LWCjg.

193 Eric Platt, "Wall Street IPO Bonanza," December 11, 2020.

194 Chris Bryant, "Hedge Funds Love SPACs But You Should Watch Out," Bloomberg, December 9, 2020, https://www.bloomberg.com/opinion/articles/2020-12-09/hedge-funds-love-spacs-but-retail-investors-should-watch-out?sref=ATN0rNv3.

195 Amrith Ramkumar, "2020 SPAC Boom Lifted Wall Street's Biggest Banks," *The Wall Street Journal,* January 5, 2021, https://www.wsj.com/articles/2020-spac-boom-lifted-wall-streets-biggest-banks-11609842601?st=lguw1ftxebizf6e&reflink=article_gmail_share.

196 Liz Myers, *Markus' Academy,* Princeton University Webinar, May 21, 2021, https://bcf.princeton.edu/events/finance-front-lines-in-2021/.

197 Darrell Duffie, *Markus' Academy,* Princeton University Webinar, June 5, 2020, 12:10, https://www.youtube.com/watch?v=04LYVyR3jog. See also comments by Jerome Powell, who stressed the centrality of the US Treasury market for the entire financial system at: Jerome Powell, *Markus' Academy,* Princeton University Webinar, January 14, 2021, https://www.youtube.com/watch?v=TEC3supZwvM.

198 Annette Vissing-Jorgensen, "The Treasury Market in Spring 2020 and the Response of the Federal Reserve," April 5, 2021, http://faculty.haas.berkeley.edu/vissing/vissing_jorgensen_bonds2020.pdf.

199 Darrell Duffie, *Markus' Academy,* June 5, 2020, 19:10 and 21:45.

200 Darrell Duffie, *Markus' Academy,* June 5, 2020, 41:12, 41:40, and 44:27.

201 Darrell Duffie, *Markus' Academy,* June 5, 2020, 44:50.

202 Darrell Duffie, *Markus' Academy,* June 5, 2020, 50:05.

203 More precisely 2.1296 percent.

204 Torsten Slok, *Markus' Academy,* Princeton University Webinar, March 20, 2020, 32:10, 38:20, and 40:30, https://www.youtube.com/watch?v=zgxDybynvNM.

205 Torsten Slok, *Markus' Academy,* March 20, 2020, 51:35 and 53:05.

206 Nellie Liang, *Markus' Academy,* Princeton University Webinar, March 6, 2020, 11:58, https://www.youtube.com/watch?v=6NjE-OOUB_E.

207 Arvind Krishnamurthy, *Markus' Academy,* Princeton University Webinar, June 29, 2020, 17:12, https://www.youtube.com/watch?v=voVh9BY3Lp4.

208 Arvind Krishnamurthy, *Markus' Academy,* June 29, 2020, 21:12.

209 Nellie Liang, *Markus' Academy,* March 6, 2020, 18:20.

210 Nellie Liang, *Markus' Academy,* March 6, 2020, 33:35.

211 Nellie Liang, *Markus' Academy,* March 6, 2020, 25:30.

212 Arvind Krishnamurthy, *Markus' Academy,* June 29, 2020.

213 Arvind Krishnamurthy, *Markus' Academy,* June 29, 2020.

214 James Politi and Colby Smith, "Federal Reserve Calls Time on Looser Capital Requirements for US Banks," *Financial Times,* March 19, 2021, https://www.ft.com/content/279c2755-acab-4d9a-9092-d55fe5f518fa.

215 Philip Lane, *Markus' Academy,* Princeton University Webinar, March 20, 2020, 1:07:20, https://www.youtube.com/watch?v=G-8-4hEkkbs.

216 Philip Lane, *Markus' Academy,* March 20, 2020, 1:04:22.

217 Philip Lane, *Markus' Academy,* March 20, 2020, 1:04:50.

218 Philip Lane, *Markus' Academy,* March 20, 2020, 58:21.

219 Philip Lane, *Markus' Academy,* March 20, 2020, 23:56.

220 Philip Lane, *Markus' Academy,* March 20, 2020, 47:28 and 48:36.

221 Philip Lane, *Markus' Academy,* March 20, 2020, 51:16.

222 Bill Dudley, *Markus' Academy,* Princeton University Webinar, June 1, 2020, 37:38 and 40:50, https://www.youtube.com/watch?v=65Y0kRJP_UY.

223 Bill Dudley, *Markus' Academy,* June 1, 2020, 41:42 and 42:32.

224 Sebastian Pellejero, "After Record U.S. Corporate-Bond Sales, Slowdown Expected," *The Wall Street Journal,* October 2, 2020, https://www.wsj.com/articles/after-record-u-s-corporate-bond-sales-slowdown-expected-11601631003.

225 Jeremy Stein, *Markus' Academy,* Princeton University Webinar, May 11, 2020, 21:58 and 22:32, https://www.youtube.com/watch?v=0iNQNzAUDiw.

226 Jeremy Stein, *Markus' Academy,* May 11, 2020, 29:01.

227 Jeremy Stein, *Markus' Academy,* May 11, 2020, 34:20.

Chapter 10

228 Philip Lane, *Markus' Academy,* Princeton University Webinar, March 20, 2020, 36:12, https://www.youtube.com/watch?v=G-8-4hEkkbs.

229 Markus Brunnermeier and Yuliy Sannikov, "Redistributive Monetary Policy," Princeton University, August 2012, https://scholar.princeton.edu/sites/default/files/04c%20Redistributive%20Monetary%20Policy.pdf.

230 Hence, net debt at first glance is significantly lower than gross debt.

231 Lawrence Summers, *Markus' Academy,* Princeton University Webinar, May 22, 2020, 1:00:14, 1:02:03, and 1:03:00, https://www.youtube.com/watch?v=cZmRtQCR2ns&list=PLPKR-Xs1slgSWqOqaXid_9sQXsPsjV_72&index=17.

232 Paul Schmelzing, "Eight Centuries of Global Real Interest Rates, R-G, and the 'Supra-Secular' Decline," Bank of England Staff Working Paper 845, (January 3, 2020): 1311–2018, https://www.bankofengland.co.uk/working-paper/2020/eight-centuries-of-global-real-interest-rates-r-g-and-the-suprasecular-decline-1311-2018.

233 Lawrence Summers, *Markus' Academy,* May 22, 2020, 1:05:55.

234 Markus Brunnermeier, Sebastian Merkel, and Yuliy Sannikov, "The Fiscal Theory of the Price Level with a Bubble," Princeton University, July 8, 2020, https://scholar.princeton.edu/sites/default/files/merkel/files/fiscaltheorybubble.pdf.

235 Formally, the real value of government debt, the ratio of nominal bonds B over the price level P, equals the expected present value of the cash flow from government debt plus the service flow: B/P = E[PV(cash flow)] + E[PV(service flow)].

236 For a formal treatment on the valuation puzzle, consult: Zhengyang Jiang, Hanno Lustig, Stijn van Nieuwerburgh, and Mindy Xiaolan, "The US Public Debt Valuation Puzzle," *NBER Working Papers*, no. 26583 (2021).

237 Some readers might be reminded of the Laffer curve. As the inflation tax gets too high, the tax base erodes so the government faces limits to debt financing here.

238 The cash flow that backs government debt is the excess of tax revenue over government spending, so called primary surplus. In recent decades, those cash flows have been low or even negative, and predictions suggest there will be low cash flows in the future. However, government debt is valuable even in the absence of primary surpluses because service flows drive government debt valuation.

239 Kenneth Rogoff, *Markus' Academy*, Princeton University Webinar, June 12, 2020, 48:40 and 50:30, https://www.youtube.com/watch?v=0uh4oPjxxq8.

Chapter 11

240 Federal Reserve Bank of New York, "SCE Household Spending Survey," April 2021, https://www.newyorkfed.org/microeconomics/sce/household-spending#/.

241 Alberto Cavallo, "Inflation with Covid Consumption Baskets," *NBER Working Papers*, no. 27352 (June 2020), https://www.nber.org/papers/w27352.

242 Tyler Cowen, *Markus' Academy*, Princeton University Webinar, April 10, 2020, https://www.youtube.com/watch?v=FPsPmkp6sdM&list=PLPKR-Xs1slgSWqOqaXid_9sQXsPsjV_72&index=28.

243 James Mackintosh, "Inflation Is Already Here—For the Stuff You Actually Want to Buy," *The Wall Street Journal*, September 26, 2020, https://www.wsj.com/articles/inflation-is-already-herefor-the-stuff-you-actually-want-to-buy-11601112630?st=r6rjsuab2ijc738&reflink=article_gmail_share.

244 Oshrat Carmiel, "Manhattan Apartments Haven't Been This Cheap to Rent in 10 Years," Bloomberg, December 10, 2020, https://www.bloomberg.com/news/articles/2020-12-10/manhattan-apartment-rents-sink-to-the-lowest-level-in-a-decade.

245 Veronica Guerrieri, *Markus' Academy,* Princeton University Webinar, June 19, 2020, 1:01:50, https://www.youtube.com/watch?v=x2npgxzuTVg.

246 Gita Gopinath, *Markus' Academy,* Princeton University Webinar, May 29, 2020, 40:35, https://www.youtube.com/watch?v=GjUBIxR5W78.

247 Raj Chetty, *Markus' Academy,* Princeton University Webinar, June 2017, 2020, https://www.youtube.com/watch?v=ip5pz7gOSwI&list=PLPKR-Xs1slgSWqOqaXid_9sQXsPsjV_72&index=11.

248 Natalie Cox, Peter Ganong, Pascal Noel, Joseph Vavra, Arlene Wong, Diana Farrell, and Fiona Greig, "Initial Impacts of the Pandemic on Consumer Behavior: Evidence from Linked Income, Spending, and Savings Data," Becker Friedman Institute Working Papers, July 2020, https://bfi.uchicago.edu/wp-content/uploads/BFI_WP_202082.pdf.

249 Bill Dudley, *Markus' Academy,* Princeton University Webinar, June 1, 2020, 31:56, https://www.youtube.com/watch?v=65Y0kRJP_UY.

250 Bill Dudley, *Markus' Academy,* June 1, 2020, 30:38.

251 Large balance sheets are here to stay. All major central banks are locked into paying interest on excess reserves (IOER). This contrasts with the traditional framework, which is characterized by careful interventions in the bank reserves market and no requirement to pay interest on excess reserves. See: Bill Dudley, *Markus' Academy,* June 1, 2020, 17:22.

252 Jerome Powell outlined the details of the new flexible inflation targeting framework in the webinar held on January 14, 2021. See: Jerome Powell, *Markus' Academy,* Princeton University Webinar, January 14, 2021, https://www.youtube.com/watch?v=TEC3supZwvM.

253 Arminio Fraga, *Markus' Academy,* Princeton University Webinar, July 13, 2020, 57:13 and 59:40, https://www.youtube.com/watch?v=mTy2X7zftCc.

254 Markus Brunnermeier, Sebastian Merkel, Jonathan Payne, and Yuliy Sannikov, "Covid-19: Inflation and Deflation Pressures," CESIFO Area Conferences, July 24, 2020, https://www.cesifo.org/sites/default/files/events/2020/mmi20-Payne.pdf.

255 Veronica Guerrieri, *Markus' Academy,* Princeton University Webinar, June 19, 2020, 16:15, https://www.youtube.com/watch?v=x2npgxzuTVg. Here is a brief outline of the model for academically minded readers: In the model, workers are specialized in one of two sectors. Markets are incomplete with a fraction of households being borrowing constrained (15:00, 33:30, and 34:45). In particular, there are two types of supply shocks. Standard supply shocks in a one-sector model lead to excess demand as the natural rate rises, whereas Keynesian supply shocks lead to insufficient demand with the natural rate falling thereby forcing agents to save more, assuming a high complementarity across goods.

256 Veronica Guerrieri, *Markus' Academy,* June 19, 2020.

257 Olivier Blanchard, "In Defense of Concerns over the $1.9 Trillion Relief Plan," Peterson Institute for International Economics, February 18, 2021, https://www.piie.com/blogs/realtime-economic-issues-watch/defense-concerns-over-19-trillion-relief-plan.

258 It might be greater than 1 if there is a second-round effect, such as household A spending a $1,400 stimulus check on a vacation in Florida. This implies $1400 more in joint income for households B and C in Florida, who are the households of the hotel owner where household A will stay, and of the restaurant owner where A will eat out. If households B and C spend some of that additional income again, the multiplier (the increase in consumption spending) will exceed $1,400.

259 Warren Buffet, Berkshire Hathaway Annual Meeting, Yahoo! Finance, May 1, 2021, https://www.youtube.com/watch?v=7t7qfOyQdQA.

260 Paul Krugman and Larry Summers, *Markus' Academy,* Princeton University Webinar, February 12, 2021, https://www.youtube.com/watch?v=EbZ3_LZxs54&t=7s.

261 Harold James, *Markus' Academy,* Princeton University Webinar, April 24, 2020, 35:16 and 35:54, https://www.youtube.com/watch?v=PVIm4BdBmTI.

262 Harold James, *Markus' Academy,* April 24, 2020, 47:40, 48:30, and 50:10.

263 Harold James, *Markus' Academy,* April 24, 2020, 36:36.

264 Jerome Powell states in his webinar presentation that central bank independence is an institutional arrangement that has served the public well. See: Jerome Powell, *Markus' Academy,* January 14, 2021.

265 Conceptually, bringing down deficits from 10 percent to 5 percent should be similarly implementable as reducing them from 6 percent to 5 percent, but political forces make the latter easier. The former requires more severe budget cuts across several departments and might therefore draw more opposition.

266 Nellie Liang, *Markus' Academy,* Princeton University Webinar, March 6, 2020, 41:05, https://www.youtube.com/watch?v=6NjE-OOUB_E.

267 This section heavily draws on Charles Goodhart's Markus' Academy webinar and the 2020 book by Charles Goodhart and Manoj Pradhan titled *The Great Demographic Reversal: Ageing Societies, Waning Inequality, and Inflation Reversal.*

268 Markus Brunnermeier and Yuliy Sannikov, "Redistributive Monetary Policy," Princeton University, August 2012, https://scholar.princeton.edu/sites/default/files/04c%20Redistributive%20Monetary%20Policy.pdf.

Chapter 12

269 Linda Carroll, "U.S. Life Expectancy Declining Due to More Deaths in Middle Age," Reuters, November 26, 2019, https://www.reuters.com/article/us-health-life-expectancy-idUSKBN1Y02C7.

270 Sendhil Mullainathan and Edgar Shafir, *Scarcity: Why Having Too Little Means So Much,* New York: Times Books, 2013.

271 Andreas Fagereng, Luigi Guso, Davide Malacrino, and Luigi Pistaferri, "Heterogeneity and Persistence in Returns on Wealth," Stanford University Working Paper, August 2019, https://web.stanford.edu/~pista/FGMP.pdf.

272 Sylvain Catherine, Max Miller, and Natasha Sarin, "Social Security and Trends in Wealth Inequality," SSRN Working Paper, February 29, 2020, https://papers.ssrn.com/sol3/papers.cfm?abstract_id=3546668.

273 *The Economist,* "Economists Are Rethinking the Numbers on Inequality," November 28, 2019, https://www.economist.com/briefing/2019/11/28/economists-are-rethinking-the-numbers-on-inequality.

274 Yu Xie and Xiang Zhou, "Income Inequality in Today's China," *Proceedings of the National Academy of Sciences* 111, no. 19 (2014): 6928-6933, https://www.pnas.org/content/111/19/6928.short.

275 Joseph Stiglitz, *Markus' Academy,* Princeton University Webinar, April 27, 2020, 16:58, https://www.youtube.com/watch?v=_6SoT97wo3g.

276 Torsten Slok, *Markus' Academy,* Princeton University Webinar, March 20, 2020, 1:00:33, https://www.youtube.com/watch?v=zgxDybynvNM.

277 Torsten Slok, *Markus' Academy,* March 20, 2020, 1:02:20.

278 Joseph Stiglitz, *Markus' Academy,* April 27, 2020, 16:58.

279 Caitlin Brown and Martin Ravallion, "Ineqaulity and the Coronavirus: Socioeconomic Covariates of Behavioral Responses and Viral Outcomes Across US Counties," *Proceedings of the National Academy of the Sciences* 111, no. 19 (May 13, 2014): 6928-6933, https://www.pnas.org/content/111/19/6928.short.

280 Kishinchand Poornima Wasdani and Ajnesh Prasad, "The Impossibility of Social Distancing among the Urban Poor: The Case of an Indian Slum in the Times of COVID-19," *Local Environment* 25, no. 5 (2020): 414-418.

281 Nora Lustig, Valentina Martinez Pabon, Federico Sanz, and Stephen Younger, "The Impact of Covid-19 Lockdowns and Expanded Social Assistance on Inequality, Poverty and Mobility in Argentina, Brazil, Colombia and Mexico," Center for Global Development Working Paper 556, October 2020, https://www.cgdev.org/sites/default/files/impact-covid-19-lockdowns-and-expanded-social-assistance.pdf.

282 Thiago Guimarães, Karen Lucas, and Paul Timms, "Understanding How Low-Income Communities Gain Access to Healthcare Services: A Qualitative Study in São Paulo, Brazil," *Journal of Transport and Health* 15 (2019): 100658.

283 ReliefWeb, "Q&A: Brazil's Poor Suffer the Most Under Covid-19," July 14, 2020, https://reliefweb.int/report/brazil/qa-brazils-poor-suffer-most-under-covid-19.

284 Raj Chetty, *Markus' Academy,* Princeton University Webinar, June 2017, 2020, https://www.youtube.com/watch?v=ip5pz7gOSwI&list=PLPKR-Xs1slgSWqOqaXid_9sQXsPsjV_72&index=11.

285 Raj Chetty, *Markus' Academy,* June 2017, 2020, 1:03:22.

286 Andrew Bacher-Hicks, Joshua Goodman, and Christine Mulhern, "Inequality in Household Adaptation to Schooling Shocks: Covid-Induced Online Learning Engagement in Real Time," *Journal of Public Economics* 193 (2021): 204345.

287 Per Engzell, Arun Freya, and Mark Verhagen, "Learning Inequality During the Covid-19 Pandemic," October 2020, https://scholar.googleusercontent.com/scholar?q=cache:Zva2ARtZvlkJ:scholar.google.com/+covid+inequality+statistics+mexico&hl=en&as_sdt=0,31&as_vis=1.

288 Angus Deaton, "Covid Shows How the State Can Address Social Inequality," *Financial Times,* January 4, 2021, https://www.ft.com/content/caa37763-9c71-4f8d-9c29-b16ccf53d780.

289 Marcelo Medeiros, "Brazil LAB at Princeton University: Inequalities: Poverty, Racism, and Social Mobility in Brazil," Princeton University Webinar, October 15, 2020, 36:00, https://www.youtube.com/watch?v=k3OSo83qFq8.

290 Alon Titan, Matthias Doepke, Jane Olmstead-Rumsey, and Michele Tertilt, "The Impact of Covid-19 on Gender Equality," *NBER Working Papers,* no. 27660 (August 2020); and Erik Hurst, *Markus' Academy,* Princeton University Webinar, March 20, 2021, https://www.youtube.com/watch?v=VG7KS5sLABY.

291 Marin Wolf, "How Coronavirus and Race Collide in the US," Bloomberg, August 11, 2020, https://www.bloombergquint.com/quicktakes/how-coronavirus-and-race-collide-in-the-u-s-quicktake.

292 Robert Fairlie, "Covid-19, Small Business Owners, and Racial Inequality," NBER, December 4, 2020, https://www.nber.org/reporter/2020number4/covid-19-small-business-owners-and-racial-inequality.

293 Kia Lilly Caldwell and Edna Maria de Araújo, "Covid-19 Is Deadlier for Black Brazilians: A Legacy of Structural Racism that Dates Back to Slavery," The Conversation, June 10, 2020, https://theconversation.com/covid-19-is-deadlier-for-black-brazilians-a-legacy-of-structural-racism-that-dates-back-to-slavery-139430.

294 Centers for Disease Control and Prevention, "Risk for COVID-19 Infection, Hospitalization, and Death by Race/Ethnicity," April 23, 2021, https://www.cdc.gov/coronavirus/2019-ncov/covid-data/investigations-discovery/hospitalization-death-by-race-ethnicity.html.

295 Lisa Cook, *Markus' Academy,* Princeton University Webinar, June 8, 2020, 53:57, 56:46, and 57:09, https://www.youtube.com/watch?v=PeKhSsJsW2w.

296 Lisa Cook, *Markus' Academy,* June 8, 2020, 36:24 and 47:18.

297 Lisa Cook, *Markus' Academy,* June 8, 2020, 49:35.

298 RSF Social Finance, "The Runway Project: Loan Provided by the Women's Capital Collaborative," https://rsfsocialfinance.org/person/the-runway-project/.

299 Gillian Tett, "Pandemic Aid Is Exacerbating US Inequality," *Financial Times,* August 6, 2020, https://www.ft.com/content/8287303f-4062-4808-8ce3-f7fa9f87e185.

300 Robert Fairlie, "Covid-19, Small Business Owners, and Racial Inequality," December 4, 2020.

301 Lisa Cook, *Markus' Academy,* June 8, 2020, 10:25 and 11:14.

302 Lisa Cook also shows that violence significantly diminishes innovation and economic activity. Missing patents—those by African Americans that didn't occur as a result of violence between 1860 and 1940—add up to about the same number of patents issued by a medium-size European country at the time. See: Lisa Cook, *Markus' Academy,* June 8, 2020, 18:48, 19:17, and 32:40.

303 Walter Scheidel, *The Great Leveler,* Princeton, NJ: Princeton University Press, 2018.

304 Claudia Goldin and Robert Margo, "The Great Compression: The Wage Structure in the United States in the Mid-Century," *Quarterly Journal of Economics* 107, no. 1 (1992): 1-34.

305 Walter Scheidel, *The Great Leveler,* 2018.

Chapter 13

306 Max Roser and Esteban Ortiz-Ospina, "Global Extreme Poverty," Our World in Data, March 27, 2017, https://ourworldindata.org/extreme-poverty.

307 Federal Reserve Bank of St. Louis, "Personal Consumption Expenditures/ Gross Domestic Product," FRED Economic Data, 2021, https://fred.stlouisfed.org/graph/?g=hh3.

308 Daron Acemoglu, Philippe Aghion, and Fabrizio Zilibotti, "Distance to Frontier, Selection and Economic Growth," *Journal of European Economic Association,* (2006): 37-74.

309 Pinelopi Goldberg, *Markus' Academy,* Princeton University Webinar, April 17, 2020, 1:08:50, https://www.youtube.com/watch?v=erq8pqBpFhI.

310 Arminio Fraga, *Markus' Academy,* Princeton University Webinar, July 13, 2020, 16:10 and 18:09, https://www.youtube.com/watch?v=mTy2X7zftCc.

311 Arminio Fraga, *Markus' Academy,* July 13, 2020, 16:10 and 18:09.

312 Arminio Fraga, *Markus' Academy,* July 13, 2020, 48:29.

313 Arminio Fraga, *Markus' Academy,* July 13, 2020, 15:17.

314 Ragani Saxena, "India's Health Time Bomb Keeps Ticking and It's Not Covid-19," Bloomberg, September 10, 2020, https://www.bloomberg.com/news/articles/2020-09-10/india-s-health-time-bomb-keeps-ticking-and-it-s-not-covid-19.

315 *The Economist,* "India's Giant Second Wave Is a Disaster for It and for the World," April 24, 2021.

316 Sneha Mordani, Haider Tanseem, and Milan Sharma, "Watch: Doctors, Nurses Attacked in Delhi Hospital as Covid Patient Dies Without Getting ICU Bed," *India Today*, April 27, 2021, https://www.indiatoday.in/cities/delhi/story/doctors-attacked-in-delhi-hospital-by-family-of-covid-patient-1795567-2021-04-27.

317 Michael Spence, *Markus' Academy,* Princeton University Webinar, July 6, 2020, 48:08 and 50:25, https://www.youtube.com/watch?v=92-vc238_nI&list=PLPKR-Xs1slgSWqOqaXid_9sQXsPsjV_72&index=6.

318 Debraj Ray and S. Subramanian, "India's Lockdown: An Interim Report," *NBER Working Papers,* no. 27282 (May 2020).

319 Michael Spence, *Markus' Academy,* July 6, 2020, 50:25; and Angus Deaton, *Markus' Academy,* Princeton University Webinar, April 13, 2020, 49:42, https://www.youtube.com/watch?v=2uzASRQz4gM.

320 Raghuram Rajan, "Raghuram Rajan on Covid-19: Is It Time to Decentralise Power?" (video), Coronanomics, July 22, 2020, 33:00, https://www.youtube.com/watch?v=VU9d5IyudYs.

321 Some observers claim India might have "bent the wrong curve." See: Raghuram Rajan, July 22, 2020, 38:42.

322 Luiz Brotherhood, Tiago Cavalcanti, Daniel Da Mata, and Cezar Santos, "Slums and Pandemics," SSRN Working Paper, August 5, 2020 (Updated January 4, 2021), https://papers.ssrn.com/sol3/papers.cfm?abstract_id=3665695.

323 Gita Gopinath, *Markus' Academy,* Princeton University Webinar, May 29, 2020, 45:35 and 46:50, https://www.youtube.com/watch?v=GjUBIxR5W78.

324 International Monetary Fund, "Fiscal Monitor Database of Country Fiscal Measures in Response to the COVID-19 Pandemic," April 2021, https://www.imf.org/en/Topics/imf-and-covid19/Fiscal-Policies-Database-in-Response-to-COVID-19.

325 International Monetary Fund, "Fiscal Monitor Database," April 2021.

326 Rachel Glennerster, "Covid-19 Pandemic in Developing Countries: Pandemic Policies for People," International Monetary Fund, September 12, 2020, https://www.imf.org/external/mmedia/view.aspx?vid=6215224981001.

327 Andrew Henley, G. Reza Arabsheibani, and Francisco G. Carneiro, "On Defining and Measuring the Informal Sector," World Bank Policy Research Working Papers, March 2006.

328 Niall McCarthy, "The Countries Most Reliant on Remittances [Infographic]," *Forbes,* April 26, 2018, https://www.forbes.com/sites/niallmccarthy/2018/04/26/the-countries-most-reliant-on-remittances-infographic/?sh=50407d577277.

329 Arminio Fraga, *Markus' Academy,* July 13, 2020, 23:32.

330 Raghuram Rajan makes the same point for India. See: "Raghuram Rajan on Covid-19," July 22, 2020, 49:40. The Brazilian primary deficit in 2020 will be 12 to 13 percent, warranting concerns of large deficits persisting for the years to come. See: Arminio Fraga, *Markus' Academy,* July 13, 2020, 53:50, 54:38, and 56:30.

331 Carlos A. Vegh, "Fiscal Policy in Emerging Markets: Procyclicality and Graduation," NBER, December 2015, https://www.nber.org/reporter/2015number4/fiscal-policy-emerging-markets-procyclicality-and-graduation.

332 The interested reader may consult the IMF's website for more details. See: International Monetary Fund, "Q&A on Special Drawing Rights," March 16, 2021, https://www.imf.org/en/About/FAQ/special-drawing-right#Q4.%20Will%20an%20SDR%20allocation%20give%20countries%20with%20poor%20governance%20money%20to%20waste.

333 Andrea Shalal and David Lawder, "Yellen Backs New Allocation of IMF's SDR Currency to Help Poor Nations," Reuters, February 25, 2021, https://www.reuters.com/article/g20-usa/update-3-yellen-backs-new-allocation-of-imfs-sdr-currency-to-help-poor-nations-idUSL1N2KV1IA.

334 Kevin Gallagher, José Antonio Ocampo, and Ulrich Volz, "It's Time for a Major Issuance of the IMF's Special Drawing Rights," *Financial Times,* March 20, 2020. https://www.ft.com/content/43a67e06-bbeb-4bea-8939-bc29ca785b0e.

335 Kevin Gallagher et al., "It's Time for a Major Issuance of the IMF's Special Drawing Rights," March 20, 2020.

336 Saumya Mitra, "Letter: Why G8 States Are Wary of Special Drawing Rights." *Financial Times.* January 22, 2021. https://www-ft-com.btpl.idm.oclc.org/content/20ca8b0f-9773-43de-9bfc-b09ab9ac5942.

337 Ezra Fieser and Oscar Medina, "Colombia Risks Forced Selling of Its Bonds After More Downgrades," Bloomberg, May 5, 2021, https://www.bloomberg.com/news/articles/2021-05-21/colombia-risks-forced-selling-of-its-bonds-after-more-downgrades?sref=ATN0rNv3.

338 Reuters, "Zambia Requests Debt Restructuring Under G20 Common Framework," February 5, 2021, https://www.reuters.com/article/us-zambia-debt-idUSKBN2A50XL.

339 Marc Jones, "Second Sovereign Downgrade Wave Coming, Major Nations at Risk," Reuters, October 16, 2020, https://www.reuters.com/article/us-global-ratings-sovereign-s-p-exclusiv-idUSKBN27126V.

340 International Monetary Fund, "The Good, the Bad, and the Ugly: 100 Years of Dealing with Public Debt Overhangs," October 8, 2012, https://www.elibrary.imf.org/view/IMF081/12743-9781616353896/12743-9781616353896/chap03.xml?rskey=VXkXsE&result=5&redirect=true&redirect=true.

341 Hyun Song Shin, *Markus' Academy,* Princeton University Webinar, April 20, 2020, 23:40, 35:20, 36:45, and 37:30, https://www.youtube.com/watch?v=LnmMRrzjNWQ.

342 The following discussion is inspired by an IMF video at: International Monetary Fund, "Analyze This! Sovereign Debt Restructuring" (Video), December 2, 2020, https://www.imf.org/external/mmedia/view.aspx?vid=6213167814001. Another excellent resources on the topic can be found at: Lee Buchheit, Guillaume Chabert, Chanda DeLong, and Joremin Zettelmeyer, "How to Restructure Sovereign Debt: Lessons from Four Decades," Peterson Institute for International Economics Working

Paper 19-8, May 2019, https://www.piie.com/publications/working-papers/how-restructure-sovereign-debt-lessons-four-decades.

343 Julianne Ams, Reza Baqir, Anna Gelpern, and Christoph Trebesch, "Chapter 7: Sovereign Default," IMF Research Department, 2018, https://www.imf.org/~/media/Files/News/Seminars/2018/091318SovDebt-conference/chapter-7-sovereign-default.ashx.

344 Renae Merle, "How One Hedge Fund Made $2 Billion from Argentina's Economic Collapse," *The Washington Post,* March 29, 2016, https://www.washingtonpost.com/news/business/wp/2016/03/29/how-one-hedge-fund-made-2-billion-from-argentinas-economic-collapse/.

345 Anne Krueger, "A New Approach to Sovereign Debt Restructuring," International Monetary Fund, April 2002, https://www.imf.org/external/pubs/ft/exrp/sdrm/eng/sdrm.pdf.

346 Anna Gelpern, Sebastian Horn, Scott Morris, Brad Parks, and Christoph Trebesch, "How China Lends: A Rare Look into 100 Debt Contracts with Foreign Governments," Peterson Institute for International Economics Working Paper 21-7, May 2021, https://www.piie.com/publications/working-papers/how-china-lends-rare-look-100-debt-contracts-foreign-governments.

347 Reuters, "Factbox: How the G20's Debt Service Suspension Initiative Works," October 15, 2020, https://www.reuters.com/article/us-imf-worldbank-emerging-debtrelief-fac/factbox-how-the-g20s-debt-service-suspension-initiative-works-idINKBN27021V.

348 Jonathan Wheatley, "Debt Dilemma: How to Avoid a Crisis in Emerging Nations," *Financial Times,* December 20, 2020, https://www.ft.com/content/de43248e-e8eb-4381-9d2f-a539d1f1662c?shareType=nongift.

349 Anne Krueger, "A New Approach to Sovereign Debt Restructuring," International Monetary Fund. April 2002. https://www.imf.org/external/pubs/ft/exrp/sdrm/eng/sdrm.pdf.

Chapter 14

350 Eric Schmidt, *Markus' Academy,* Princeton University Webinar, July 27, 2020, 12:14, https://www.youtube.com/watch?v=726B0y1D5ZM&t=31s.

351 Emma Graham-Harrison and Tom Phillips, "China Hopes 'Vaccine Diplomacy' Will Restore Its Image and Boost Its Influence," *The Guardian,* November 29, 2020, https://www.theguardian.com/world/2020/nov/29/

china-hopes-vaccine-diplomacy-will-restore-its-image-and-boost-its-influence.

352 Niall McCarthy, "America First? Covid-19 Production & Exports," Statista, March 31, 2021, https://www.statista.com/chart/24555/vaccine-doses-produced-and-exported/.

353 Carmen Aguilar Garcia and Ganesh Rao, "Covid-19: India's Vaccine Export Ban Could Send Shockwaves Worldwide. Should the UK Step in to Help?" Sky News, April 30, 2021, https://news.sky.com/story/covid-19-how-does-indias-pause-on-vaccine-export-hurt-other-nations-12290300.

354 Dani Rodrik, *Markus' Academy,* Princeton University Webinar, May 5, 2020, 1:10:00 onward, https://www.youtube.com/watch?v=3cRlHugFBq8.

355 William Nordhaus proposes a club structure for countries in order to internalize externalities. See: William Nordhaus, *Markus' Academy,* Princeton University Webinar, January 28, 2021, https://www.youtube.com/watch?v=QaXZx_nJ_3I.

356 Michael Kremer, *Markus' Academy,* Princeton University Webinar, May 1, 2020, 37:15, 37:40, 40:00, and 41:05, https://www.youtube.com/watch?v=C8W8JQLTECc.

357 Bill Gates, "How the Pandemic Will Shape the Near Future," TED, July 6, 2020, 19:30 and 27:00, https://www.youtube.com/watch?v=jmQWOPDqxWA.

358 Stephanie Nebehay and Kate Kelland, "COVAX Programme Doubles Global Vaccine Supply Deals to 2 Billion Doses," Reuters, December 18, 2020, https://www.reuters.com/article/us-health-coronavirus-covax/covax-programme-doubles-global-vaccine-supply-deals-to-2-billion-doses-idUSKBN28S1PW.

359 CBC, "Canada Could Share Any Excess Vaccine Supply with Poorer Countries: Reuters Sources," November 18, 2020, https://www.cbc.ca/news/health/canada-vaccine-supply-share-1.5807679.

360 Lawrence Summers, *Markus' Academy,* Princeton University Webinar, May 22, 2020, 30:14, 31:55, 32:40, and 40:30, https://www.youtube.com/watch?v=cZmRtQCR2ns&list=PLPKR-Xs1slgSWqOqaXid_9sQXsPsjV_72&index=17.

361 Mercedes Ruehl, Stephanie Findlay, and James Kynge, "Tech Cold War Comes to India: Silicon Valley Takes on Alibaba and Tencent," *Financial Times,* August 3, 2020, https://www.ft.com/content/b1df5dfd-36c4-49e6-bc56-506bf3ca3444?shareType=nongift.

362 Lawrence Summers, *Markus' Academy,* May 22, 2020, 30:10.

363 Organization for Economic Cooperation and Development, "China's Belt and Road Initiative in the Global Trade, Investment and Finance Landscape," 2018, https://www.oecd.org/finance/Chinas-Belt-and-Road-Initiative-in-the-global-trade-investment-and-finance-landscape.pdf.

364 Derek Grossman, "The Quad Is Poised to Become Openly Anti-China Soon" (Blog), The RAND Corporation, July 28, 2020, https://www.rand.org/blog/2020/07/the-quad-is-poised-to-become-openly-anti-china-soon.html.

365 Kimberly Amadeo, "Trans-Pacific Partnership Summary, Pros and Cons," The Balance, February 10, 2021, https://www.thebalance.com/what-is-the-trans-pacific-partnership-3305581.

366 Alexander Chipman Koty, "What Is the China Standards 2035 Plan and How Will It Impact Emerging Industries?" *China Briefing,* July 2, 2020, https://www.china-briefing.com/news/what-is-china-standards-2035-plan-how-will-it-impact-emerging-technologies-what-is-link-made-in-china-2025-goals/.

367 Demetri Sevastopulo and Amy Kazmin, "US and Asia Allies Plan Covid Vaccine Strategy to Counter China," *Financial Times,* March 3, 2021, https://www.ft.com/content/1dc04520-c2fb-4859-9821-c405f51f8586.

368 Stephanie Findlay, "India Eyes Global Vaccine Drive to Eclipse Rival China," *Financial Times,* January 31, 2021, https://www.ft.com/content/1bb8b97f-c046-4d0c-9859-b7f0b60678f4.

369 Tyler Cowen, *Markus' Academy,* Princeton University Webinar, April 10, 2020, 15:56, https://www.youtube.com/watch?v=FPsPmkp6sdM&list=PLPKR-Xs1slgSWqOqaXid_9sQXsPsjV_72&index=28.

370 Alicia Chen and Vanessa Molter, "Mask Diplomacy: Chinese Narratives in the COVID Era," Stanford University (blog), June 16, 2020, https://fsi.stanford.edu/news/covid-mask-diplomacy.

371 Frank Chen, "China's e-RMB Era Comes into Closer View," *Asia Times,* October 28, 2020, https://asiatimes.com/2020/10/chinas-e-rmb-era-comes-into-closer-view/.

372 Erika Solomon and Guy Chazan, "'We Need a Real Policy for China': Germany Ponders Post-Merkel Shift," *Financial Times,* January 5, 2021, https://www.ft.com/content/0de447eb-999d-452f-a1c9-d235cc5ea6d9.

373 Erika Solomon, "'We Need a Real Policy for China,'" January 5, 2021.

374 Erika Solomon, "'We Need a Real Policy for China,'" January 5, 2021.

375 Robin Emmott and Jan Strupczewski, "EU and India Agree to Resume Trade Talks at Virtual Summit," Reuters, May 8, 2021, https://www.reuters.com/world/europe/eu-india-re-launch-trade-talks-virtual-summit-2021-05-08/.

376 Gita Gopinath, Emine Boz, Federico Diez, Pierre-Olivier Gourinchas, and Mikkel Plagborg-Moller, "Dominant Currency Paradigm," Harvard University Department of Economics, June 12, 2019, https://scholar.harvard.edu/gopinath/publications/dominant-currency-paradigm-0.

377 Jonathan Wheatley, "Foreign Investors Dash into Emerging Markets at Swiftest Pace since 2013, *Financial Times,* December 17, 2020, https://www.ft.com/content/e12a1eee-2571-4ae5-bc91-cc17ee7f40d0?shareType=nongift.

378 Jonathan Wheatley, "Emerging Markets Attract $17bn of Inflows in First Three Weeks of 2021," *Financial Times,* January 22, 2021, https://www.ft.com/content/f9b94ac9-1df1-4d89-b129-5b30ff98e715?shareType=nongift.

379 Markus Brunnermeier, Sam Langfield, Marco Pagano, Ricardo Reis, Stijn Van Nieuwerburh, and Dimitri Vayanos, "ESBies: Safety in the Tranches," VoxEU, September 20, 2016, https://voxeu.org/article/esbies-safety-tranches.

380 Research by the Global Capital Allocation Project quantifies these flows. The interested reader may consult their project website: https://www.globalcapitalallocation.com. They highlight that beyond direct capital flows from the US to other parts of the world, there are also many indirect capital flows where dollar-denominated bonds, for example, are setup via London, Luxemburg, the Netherlands, or the Cayman Islands. These constructs are not necessarily illegal.

381 Saleem Bahaj and Ricardo Reis, "Central Bank Swap Lines: Evidence on the Effects of the Lender of Last Resort," IMES Discussion Paper Series, 2019.

382 Markus Brunnermeier and Luang Huang, "A Global Safe Asset from and for Emerging Economies," In *Monetary Policy and Financial Stability: Transmission Mechanisms and Policy Implications,* 111-167, Central Bank of Chile, 2019.

383 Markus Brunnermeier et al., "ESBies: Safety in the Tranches," September 20, 2016.
Markus K Brunnermeier, Sam Langfield, Marco Pagano, Ricardo Reis, Stijn Van Nieuwerburgh, Dimitri Vayanos, ESBies: safety in the tranches, *Economic Policy*, Volume 32, Issue 90, April 2017, Pages 175–219, https://doi.org/10.1093/epolic/eix004

384 For more detail on these effects see: Markus Brunnermeier, Harold James, and Jean-Pierre Landau, "Digital Currency Areas," VoxEU, July 3, 2019, https://voxeu.org/article/digital-currency-areas.

385 Frank Chen, "China's e-RMB Era Comes into Closer View," October 28, 2020.

386 Pinelopi Goldberg, *Markus' Academy,* Princeton University Webinar, April 17, 2020, 18:30, https://www.youtube.com/watch?v=erq8pqBpFhI.

387 Pol Antras, "De-Globalisation? Global Value Chains in the Post-COVID-19 Age," PowerPoint presented at the ECB Forum in November 2020, https://www.ecb.europa.eu/pub/conferences/shared/pdf/20201111_ECB_Forum/presentation_Antras.pdf.

388 Susan Lund, "Central Banks in a Shifting World," European Central Bank, November 2020, https://www.ecb.europa.eu/pub/conferences/html/20201111_ecb_forum_on_central_banking.en.html.

389 Andrew Hill, "People: The Strongest Link in the Strained Supply Chain," *Financial Times,* March 8, 2021, https://www.ft.com/content/ef937903-ed1d-4625-b2ba-d682318a314f?shareType=nongift.

390 Susan Lund, "Central Banks in a Shifting World," November 2020.

391 Rai Saritha, "Wall Street Giants Get Swept Up by India's Brutal Covid Wave," Bloomberg, May 6, 2021, https://www.bloomberg.com/news/articles/2021-05-06/wall-street-giants-get-swept-up-by-india-s-brutal-covid-wave?utm_medium=social&utm_campaign=socialflow-organic&utm_content=markets&utm_source=twitter&cmpid=socialflow-twitter-business&cmpid%3D=socialflow-.

392 Pinelopi Goldberg, *Markus' Academy,* Princeton University Webinar, April 17, 2020, 1:10:20, https://www.youtube.com/watch?v=erq8pqBpFhI.

393 Bomin Jiang, Daniel Rigebon, and Roberto Rigebon, "From Just in Time, to Just in Case, to Just in Worst-Case," International Monetary Fund Conference Paper, October 12, 2020, https://www.imf.org/-/media/Files/Conferences/2020/ARC/Rigobon-Daniel-et-al.ashx.

394 Pinelopi Goldberg, *Markus' Academy,* April 17, 2020, 46:25.

395 Pinelopi Goldberg, *Markus' Academy,* April 17, 2020, 54:30.

396 Joseph Stiglitz, *Markus' Academy,* Princeton University Webinar, April 27, 2020, 51:45 and 52:04, https://www.youtube.com/watch?v=_6SoT97wo3g.

397 Adam Posen, *Markus' Academy* (Lecture Slides), Princeton University Webinar, December 10, 2020, https://bcf.princeton.edu/wp-content/uploads/2020/12/posenslides.pdf.

398 Pinelopi Goldberg, *Markus' Academy,* April 17, 2020, 1:07:25.

399 Tyler Cowen, *Markus' Academy,* April 10, 2020, 41:55.

400 David Autor, David Dorn, and Gordon Hanson, "The China Shock: Learning from Labor Market Adjustment to Large Changes in Trade," *NBER Working Papers*, no. 21906 (2016).

401 Dani Rodrik, *Markus' Academy,* May 5, 2020, 36:10.

402 Giovanni Maggi and Ralph Ossa, "The Political Economy of Deep Integration," *NBER Working Papers,* no. 28190 (December 2020), https://www.nber.org/papers/w28190.

403 Martin Sandbu, "Globalisation Does Not Mean Deregulation," *Financial Times,* August 20, 2020, https://www.ft.com/content/a04c186b-ab3f-4df3-99fb-638b5aa1ce50?shareType=nongift.

404 Giovanni Maggi and Ralph Ossa, "The Political Economy of Deep Integration," December 2020.

405 Giovanni Maggi and Ralph Ossa, "The Political Economy of Deep Integration," December 2020.

406 Dani Rodrik, *Markus' Academy,* May 5, 2020, 42:15.

407 Eric Schmidt, *Markus' Academy,* July 27, 2020, 57:10.

408 Dani Rodrik, *Markus' Academy,* May 5, 2020, 52:40 and 55:30.

409 Dani Rodrik, *Markus' Academy,* May 5, 2020, 34:30 and 34:55.

410 Alexander Chipman Koty, "What Is the China Standards 2035 Plan," July 2, 2020.

Chapter 15

411 Piers Forster, "Covid-19 Paused Climate Emissions—But They're Rising Again," BBC. March 12, 2021, https://www.bbc.com/future/article/20210312-covid-19-paused-climate-emissions-but-theyre-rising-again.

412 Richard Zeckhauser, *Markus' Academy,* Princeton University Webinar, July 17, 2020, 23:20 and 24:16, https://www.youtube.com/watch?v=jHTRFizTsFE&list=PLPKR-Xs1slgSWqOqaXid_9sQXsPsjV_72&index=3.

413 Klaus Desmet, Dávid Krisztián Nagy, and Esteban Rossi-Hansberg, "The Geography of Development," *Journal of Political Economy* 126, no. 3 (2018): 903-983.

414 Paul Bolton, "UK and Global Emissions and Temperature Trends," UK Parliament, House of Commons Library, June 2, 2021, https://commonslibrary.parliament.uk/uk-and-global-emissions-and-temperature-trends/#:~:text=Taken%20together%20these%20countries%20accounted,changing%20emission%20levels%20over%20time.

415 Covid can serve as a coordination device when implementing the switch from an oil driven to a green economy, and to the remodeling of cities and public transportation systems. See: Richard Zeckhauser, *Markus' Academy,* July 17, 2020, 9:45.

416 William Nordhaus, "Climate Clubs: Overcoming Free-Riding in International Climate Policy," *American Economic Review* 105, no. 4 (2015): 1339-70, https://pubs.aeaweb.org/doi/pdfplus/10.1257/aer.15000001.

417 William Nordhaus, *Markus' Academy,* Princeton University Webinar, January 28, 2021, 43:00, https://www.youtube.com/watch?v=QaXZx_nJ_3I.

418 Hans-Werner Sin, *The Green Paradox,* Cambridge, MA: MIT Press, 2012.

419 Esteban Rossi-Hansberg, *Markus' Academy,* Princeton University Webinar, October 1, 2020, 58:00, https://www.youtube.com/watch?v=ZsfKRrI2yB4.

420 Leigh Collins, "'World first' As Hydrogen Used to Power Commercial Steel Production," Recharge, April 28, 2020, https://www.rechargenews.com/transition/-world-first-as-hydrogen-used-to-power-commercial-steel-production/2-1-799308.

421 This proposal was put forward by French economist, Jacque Delpla. See: Jaques Delpla, "The Case for Creating a CO2 Central Bank," WorldCrunch, November 12, 2019, https://worldcrunch.com/world-affairs/the-case-for-creating-a-co2-central-bank.

Conclusion and Outlook

422 Lauren Fedor, Myles McCormick, and Hannah Murphy, "Cyberattack Shuts Major US Pipeline System," *Financial Times,* May 8, 2021, https://www.ft.com/content/2ce0b1fe-9c3f-439f-9afa-78d77849dd92.

423 Lawrence Summers, *Markus' Academy,* Princeton University Webinar, May 22, 2020, 1:25:24 and 1:25:47, https://www.youtube.com/watch?v=cZmRtQCR2ns&list=PLPKR-Xs1slgSWqOqaXid_9sQXsPsjV_72&index=17.

424 Nick Bostrom, "The Vulnerable World Hypothesis," *Global Policy* 10, no. 4 (November 2019): 455-476. https://nickbostrom.com/papers/vulnerable.pdf.

Bibliography

Acemoglu, Daron, Philippe Aghion, and Fabrizio Zilibotti. "Distance to Frontier, Selection and Economic Growth." *Journal of European Economic Association,* (2006): 37-74.

Acemoglu, Daron, Victor Chernozukhov, Ivan Werning, and Michael Whinston. "Optimal Targeted Lockdowns." MIT Economics Department. May 2020. economics.mit.edu/files/19698.

Acemoglu, Daron. *Markus' Academy.* Princeton University Webinar. May 8, 2020. https://www.youtube.com/watch?v=NqtS8MZBuZ0&list=PLPKR-Xs1slgSWqOqaXid_9sQXsPsjV_72&index=20.

Acharya, Viral, and Sascha Steffen. 2020. "The Risk of Being a Fallen Angel and the Corporate Dash for Cash in the Midst of COVID." *NBER Working Papers,* no. 2760127601 (July 2020). https://www.nber.org/papers/w27601.

Adelstein, Jake and Nathaly-Kyoko Stucky. "Japan's Finance Minister Commits Suicide on World Suicide Prevention Day." *The Atlantic.* September 10, 2012. https://www.theatlantic.com/international/archive/2012/09/japans-finance-minister-commits-suicide-world-suicide-prevention-day/323787/.

Aguiar, Mark, Mark Blis, Kofi Kerwin, and Erik Hurst. "Leisure Luxuries and the Labor Supply of Young Men." *Journal of Political Economy,* (2021): 337-382.

Aliprantis, Dionissi, Daniel R Carroll, and Eric R. Young. "The Dynamics of the Racial Wealth Gap." SSRN. FRB of Cleveland Working Paper 19-18, October 2019.

Alon, Titan, Matthias Doepke, Jane Olmstead-Rumsey, and Michele Tertilt. "This Time It's Different: The Role of Women's Employment in a Pandemic Recession." *NBER Working Papers,* no. 27660 (2020).

Amadeo, Kimberly. "Trans-Pacific Partnership Summary, Pros and Cons." The Balance. February 10, 2021. https://www.thebalance.

com/what-is-the-trans-pacific-partnership-3305581.

Ams, Julianne, Reza Baqir, Anna Gelpern, and Christoph Trebesch. "Chapter 7: Sovereign Default." IMF Research Department. 2018. https://www.imf.org/~/media/Files/News/Seminars/2018/091318SovDebt-conference/chapter-7-sovereign-default.ashx.

Antras, Pol. "De-Globalisation? Global Value Chains in the Post-COVID-19 Age." PowerPoint presented at the ECB Forum in November 2020. https://www.ecb.europa.eu/pub/conferences/shared/pdf/20201111_ECB_Forum/presentation_Antras.pdf.

Arkenberg, Chris. "Will Gaming Keep Growing When the Lockdowns End?" Deloitte. July 8, 2020. https://www2.deloitte.com/be/en/pages/technology-media-and-telecommunications/articles/video-game-industry-trends.html.

Arnaout, Abdelraouf. "Netanyahu to Be First Israeli to Take Covid-19 Vaccine." *Anadolu Agency*. December 9, 2020. https://www.aa.com.tr/en/middle-east/netanyahu-to-be-first-israeli-to-take-covid-19-vaccine/2070779.

Arnold, Veronika. "Ansturm auf Skigebiete trotz Lockdown: Nächster Wintersport-Ort nun abgeriegelt – 'Wurden überrannt.'" Merkur. January 5, 2021. https://www.merkur.de/welt/coronavirus-skigebiete-lockdown-oberhof-deutschland-ansturm-nrw-willingen-eifel-winterberg-90157267.html.

Asgari, Nikou, Joe Rennison, Philip Stafford, and Hudson Lockett. "Companies Raise $400bn Over Three Weeks in Blistering Start to 2021." *Financial Times*. January 26, 2021. https://www.ft.com/content/45770ddb-29e0-41c2-a97a-60ce13810ff2?shareType=nongift.

Autor, David, David Dorn, and Gordon Hanson. "The China Shock: Learning from Labor Market Adjustment to Large Changes in Trade." *NBER Working Papers*, no. 21906 (2016).

Bacher-Hicks, Andrew, Joshua Goodman, and Christine Mulhern. "Inequality in Household Adaptation to Schooling Shocks: Covid-Induced Online Learning Engagement in Real Time." *Journal of Public Economics* 193 (2021): 204345.

Bahaj, Saleem, and Ricardo Reis. "Central Bank Swap Lines: Evidence on the Effects of the Lender of Last Resort." IMES Discussion Paper Series, 2019.

Ball, Sam. "'I Won't Take the Risk': France Leads the World in Covid-19 Vaccine Scepticism." France24. November 20, 2020. https://www.france24.com/en/france/20201120-i-won-t-take-the-risk-france-leads-the-world-in-covid-19-vaccine-scepticism.

Banerjee, Abhijit, Marcella Alsam, Emily Breza, Arun Chandrasekhar, Abhijit Chowdhury, Esther Dufo, Paul Goldsmith Pinkham, and Benjamin Olken. "Messages on Covid-19 Prevention Increased Symptoms Reporting and Adherence to Preventative Behaviors Among 25 Million Recipients with Similar Effects on Non-Recipient Members of Their Communities." *NBER Working Papers,* no. 27496 (July 2020). https://www.nber.org/system/files/working_papers/w27496/w27496.pdf.

Barrero, Jose Maria, Nick Bloom, and Stephen Davis. "Why Working from Home Will Stick." Stanford Working Paper, April 2021. https://nbloom.people.stanford.edu/sites/g/files/sbiybj4746/f/why_wfh_will_stick_21_april_2021.pdf.

Barrero, Jose Maria, Nick Bloom, and Steven J Davis. "COVID-19 Is also a Reallocation Shock." Brookings Institute. June 25, 2020. https://www.brookings.edu/wp-content/uploads/2020/06/Barrero-et-al-conference-draft.pdf.

BBC. "Coronavirus: Under Surveillance and Confined at Home in Taiwan." March 24, 2020. https://www.bbc.co.uk/news/technology-52017993.

BBC. "Covid: EU Plans Rollout of Travel Certificate before Summer." March 18, 2020. https://www.bbc.co.uk/news/world-europe-56427830.

Beaumont, Peter. "Tanzania's President Shrugs Off Covid-19 Risk After Sending Fruit for Tests." *The Guardian.* May 19, 2020. https://www.theguardian.com/global-development/2020/may/19/tanzanias-president-shrugs-off-covid-19-risk-after-sending-fruit-for-tests.

Birtles, Bill. "China Embraces Coronavirus Vaccine Passports for Overseas Travel, but Other Countries Foresee Concerns." *ABC News.* March 17, 2021. https://www.abc.net.au/news/2021-03-17/china-embraces-vaccine-passports-while-the-west-mulls-ethics/13252588.

Blanchard, Olivier, and Lawrence Summers. "Hysteresis in Unemployment." *European Economic Review,* (1987): 288-295.

Blanchard, Olivier. "Should We Reject the Natural Rate Hypothesis." *Journal of Economic Perspectives* 32, no. 1 (2018): 97-120.

Blanchard, Olivier. "In Defense of Concerns over the $1.9 Trillion Relief Plan." Peterson Institute for International Economics. February 18, 2021. https://www.piie.com/blogs/realtime-economic-issues-watch/defense-concerns-over-19-trillion-relief-plan.

Bloom, Nick, James Liang, John Roberts, and Zhichun Jenny Ying. "Does Working from Home Work? Evidence from a Chinese Experiment." *Quarterly Journal of Economics* 130, no. 1 (2015): 165-218

Bloom, Nick. *Markus' Academy.* Princeton University Webinar. December 3, 2020. https://www.youtube.com/watch?v=N8_rvy-hqUs.

Bloomberg. "Covid-19 Deals Tracker." March 3, 2021. https://www.bloomberg.com/graphics/covid-vaccine-tracker-global-distribution/contracts-purchasing-agreements.html.

Boakye-Adjei, Nana Yaa. "Covid-19: Boon and Bane for Digital Payments and Financial Inclusion." Bank for International Settlements. Financial Stability Institute, July 2020. https://www.bis.org/fsi/fsibriefs9.pdf.

Bolton, Paul. "UK and Global Emissions and Temperature Trends." UK Parliament. House of Commons Library, June 2, 2021. https://commonslibrary.parliament.uk/uk-and-global-emissions-and-temperature-trends/#:~:text=Taken%20together%20these%20countries%20accounted,changing%20emission%20levels%20over%20time.

Bostrom, Nick. "The Vulnerable World Hypothesis." *Global Policy* 10, no. 4 (November 2019): 455-476. https://nickbostrom.com/papers/vulnerable.pdf.

Bourke, Latika. "International Borders Might Not Open Even If Whole Country Is Vaccinated." *The Sydney Morning Herald.* April 13, 2021. https://www.smh.com.au/politics/federal/international-borders-might-not-open-even-if-whole-country-is-vaccinated-greg-hunt-20210413-p57ixi.html.

Brooks, David. *Munk Dialogues.* Peter and Melanie Munk Charitable Foundation. July 22, 2020. https://www.youtube.com/watch?v=W0dbDFJR3A4&feature=youtu.be].

Brotherhood, Luiz, Tiago Cavalcanti, Daniel Da Mata, and Cezar Santos. "Slums and Pandemics." SSRN Working Paper, August 5, 2020 (Updated January 4, 2021). https://papers.ssrn.com/sol3/papers.cfm?abstract_id=3665695.

Brown, Caitlin, and Martin Ravallion. "Inequality and the Coronavirus: Socioeconomic Covariates of Behavioral Responses and Viral Outcomes Across US Counties." *Proceedings of the National Academy of the Sciences* 111, no. 19 (May 13, 2014): 6928-6933. https://www.pnas.org/content/111/19/6928.short.

Brunnermeier, Markus, and Jonathan Parker. "Optimal Expectations." *American Economic Review* 95, no. 4 (2005): 1092-1118.

Brunnermeier, Markus, and Luang Huang. "A Global Safe Asset from and for Emerging Economies." In *Monetary Policy and Financial Stability: Transmission Mechanisms and Policy Implications,* 111-167. Central Bank of Chile, 2019.

Brunnermeier, Markus, and Yuliy Sannikov. "Redistributive Monetary Policy." Princeton University, August 2012. https://scholar.princeton.edu/sites/default/files/04c%20Redistributive%20Monetary%20Policy.pdf.

Brunnermeier, Markus, Harold James, and Jean-Pierre Landau. "The Digitalization of Money." Princeton University Working Paper, 2019.

Brunnermeier, Markus, Harold James, and Jean-Pierre Landau. "Digital Currency Areas." VoxEU. July 3, 2019. https://voxeu.org/article/digital-currency-areas.

Brunnermeier, Markus, Rohit Lamba, and Carlos Segura Rodriguez. "Inverse selection." SSRN Working Paper, May 21, 2020. https://papers.ssrn.com/sol3/papers.cfm?abstract_id=3584331.

Brunnermeier, Markus, Sam Langfield, Marco Pagano, Ricardo Reis, Stijn Van Nieuwerburh, and Dimitri Vayanos. "ESBies: Safety in the tranches." *VoxEU.* September 20, 2016. https://voxeu.org/article/esbies-safety-tranches.

Brunnermeier, Markus, Sebastian Merkel, and Yuliy Sannikov. "A Safe-Asset Perspective for an Integrated Policy Framework." Princeton University, May 29, 2020. https://scholar.princeton.edu/sites/default/files/markus/files/safeassetinternational.pdf.

Brunnermeier, Markus, Sebastian Merkel, and Yuliy Sannikov. "The Fiscal Theory of the Price Level with a Bubble." Princeton University, July 8, 2020. https://scholar.princeton.edu/sites/default/files/merkel/files/fiscaltheorybubble.pdf.

Brunnermeier, Markus, Sebastian Merkel, Jonathan Payne, and Yuliy Sannikov. "Covid-19: Inflation and Deflation Pressures." CESIFO Area Conferences, July 24, 2020. https://www.cesifo.org/sites/default/files/events/2020/mmi20-Payne.pdf.

Brunnermeier, Markus. "Money in the Digital Age." Speech delivered at the EBA Research Workshop, November 25, 2020. *https://www.youtube.com/watch?v=QdlSzTnOlkg.*

Bryant, Chris. "Hedge Funds Love SPACs But You Should Watch Out." Bloomberg. December 9, 2020. https://www.bloomberg.com/opinion/articles/2020-12-09/hedge-funds-love-spacs-but-retail-investors-should-watch-out?sref=ATN0rNv3.

Buchheit, Lee, Guillaume Chabert, Chanda DeLong, and Joremin Zettelmeyer. "How to Restructure Sovereign Debt: Lessons from Four Decades." Peterson Institute for International Economics Working Paper 19-8, May 2019. https://www.piie.com/publications/working-papers/how-restructure-sovereign-debt-lessons-four-decades.

Buffet, Warren. Berkshire Hathaway Annual Meeting. Yahoo Finance. May 1, 2021. https://www.youtube.com/watch?v=7t7qfOyQdQA.

Caballero, Ricardo, Takeo Hoshi, and Anil Kashyap. "Zombie Lending and Depressed Restructuring in Japan." *American Economic Review* 98, no. 5 (2008): 1943-77.

Caldwell, Kia Lilly, and Edna Maria de Araújo. "Covid-19 Is Deadlier for Black Brazilians: A Legacy of Structural Racism that Dates Back to Slavery." The Conversation. June 10, 2020. https://

theconversation.com/covid-19-is-deadlier-for-black-brazilians-a-legacy-of-structural-racism-that-dates-back-to-slavery-139430.

Carmiel, Oshrat. "Manhattan Apartments Haven't Been This Cheap to Rent in 10 Years." Bloomberg. December 10, 2020. https://www.bloomberg.com/news/articles/2020-12-10/manhattan-apartment-rents-sink-to-the-lowest-level-in-a-decade.

Carroll, Linda. "U.S. Life Expectancy Declining Due to More Deaths in Middle Age." Reuters. November 26, 2019. https://www.reuters.com/article/us-health-life-expectancy-idUSKBN1Y02C7.

Carter, Devon. "Can mRNA Vaccines Be Used in Cancer Care?" MD Anderson Cancer Center, January 25, 2021. https://www.mdanderson.org/cancerwise/can-mrna-vaccines-like-those-used-for-covid-19-be-used-in-cancer-care.h00-159457689.html.

Catherine, Sylvain, Max Miller, and Natasha Sarin. "Social Security and Trends in Wealth Inequality." SSRN Working Paper, February 29, 2020. https://papers.ssrn.com/sol3/papers.cfm?abstract_id=3546668.

Cavallo, Alberto. "Inflation with Covid Consumption Baskets." *NBER Working Papers*, no. 27352 (June 2020). https://www.nber.org/papers/w27352.

CBC. "Canada Could Share Any Excess Vaccine Supply with Poorer Countries: Reuters Sources." November 18, 2020. https://www.cbc.ca/news/health/canada-vaccine-supply-share-1.5807679.

Centers for Disease Control and Prevention. "Risk for COVID-19 Infection, Hospitalization, and Death by Race/Ethnicity." April 23, 2021. https://www.cdc.gov/coronavirus/2019-ncov/covid-data/investigations-discovery/hospitalization-death-by-race-ethnicity.html.

Chen, Alicia, and Vanessa Molter. "Mask Diplomacy: Chinese Narratives in the COVID Era." Stanford University (blog), June 16, 2020. https://fsi.stanford.edu/news/covid-mask-diplomacy.

Chen, Frank. "China's e-RMB Era Comes into Closer View." *Asia Times*. October 28, 2020. https://asiatimes.com/2020/10/chinas-e-rmb-era-comes-into-closer-view/.

Chetty, Raj, John N. Friedman, Nathaniel Hendren, and Michael Stepner. "The Economic Impacts of COVID-19: Evidence from a New Public Database Built Using Private Sector Data." Opportunity Insights. November 5, 2020. https://opportunityinsights.org/wp-content/uploads/2020/05/tracker_paper.pdf.

Chetty, Raj. *Markus' Academy.* Princeton University Webinar. June 2017, 2020. https://www.youtube.com/watch?v=ip5pz7gOSwI&list=PLPKR-Xs1slgSWqOqaXid_9sQXsPsjV_72&index=11.

Cochrane, John. *Markus' Academy.* Princeton University Webinar. May 18, 2020. https://www.youtube.com/watch?v=H6sSvqD9Xsw&list=PLPKR-Xs1slgSWqOqaXid_9sQXsPsjV_72&index=18.

Coibion, Olivier, Yuriy Goridnichenko, and Michael Weber. "How Did US Consumers Use Their Stimulus Payments?" *NBER Working Papers,* no. 27693 (August 2020). *https://www.nber.org/papers/w27693.*

Collins, Leigh. "'World first' As Hydrogen Used to Power Commercial Steel Production." Recharge. April 28, 2020. https://www.rechargenews.com/transition/-world-first-as-hydrogen-used-to-power-commercial-steel-production/2-1-799308.

Columbia University Irving Medical Center. "Long Haul Covid: Columbia Physicians Review What's Known." March 22, 2021. https://www.cuimc.columbia.edu/news/long-haul-covid-columbia-physicians-review-whats-known.

Cook, Lisa. *Markus' Academy.* Princeton University Webinar. June 8, 2020. https://www.youtube.com/watch?v=PeKhSsJsW2w.

Cowen, Tyler. *Markus' Academy.* Princeton Webinar. April 10, 2020. https://www.youtube.com/watch?v=FPsPmkp6sdM&list=PLPKR-Xs1slgSWqOqaXid_9sQXsPsjV_72&index=28.

Cox, Natalie, Peter Ganong, Pascal Noel, Joseph Vavra, Arlene Wong, Diana Farrell, and Fiona Greig. "Initial Impacts of the Pandemic on Consumer Behavior: Evidence from Linked Income, Spending, and Savings Data." Becker Friedman Institute Working Papers, July 2020. https://bfi.uchicago.edu/wp-content/uploads/BFI_WP_202082.pdf.

CPB Netherlands Bureau for Economic Policy Analysis. "World Trade Monitor." 2021. https://www.cpb.nl/en/worldtrademonitor.

Cundy, Antonia. "The Home Buyers Making Their Tuscan Dream a Reality." *Financial Times.* August 19, 2020. https://www.ft.com/content/2a127c83-08ba-4ad7-8a1b-19dcaee5c6ae.

Davies, Gavyn. "The Anatomy of a Very Brief Bear Market." *Financial Times.* August 2, 2020. https://www.ft.com/content/cd8e2299-161b-4f17-adad-ac6d8a730049.

de Bolle, Monica. *Markus' Academy.* Princeton University Webinar. February 25, 2021. https://www.youtube.com/watch?v=Ptsg_EjCXxw.

Deaton, Angus. "Covid Shows How the State Can Address Social Inequality." *Financial Times.* January 4, 2021. https://www.ft.com/content/caa37763-9c71-4f8d-9c29-b16ccf53d780.

Deaton, Angus. *Markus' Academy.* Princeton University Webinar. April 13, 2020. https://www.youtube.com/watch?v=2uzASRQz4gM.

Delpla, Jacques. "The Case for Creating a CO2 Central Bank." WorldCrunch. November 12, 2019. https://worldcrunch.com/world-affairs/the-case-for-creating-a-co2-central-bank.

DeMarzo, Peter, Dimitri Vayanos, and Jeffrey Zwiebel. "Persuasion Bias, Social Influence, and Unidimensional Opinions." *Quarterly Journal of Economics* 118, no. 3 (2003): 909-968.

Desmet, Klaus, Dávid Krisztián Nagy, and Esteban Rossi-Hansberg. 2018. "The Geography of Development." *Journal of Political Economy* 126, no. 3 (2018): 903-983.

Destatis. "Mortality Figures in Week 50 of 2020: 23% Above the Average of Previous Years." Statistisches Bundesamt. January 28, 2021. https://www.destatis.de/EN/Press/2021/01/PE21_014_12621.html;jsessionid=CE5D09E9528E1803D00E12AF9A9D0300.internet8741.

Dingel, Jonathan, and Brent Neiman. "How many Jobs Can be Done at Home?" Becker Friedman Institute for Economics Working Paper, June 19, 2020. https://bfi.uchicago.edu/wp-content/

uploads/BFI_White-Paper_Dingel_Neiman_3.2020.pdf.

Dudley, Bill. *Markus' Academy.* Princeton University Webinar. June 1, 2020. https://www.youtube.com/watch?v=65Y0kRJP_UY.

Duffie, Darrell. *Markus' Academy.* Princeton University Webinar. June 5, 2020. https://www.youtube.com/watch?v=04LYVyR3jog.

Duflo, Esther. *Markus' Academy.* Princeton University Webinar. February 11, 2021. https://www.youtube.com/watch?v=15PMtvJBI-s.

Econreporter. "US Needs Large-Scale Covid Testing Urgently: Nobel Winning Economist Paul Romer." June 28, 2020. https://en.econreporter.com/2020/06/its-intellectual-failure-nobel-economics-winner-paul-romer-on-why-us-needs-large-scale-COVID-testing-urgently/.

Ellyatt, Holly. "Covid Variant in South Africa Is 'More of a Problem' Than the One in UK, Official Says." CNBC. January 4, 2021. https://www.cnbc.com/2021/01/04/south-african-coronavirus-variant-more-of-a-problem-than-uk-one.html.

Emmott, Robin and Jan Strupczewski. "EU and India Agree to Resume Trade Talks at Virtual Summit." Reuters. May 8, 2021. https://www.reuters.com/world/europe/eu-india-re-launch-trade-talks-virtual-summit-2021-05-08/.

Engzell, Per, Arun Freya, and Mark Verhagen. "Learning Inequality During the Covid-19 Pandemic." October 2020. https://scholar.googleusercontent.com/scholar?q=cache:Zva2ARtZvlkJ:scholar.google.com/+covid+inequality+statistics+mexico&hl=en&as_sdt=0,31&as_vis=1.

European Central Bank. "Annual Consolidated Balance Sheet of the Eurosystem." 2021. https://www.ecb.europa.eu/pub/annual/balance/html/index.en.html.

Fagereng, Andreas, Luigi Guso, Davide Malacrino, and Luigi Pistaferri. "Heterogeneity and Persistence in Returns on Wealth." Stanford University Working Paper, August 2019. https://web.stanford.edu/~pista/FGMP.pdf.

Fähnders, Till. "Warum Indonesien Zuerst die Jungen Impft." *Frankffurter Allgemeine.* January 13, 2021. https://www.faz.net/aktuell/politik/ausland/

corona-impfstart-in-indonesien-die-arbeitsfaehigen-zuerst-17144460.html.

Fairlie, Robert. "Covid-19, Small Business Owners, and Racial Inequality." NBER. December 4, 2020. https://www.nber.org/reporter/2020number4/covid-19-small-business-owners-and-racial-inequality.

Falato, Antonio, Itay Goldstein, and Ali Hortacsu. "Financial Fragility in the COVID-19 Crisis: The Case of Investment Funds in Corporate Bond Markets." *NBER Working Papers,* no. 27559 (July 2020). https://www.nber.org/papers/w27559.

Farr, Christina and Michelle Gao. "How Taiwan Beat the Coronavirus." CNBC. July 15, 2020. https://www.cnbc.com/2020/07/15/how-taiwan-beat-the-coronavirus.html.

Federal Reserve Bank of New York. "SCE Household Spending Survey." April 2021. https://www.newyorkfed.org/microeconomics/sce/household-spending#/.

Federal Reserve Bank of New York. "Survey of Consumer Expectations." February 2021. https://www.newyorkfed.org/microeconomics/sce#indicators/inflation-expectations/g1.

Federal Reserve Bank of Philadelphia. "Survey of Professional Forecasters." 2020. https://www.philadelphiafed.org/surveys-and-data/real-time-data-research/survey-of-professional-forecasters.

Federal Reserve Bank of St. Louis. "Personal Consumption Expenditures/Gross Domestic Product." FRED Economic Data. 2021. https://fred.stlouisfed.org/graph/?g=hh3.

Federal Reserve Bank of St. Louis. FRED Economic Data. 2021. https://fred.stlouisfed.org/.

Fedor, Lauren, Myles McCormick, and Hannah Murphy. "Cyberattack Shuts Major US Pipeline System." *Financial Times.* May 8, 2021. https://www.ft.com/content/2ce0b1fe-9c3f-439f-9afa-78d77849dd92.

Fehr, Mark. "Zombiefirmen könnten Insolvenzwelle auslösen." Frankfurter Allgemeine Zeitung, April 29, 2021.

Federal Reserve Board of Governors. "Survey of Consumer Finances." 2021. https://www.federalreserve.gov/econres/scfindex.htm.

Fieser, Ezra, and Oscar Medina. "Colombia Risks Forced Selling of Its Bonds After More Downgrades." Bloomberg. May 5, 2021. https://www.bloomberg.com/news/articles/2021-05-21/colombia-risks-forced-selling-of-its-bonds-after-more-downgrades?sref=ATN0rNv3.

Financial Times. "Hotspots of Resurgent Covid Erode Faith in Herd Immunity." October 9, 2020. https://www.ft.com/content/5b96ee2d-9ced-46ae-868f-43c9d8df1ecb.

Findlay, Stephanie. "India Eyes Global Vaccine Drive to Eclipse Rival China." *Financial Times.* January 31, 2021. https://www.ft.com/content/1bb8b97f-c046-4d0c-9859-b7f0b60678f4.

Forster, Piers. "Covid-19 Paused Climate Emissions—But They're Rising Again." BBC. March 12, 2021. https://www.bbc.com/future/article/20210312-covid-19-paused-climate-emissions-but-theyre-rising-again.

Fraga, Arminio. *Markus' Academy.* Princeton University Webinar. July 13, 2020. https://www.youtube.com/watch?v=mTy2X7zftCc.

Gallagher, Kevin, José Antonio Ocampo, and Ulrich Volz. "It's Time for a Major Issuance of the IMF's Special Drawing Rights." *Financial Times.* March 20, 2020. https://www.ft.com/content/43a67e06-bbeb-4bea-8939-bc29ca785b0e.

Garcia, Carmen Aguilar, and Ganesh Rao. "Covid-19: India's Vaccine Export Ban Could Send Shockwaves Worldwide. Should the UK Step in to Help?" Sky News. April 30, 2021. https://news.sky.com/story/covid-19-how-does-indias-pause-on-vaccine-export-hurt-other-nations-12290300.

Gates, Bill. "How the Pandemic Will Shape the Near Future." TED. July 6, 2020. https://www.youtube.com/watch?v=jmQWOPDqxWA.

Gelpern, Anna, Sebastian Horn, Scott Morris, Brad Parks, and Christoph Trebesch. "How China Lends: A Rare Look into 100 Debt Contracts with Foreign Governments." Peterson Institute for International Economics Working Paper 21-7, May 2021. https://www.piie.com/publications/working-papers/how-china-lends-rare-look-100-debt-contracts-foreign-governments.

Gennaiolo, Nicola, Andei Shleifer, and Robert Vishny. "Neglected Risks: The Psychology of Financial Crises." *American Economic Review* 105, no. 5 (2015): 310-14.

Glennerster, Rachel, and IMF. "Covid-19 Pandemic in Developing Countries: Pandemic Policies for People." International Monetary Fund. September 12, 2020. https://www.imf.org/external/mmedia/view.aspx?vid=6215224981001.

Godeluck, Solveig. "Cette Épargne des Ménages qui Menace de Nuire à la Reprise." LesEchos. July 29, 2020. https://www.lesechos.fr/economie-france/social/Covid-cette-epargne-des-menages-qui-menace-de-nuire-a-la-reprise-1227200.

Goldberg, Pinelopi. *Markus' Academy.* Princeton University Webinar. April 17, 2020. https://www.youtube.com/watch?v=erq8pqBpFhI.

Goldin, Claudia, and Robert Margo. "The Great Compression: The Wage Structure in the United States in the Mid-Century." *Quarterly Journal of Economics* 107, no. 1 (1992): 1-34.

Google. Google Covid Case Tracker, South Dakota. 2021. https://www.google.com/search?q=covid+cases+in+south+dakota&oq=covid+cases+in+south+dakota&aqs=chrome..69i57j0l2j0i395l7.4013j1j7&sourceid=chrome&ie=UTF-8.

Gopinath, Gita, Emine Boz, Federico Diez, Pierre-Olivier Gourinchas, and Mikkel Plagborg-Moller. "Dominant Currency Paradigm." Harvard University Department of Economics. June 12, 2019. https://scholar.harvard.edu/gopinath/publications/dominant-currency-paradigm-0.

Gopinath, Gita. 2020. *Markus' Academy.* Princeton University Webinar. May 29, 2020. https://www.youtube.com/watch?v=GjUBIxR5W78.

Gormsen, Niels, and Ralph Koijen. "Coronavirus: Impact on Stock Prices and Growth Expectations." *NBER Working Papers,* no. 27387 (June 2020). https://www.nber.org/papers/w27387.

Gould, Elise, and Valerie Wilson. "Black Workers Face Two of the Most Lethal Preexisting Conditions for Coronavirus—Racism and Economic Inequality." Economic Policy Institute. June 1, 2020. https://www.epi.org/publication/black-workers-covid/.

Graham-Harrison, Emma and Tom Phillips. "China Hopes 'Vaccine Diplomacy' Will Restore Its Image and Boost Its Influence." *The Guardian*. November 29, 2020. https://www.theguardian.com/world/2020/nov/29/china-hopes-vaccine-diplomacy-will-restore-its-image-and-boost-its-influence.

Green, Adam. "Covid-19 Pandemic Accelerates Digital Health Reforms." *Financial Times.* May 17, 2020. https://www.ft.com/content/31c927c6-684a-11ea-a6ac-9122541af204.

Greenwood, Robin, Benjamin Iverson, and David Thesmar. "Sizing Up Corporate Restructuring in the Covid crisis." Brookings. September 23, 2020. https://www.brookings.edu/bpea-articles/sizing-up-corporate-restructuring-in-the-covid-crisis/.

Griffin, Riley and Drew Armstrong. "Pfizer Vaccine's Funding Came from Berlin, not Washington." Bloomberg. September 11, 2020. https://www.bloomberg.com/news/articles/2020-11-09/pfizer-vaccine-s-funding-came-from-berlin-not-washington.

Grossman, Derek. "The Quad Is Poised to Become Openly Anti-China Soon" (Blog). The RAND Corporation. July 28, 2020. https://www.rand.org/blog/2020/07/the-quad-is-poised-to-become-openly-anti-china-soon.html.

Grossman, Gene, and Elhanan Helpman. "Identity Politics and Trade Policy." Princeton University. July 2019. https://www.princeton.edu/~grossman/SocialIdentityJuly2019..pdf.

Guerrieri, Veronica. *Markus' Academy.* Princeton University Webinar. June 19, 2020. https://www.youtube.com/watch?v=x2npgxzuTVg.

Guimarães, Thiago, Karen Lucas, and Paul Timms. "Understanding How Low-Income Communities Gain Access to Healthcare Services: A Qualitative Study in São Paulo, Brazil." *Journal of Transport and Health* 15 (2019): 100658.

Gurk, Christoph. "Lateinamerika wird zum Testfeld für die Pharmaindustrie." Süddeutsche Zeitung. August 3,

2020. https://www.sueddeutsche.de/politik/coronavirus-impfstoff-lateinamerika-pharmaindustrie-1.4986326.

Hall, Robert, and Marianna Kudlyak. "The Inexorable Recoveries of US Unemployment." *NBER Working Papers*, no. 28111 (November 2020). *https://sites.google.com/site/mariannakudlyak/home/inexorable_recoveries*.

Haltiwanger, John C. "John Haltiwanger Describes How New Business Applications Surged during the Pandemic." NBER. July 12, 2021. *https://www.nber.org/affiliated-scholars/researchspotlight/john-haltiwanger-describes-how-new-business-applications-surged-during-pandemic*.

Handfield, Robert. "Automation in the Meatpacking Industry Is on the Way." Supply Chain Resource Cooperative. July 9, 2020. https://scm.ncsu.edu/scm-articles/article/automation-in-the-meat-packing-industry-is-on-the-horizon.

Harford, Tim. "Statistics, Lies, and the Virus: Tim Harford's Five Lessons from a Pandemic" (Blog). September 17, 2020. https://timharford.com/2020/09/statistics-lies-and-the-virus-five-lessons-from-a-pandemic/.

Healy, Andrew, and Neal Malhotra. "Myopic Voters and Natural Disaster Policy." *American Political Science Review* 103, no. 3 (2009): 387-406.

Heathcote, Jonathan, Fabrizio Perri, and Giovannia Violante. "The Rise of US Earnings Inequality: Does the Cycle Drive the Trend?" Princeton University. May 31, 2020. http://violante.mycpanel.princeton.edu/Journals/Draft_05-31-20_JH.pdf.

Heimbach, Tobias. "Biden, Netanjahu & Co.: Spitzenpolitiker weltweit lassen sich öffentlich impfen – wann kommt Merkel an die Reihe?" Business Insider. December 23, 2020. https://www.businessinsider.de/politik/deutschland/corona-impfung-joe-biden-wurde-geimpft-merkel/.

Helmore, Edward. "How GameStop Found Itself at the Center of a Groundbreaking Battle between Wall Street and Small Investors." *The Guardian*. January 27, 2021. https://www.theguardian.com/business/2021/jan/27/gamestop-stock-market-retail-wall-street.

Henderson, Richard. "Retail Investors Bet on Bankrupt US Companies Rising Again." *Financial Times*. June 9, 2020. https://

www.ft.com/content/b592847a-2061-4460-8aa5-3b22a2153210.

Henley, Andrew, G. Reza Arabsheibani, and Francisco G. Carneiro. "On Defining and Measuring the Informal Sector." World Bank Policy Research Working Papers, March 2006.

Hill, Andrew. "People: The Strongest Link in the Strained Supply Chain." *Financial Times.* March 8, 2021. https://www.ft.com/content/ef937903-ed1d-4625-b2ba-d682318a314f?shareType=nongift.

Holmstrom, Bengt. "The Seasonality of Covid-19." Princeton Bendheim Center for Finance (Webinar). October 22, 2020. https://www.youtube.com/watch?v=z95U8FU9gMQ.

http://documents1.worldbank.org/curated/en/940751468021241000/pdf/wps3866.pdf.

Hurst, Erik. *Markus' Academy.* Princeton University Webinar. March 20, 2021. https://www.youtube.com/watch?v=VG7KS5sLABY.

Hutt, David. "EU Split Over China's 'Face Mask' Diplomacy." *Asia Times.* March 28, 2020. https://asiatimes.com/2020/03/eu-split-over-chinas-face-mask-diplomacy/.

Ifo Institut. "Handel mit Bekleidung Wanderts ins Internet ab." April 23, 2021. https://www.ifo.de/node/62942?eNLifo-202104.

International Monetary Fund. "Analyze This! Sovereign Debt Restructuring" (Video). December 2, 2020. https://www.imf.org/external/mmedia/view.aspx?vid=6213167814001.

International Monetary Fund. "Fiscal Monitor Database of Country Fiscal Measures in Response to the COVID-19 Pandemic." April 2021. https://www.imf.org/en/Topics/imf-and-covid19/Fiscal-Policies-Database-in-Response-to-COVID-19.

International Monetary Fund. "Q&A on Special Drawing Rights." March 16, 2021. https://www.imf.org/en/About/FAQ/special-drawing-right#Q4.%20Will%20an%20SDR%20allocation%20give%20countries%20with%20poor%20governance%20money%20to%20waste.

International Monetary Fund. "Questions and Answers on Sovereign Debt Issues." April 8, 2021. https://www.imf.org/en/About/FAQ/sovereign-debt#Section%205.

International Monetary Fund. "The Good, the Bad, and the Ugly: 100 Years of Dealing with Public Debt Overhangs." October 8, 2012. https://www.elibrary.imf.org/view/IMF081/12743-9781616353896/12743-9781616353896/chap03.xml?rskey=VXkXsE&result=5&redirect=true&redirect=true.

James, Harold. *Markus' Academy.* Princeton University Webinar. April 24, 2020. https://www.youtube.com/watch?v=PVIm4BdBmTI.

Jiang, Bomin, Daniel Rigebon, and Roberto Rigebon. "From Just in Time, to Just in Case, to Just in Worst-Case." International Monetary Fund Conference Paper. October 12, 2020. https://www.imf.org/-/media/Files/Conferences/2020/ARC/Rigobon-Daniel-et-al.ashx.

Jiang, Zhengyang, Hanno Lustig, and Stijn, Xiaolan, Mindy van Nieuwerburgh. "The US Public Debt Valuation Puzzle." *NBER Working Papers,* no. 26583 (2021).

Johnston, Louis, and Samuel H. Williamson. "What Was the U.S. GDP Then?" MeasuringWorth. 2021

Jones, Marc. "Second Sovereign Downgrade Wave Coming, Major Nations at Risk." Reuters. October 16, 2020. https://www.reuters.com/article/us-global-ratings-sovereign-s-p-exclusiv-idUSKBN27126V.

Kluth, Andreas. "Like a Virus, QAnon Spreads from the U.S. to Germany." Bloomberg. September 21, 2020. https://www.bloomberg.com/opinion/articles/2020-09-22/like-a-virus-qanon-spreads-from-the-u-s-to-europe-germany?sref=ATN0rNv3.

Kotowski, Timo. "So Soll der Sommerurlaub Funktionieren." *Frankffurter Allgemeine.* March 19, 2021. https://www.faz.net/aktuell/gesellschaft/gesundheit/coronavirus/testen-statt-quarantaene-konzeptpapier-fuer-corona-sommerurlaub-17253631.html.

Koty, Alexander Chipman. "What Is the China Standards 2035 Plan and How Will It Impact Emerging Industries?" *China*

Briefing. July 2, 2020. https://www.china-briefing.com/news/what-is-china-standards-2035-plan-how-will-it-impact-emerging-technologies-what-is-link-made-in-china-2025-goals/.

Kozlowski, Julian, Venky Venkateswaran, and Laura Veldkamp. "The Tail That Wags the Economy: Beliefs and Persistent Stagnation." *Journal of Political Economy* 128, no. 8 (2020): 2839-2879.

Kozlowski, Julian, Venky Venkateswaran, and Laura Veldkamp. "Scarring Body and Mind: The Long-Term Belief-Scarring Effects of Covid-19." *NBER Working Papers,* no. 27439 (June 2020). https://www.nber.org/papers/w27439.

Kremer, MIchael. *Markus' Academy.* Princeton University Webinar. May 1, 2020. https://www.youtube.com/watch?v=C8W8JQLTECc.

Kresge, Naomi. "Pfizer-BioNTech Covid Vaccine Blocks Most Spread in Israel Study." Bloomberg. March 11, 2021. https://www.bloomberg.com/news/articles/2021-03-11/pfizer-biontech-covid-vaccine-blocks-most-spread-in-israel-study.

Krishnamurthy, Arvind. *Markus' Academy.* Princeton University Webinar. June 29, 2020. https://www.youtube.com/watch?v=voVh9BY3Lp4.

Krueger, Anne. "A New Approach to Sovereign Debt Restructuring." International Monetary Fund. April 2002. https://www.imf.org/external/pubs/ft/exrp/sdrm/eng/sdrm.pdf.

Krugman, Paul and Larry Summers. *Markus' Academy.* Princeton University Webinar. February 12, 2021. https://www.youtube.com/watch?v=EbZ3_LZxs54&t=7s.

Krugman, Paul. *Markus' Academy.* Princeton University Webinar. May 16, 2020. https://www.youtube.com/watch?v=h1ZiTIou0_8&list=PLl1591lvzxc3xwUuEkOVl1PNngFm9cZnH&index=17.

Lane, Philip. *Markus' Academy.* Princeton University Webinar. March 20, 2020. https://www.youtube.com/watch?v=G-8-4hEkkbs.

Laxminarayan, Ramanan. *Markus' Academy.* Princeton University Webinar. March 30, 2020. https://www.youtube.com/watch?v=z1yHjM7szBk&list=PLPKR-Xs

1slgSWqOqaXid_9sQXsPsjV_72&index=31.

LE News. "The Swiss National Bank Owns More A-Class Facebook Shares than Zuckerberg." April 4, 2018. https://lenews.ch/2018/04/04/the-swiss-national-bank-owns-more-a-class-facebook-shares-than-zuckerberg/.

Lee, Ming Jeong and Toshiro Hasegawa. "BOJ Becomes Biggest Japan Stock Owner with ¥45.1 Trillion Hoard." *The Japan Times*. December 7, 2020. https://www.japantimes.co.jp/news/2020/12/07/business/boj-japan-biggest-stock-owner/.

Leibowitz, Stan, and Stephen E. Margolis. "The Fable of Keys." *Journal of Law and Economics* 33, no. 1 (1990): 1-25.

Liang, Nellie. *Markus' Academy*. Princeton University Webinar. March 6, 2020. https://www.youtube.com/watch?v=6NjE-OOUB_E.

Lombrana, Laura. "An Urban Planner's Trick to Making Bikeable Cities." Bloomberg. August 5, 2020. https://www.bloomberg.com/news/articles/2020-08-05/an-urban-planner-s-trick-to-making-bike-able-cities?sref=ATN0rNv3.

Lund, Susan, Anu Madgavkar, James Manyika, and Sven Smit. "What's Next for Remote Work: An Analysis of 2000 Tasks, 800 Jobs, and Nine Countries." McKinsey Global Institute. November 23, 2020. https://www.mckinsey.com/featured-insights/future-of-work/whats-next-for-remote-work-an-analysis-of-2000-tasks-800-jobs-and-nine-countries?sid=blankform&sid=cd37a5db-95fb-4455-8ed2-f6b0596b8bcb#.

Lund, Susan. "Central Banks in a Shifting World." European Central Bank. November 2020. https://www.ecb.europa.eu/pub/conferences/html/20201111_ecb_forum_on_central_banking.en.html.

Lustig, Nora, Valentina Martinez Pabon, Federico Sanz, and Stephen Younger. "The Impact of Covid-19 Lockdowns and Expanded Social Assistance on Inequality, Poverty and Mobility in Argentina, Brazil, Colombia and Mexico." Center for Global Development Working Paper 556, October 2020. https://www.cgdev.org/sites/default/files/impact-covid-19-lockdowns-and-expanded-social-assistance.pdf.

MacKay, Kath. "UK Life Science Is Proving That It's Been Worth the Investment." *Forbes.* May 1, 2020. https://www.forbes.com/sites/drkathmackay/2020/05/01/uk-life-science-is-proving-that-its-been-worth-the-investment/?sh=39c104801771.

Mackintosh, James. "Inflation Is Already Here—For the Stuff You Actually Want to Buy." *The Wall Street Journal.* September 26, 2020. https://www.wsj.com/articles/inflation-is-already-herefor-the-stuff-you-actually-want-to-buy-11601112630?st=r6rjsuab2ijc738&reflink=article_gmail_share.

Maggi, Giovanni, and Ralph Ossa. "The Political Economy of Deep Integration." *NBER Working Papers,* no. 28190 (December 2020). https://www.nber.org/papers/w28190.

Malmendier, Ulrike, and Stefan Nagel. "Depression Babies: Do Macroeconomic Experiences Affect Risk Taking?" *The Quarterly Journal of Economics* 126, no. 1 (2011): 373-416.

Matrajt, Laura, Julia Eaton, Tiffany Leung, and Elizabeth Brown. 2021 "Vaccine Optimization for Covid-19: Who to Vaccinate First?" Science Advances. 2021.

McCarthy, Niall. "America First? Covid-19 Production & Exports." Statista. March 31, 2021. https://www.statista.com/chart/24555/vaccine-doses-produced-and-exported/.

McCarthy, Niall. "The Countries Most Reliant on Remittances [Infographic]." *Forbes.* April 26, 2018. https://www.forbes.com/sites/niallmccarthy/2018/04/26/the-countries-most-reliant-on-remittances-infographic/?sh=50407d577277.

McGuire, David, James EA Cunningham, Kae Reynolds, and Gerri Matthews-Smith. "Beating the Virus: An Examination of the Crisis Communication Approach Taken by New Zealand Prime Minister Jacinda Ardern During the Covid-19 Pandemic." *Human Resource Development International* 23, no. 4 (2020): 361-379.

Medeiros, Marcelo. "Brazil LAB at Princeton University: Inequalities: Poverty, Racism, and Social Mobility in Brazil." Princeton University Webinar. October 15, 2020. https://

www.youtube.com/watch?v=k3OSo83qFq8.

Merle, Renae. "How One Hedge Fund Made $2 Billion from Argentina's Economic Collapse." *The Washington Post.* March 29, 2016. https://www.washingtonpost.com/news/business/wp/2016/03/29/how-one-hedge-fund-made-2-billion-from-argentinas-economic-collapse/.

Meyer, Theodoric. "Four Ways the Government Subsidizes Risky Coastal Building." ProPublica. June 9, 2013. https://www.propublica.org/article/four-ways-the-government-subsidizes-risky-coastal-rebuilding.

Michaelson, Ruth. "'Vaccine Diplomacy' Sees Egypt Roll out Chinese Coronavirus Jab." *The Guardian.* December 30, 2020. https://www.theguardian.com/global-development/2020/dec/30/vaccine-diplomacy-sees-egypt-roll-out-chinese-coronavirus-jab.

Miller, Joe. "Inside the Hunt for a Covid-19 Vaccine: How BioNTech Made the Breakthrough." *Financial Times.* November 13, 2020. https://www.ft.com/content/c4ca8496-a215-44b1-a7eb-f88568fc9de9.

Mills, Claire Kramer, and Jessica Battisto. "Double Jeopardy: Covid-19's Concentrated Health and Wealth Effects in Black Communities." Federal Reserve Bank of New York. August 2020. https://www.newyorkfed.org/medialibrary/media/smallbusiness/DoubleJeopardy_COVID19andBlackOwnedBusinesses.

Mitteldeutscher Rundfunk. "Verschwörungstheorien in Sachsen: Ein wilder." Legenden-Mix. April 27, 2020. https://www.mdr.de/nachrichten/sachsen/corona-verschwoerungstherorien-populismus-100.html.

Mitra, Saumya. "Letter: Why G8 States Are Wary of Special Drawing Rights." *Financial Times.* January 22, 2021. https://www-ft-com.btpl.idm.oclc.org/content/20ca8b0f-9773-43de-9bfc-b09ab9ac5942.

Mordani, Sneha, Haider Tanseem, and Milan Sharma. "Watch: Doctors, Nurses Attacked in Delhi Hospital as Covid Patient Dies Without Getting ICU Bed." *India Today.* April 27, 2021. https://www.indiatoday.in/cities/delhi/story/doctors-attacked-in-delhi-hospital-by-family-of-covid-patient-1795567-2021-04-27.

Mullainathan, Sendhil and Edgar Shafir. *Scarcity: Why Having Too Little Means So Much.* New York: Times Books, 2013.

NBER. *NBER Digest.* August 8, 2020. https://www.nber.org/digest-2020-08.

Nebehay, Stephanie and Kate Kelland. "COVAX Programme Doubles Global Vaccine Supply Deals to 2 Billion Doses." Reuters. December 18, 2020. https://www.reuters.com/article/us-health-coronavirus-covax/covax-programme-doubles-global-vaccine-supply-deals-to-2-billion-doses-idUSKBN28S1PW.

Nonnemacher, Ursula. "Brandenburger Kreise Haben bis zur 200er-Inzidenz Freie Hand." RBB. March 15, 2021. https://www.rbb24.de/studiocottbus/panorama/coronavirus/beitraege_neu/2021/03/elbe-elster-corona-inzidenz-massnahmen-eingriff-land-brandenburg.html.

Nordhaus, William. "Climate Clubs: Overcoming Free-Riding in International Climate Policy." *American Economic Review* 105, no. 4 (2015): 1339-70. https://pubs.aeaweb.org/doi/pdfplus/10.1257/aer.15000001.

Nordhaus, William. *Markus' Academy.* Princeton University Webinar. January 28, 2021. https://www.youtube.com/watch?v=QaXZx_nJ_3I.

Officer, Lawrence H. and Samuel H. Williamson. "The Annual Consumer Price Index for the United States, 1774-Present." MeasuringWorth. 2021.

Opportunity Insights Economic Tracker. 2021. https://tracktherecovery.org.

Oreopoulos, Philip, Till Von Wachter, and Andrew Heisz. "The Short-and Long-Term Career Effects of Graduating in a Recession." *American Economic Journal: Applied Economics* 4, no. 1 (2012): 1-29.

Organization for Economic Cooperation and Development. "China's Belt and Road Initiative in the Global Trade, Investment and Finance Landscape." 2018. https://www.oecd.org/finance/Chinas-Belt-and-Road-Initiative-in-the-global-trade-investment-and-finance-landscape.pdf.

Organization for Economic Cooperation and Development. "The Face Mask Global Value Chain in the Covid-19 Outbreak: Evidence and Policy Lessons." May 4, 2020. http://www.oecd.org/coronavirus/policy-responses/the-face-mask-global-value-chain-in-the-COVID-

19-outbreak-evidence-and-policy-lessons-a4df866d/#endnotea0z8.

Our World in Data. "Covid-19 Stringency Index." June 1, 2021. https://ourworldindata.org/grapher/Covid-stringency-index.

Oxfam International. "Sanofi/GSK Vaccine Delay a Bitter Blow for World's Poorest Countries." December 11, 2020. https://www.oxfam.org/en/press-releases/sanofigsk-vaccine-delay-bitter-blow-worlds-poorest-countries.

Pedersen, Lasse. *Markus' Academy.* Princeton University Webinar. February 19, 2021. https://www.youtube.com/watch?v=ADnRm5LWCjg.

Peel, Michael and Joe Miller. "EU Hits Back as Blame Game Over Vaccine Procurement Intensifies." *Financial Times.* January 7, 2021. https://www.ft.com/content/c1575e05-70e5-4e5f-b58c-cde5c99aba5f.

Pellejero, Sebastian. "After Record U.S. Corporate-Bond Sales, Slowdown Expected." *The Wall Street Journal.* October 2, 2020. https://www.wsj.com/articles/after-record-u-s-corporate-bond-sales-slowdown-expected-11601631003.

Perchet, Vianney, Philippe Rigollet, Sylvain Chassang, and Erik Snowberg. "Batched Bandit Problems." *Annals of Statistics* 44, no. 2 (2016): 660-681. https://arxiv.org/abs/1505.00369.

Phillips, Toby. "Eat Out to Help Out: Crowded Restaurants May Have Driven UK Coronavirus Spike: New Findings." The Conversation. September 10, 2020. https://theconversation.com/eat-out-to-help-out-crowded-restaurants-may-have-driven-uk-coronavirus-spike-new-findings-145945.

Platt, Eric, David Carnevali, and Michael Mackenzie. "Wall Street IPO Bonanza Stirs Uneasy Memories of 90s Dotcom Mania." *Financial Times.* December 11, 2020. https://www.ft.com/content/cfdab1d0-ee5a-4e4a-a37b-20acfc0628e3?shareType=nongift.

Politi, James and Colby Smith. "Federal Reserve Calls Time on Looser Capital Requirements for US Banks." *Financial Times.* March 19, 2021. https://www.ft.com/content/279c2755-acab-4d9a-9092-d55fe5f518fa.

Posen, Adam. *Markus' Academy* (Lecture Slides). Princeton Bendheim Center for Finance. December 10, 2020. https://bcf.

princeton.edu/wp-content/uploads/2020/12/posenslides.pdf.

Powell, Jerome. *Markus' Academy.* Princeton University Webinar. January 14, 2021. https://www.youtube.com/watch?v=TEC3supZwvM.

Rai, Saritha. "Apple Alum Builds App to Help Millions in Indian Slums Find Jobs." Bloomberg. August 13, 2020. https://www.bloomberg.com/news/articles/2020-08-14/apna-job-app-aims-to-connect-india-s-workers-with-employees?sref=ATN0rNv3.

Rajan, Raghuram. "Raghuram Rajan on Covid-19: Is It Time to Decentralise Power?" (Video). Coronanomics. July 22, 2020. https://www.youtube.com/watch?v=VU9d5IyudYs.

Ramkumar, Amrith. "2020 SPAC Boom Lifted Wall Street's Biggest Banks." *The Wall Street Journal.* January 5, 2021. https://www.wsj.com/articles/2020-spac-boom-lifted-wall-streets-biggest-banks-11609842601?st=lguw1ftxebizf6e&reflink=article_gmail_share.

Ray, Debraj and S. Subramanian. "India's Lockdown: An Interim Report." *NBER Working Papers,* no. 27282 (May 2020).

ReliefWeb. "Q&A: Brazil's Poor Suffer the Most Under Covid-19." July 14, 2020. https://reliefweb.int/report/brazil/qa-brazils-poor-suffer-most-under-covid-19.

République Française. "Non-Respect de l'Obligation de Port du Masque: Quelles sont les Règles? October 21, 2020. https://www.service-public.fr/particuliers/vosdroits/F35351.

Reuters. "Factbox: How the G20's Debt Service Suspension Initiative Works." October 15, 2020. https://www.reuters.com/article/us-imf-worldbank-emerging-debtrelief-fac/factbox-how-the-g20s-debt-service-suspension-initiative-works-idINKBN27021V.

Reuters. "Germany to Extend Insolvency Moratorium for Virus-Hit Companies." August 25, 2020. https://www.reuters.com/article/healthcoronavirus-germany-bankruptcy-idUSL8N2FR36J.

Reuters. "Zambia Requests Debt Restructuring Under G20 Common Framework." February 5, 2021. https://www.reuters.

com/article/us-zambia-debt-idUSKBN2A50XL.

Robert Koch Institut. "Daily Situation Report of the Robert Koch Institute. December 29, 2020. https://www.rki.de/DE/Content/InfAZ/N/Neuartiges_Coronavirus/Situationsberichte/Dez_2020/2020-12-29-en.pdf?__blob=publicationFile.

Rodrik, Dani. *Markus' Academy.* Princeton University Webinar. May 5, 2020. https://www.youtube.com/watch?v=3cRlHugFBq8.

Rogoff, Kenneth. *Markus' Academy.* Princeton University Webinar. June 12, 2020. https://www.youtube.com/watch?v=0uh4oPjxxq8.

Romer, Paul. *Markus' Academy.* Princeton University Webinar. April 3, 2020. https://www.youtube.com/watch?v=q9z0eu4piHw&list=PLPKR-Xs1slgSWqOqaXid_9sQXsPsjV_72&index=30.

Roosevelt, Franklin Delano. "'Only Thing We Have to Fear Is Fear Itself': FDR's First Inaugural Address." History Matters. 1933. historymatters.gmu/edu/d/5057.

Rosenberg, Daniel. "How Digital Coupons Fuel China's Economic Recovery." Luohan Academy. May 27, 2020. https://www.luohanacademy.com/insights/e0d638c3f840e3be.

Roser, Max, and Esteban Ortiz-Ospina. "Global Extreme Poverty." Our World in Data. March 27, 2017. https://ourworldindata.org/extreme-poverty.

Rossi-Hansberg, Esteban. *Markus' Academy.* Princeton University Webinar. October 1, 2020. https://www.youtube.com/watch?v=ZsfKRrI2yB4.

RSF Social Finance. "The Runway Project: Loan Provided by the Women's Capital Collaborative." https://rsfsocialfinance.org/person/the-runway-project/.

Ruehl, Mercedes, Stephanie Findlay, and James Kynge. "Tech Cold War Comes to India: Silicon Valley Takes on Alibaba and Tencent." *Financial Times.* August 3, 2020. https://www.ft.com/content/b1df5dfd-36c4-49e6-bc56-506bf3ca3444?shareType=nongift.

Samson, Adam. "Bitcoin's Revival: Boom or Bubble?"

Financial Times. November 18, 2020. https://www.ft.com/content/a47090ee-fdf5-4cfa-9d17-47c56afad8c3.

Sandbu, Martin. "Globalisation Does Not Mean Deregulation." *Financial Times.* August 20, 2020. https://www.ft.com/content/a04c186b-ab3f-4df3-99fb-638b5aa1ce50?shareType=nongift.

Saritha, Rai. "Wall Street Giants Get Swept Up by India's Brutal Covid Wave." Bloomberg. May 6, 2021. https://www.bloomberg.com/news/articles/2021-05-06/wall-street-giants-get-swept-up-by-india-s-brutal-covid-wave?utm_medium=social&utm_campaign=socialflow-organic&utm_content=markets&utm_source=twitter&cmpid=socialflow-twitter-business&cmpid%3D=socialflow-.

Saxena, Ragani. "India's Health Time Bomb Keeps Ticking and It's Not Covid-19. Bloomberg. September 10, 2020. https://www.bloomberg.com/news/articles/2020-09-10/india-s-health-time-bomb-keeps-ticking-and-it-s-not-covid-19.

Saxony Government. "Infektionsfälle in Sachsen." March 18, 2021. https://www.coronavirus.sachsen.de/infektionsfaelle-in-sachsen-4151.html.

Scheidel, Walter. *The Great Leveler.* Princeton, NJ: Princeton University Press, 2018.

Schmelzing, Paul. "Eight Centuries of Global Real Interest Rates, R-G, and the 'Supra-Secular' Decline." Bank of England Staff Working Paper 845, (January 3, 2020): 1311–2018. https://www.bankofengland.co.uk/working-paper/2020/eight-centuries-of-global-real-interest-rates-r-g-and-the-suprasecular-decline-1311-2018.

Schmidt, Eric. *Markus' Academy.* Princeton University Webinar. July 27, 2020. https://www.youtube.com/watch?v=726B0y1D5ZM&t=31s.

Schulze, Elizabeth. "Robert Shiller Warns that Urban Home Prices Could Decline. CNBC. July 13, 2020. https://www.cnbc.com/2020/07/13/robert-shiller-warns-that-urban-home-prices-could-decline.html.

Sevastopulo, Demetri and Amy Kazmin. "US and Asia Allies Plan Covid Vaccine Strategy to Counter China." *Financial Times.* March 3, 2021.

https://www.ft.com/content/1dc04520-c2fb-4859-9821-c405f51f8586.

Shalal, Andrea and David Lawder. "Yellen Backs New Allocation of IMF's SDR Currency to Help Poor Nations." Reuters. February 25, 2021. https://www.reuters.com/article/g20-usa/update-3-yellen-backs-new-allocation-of-imfs-sdr-currency-to-help-poor-nations-idUSL1N2KV1IA.

Shayo, Moses. "A Model of Social Identity with an Application to Political Economy: Nation, Class, and Redistribution." *American Political Science Review* (2009): 147-174.

Shiller, Robert. *Markus' Academy.* Princeton University Webinar. July 10, 2020. https://www.youtube.com/watch?v=ak5xX8PEGAI.

Shin, Hyun Song. *Markus' Academy.* Princeton University Webinar. April 20, 2020. https://www.youtube.com/watch?v=LnmMRrzjNWQ.

Siedenbiedel, Christian. "In der Krise Horten die Menschen Bargeld." *Frankfurter Allgemeine.* September 24, 2020. https://www.faz.net/aktuell/finanzen/meine-finanzen/sparen-und-geld-anlegen/ezb-wirtschaftsbericht-in-der-krise-wird-bargeld-gehortet-16969517.html.

Sina, Ralph and Dominik Lauck. "Warum Israel Genug Impfstoff Hat." Tagesschau. January 23, 2021. https://www.tagesschau.de/ausland/impfstoff-israel-biontech-101.html.

Sinn, Hans-Werner. *The Green Paradox.* Cambridge, MA: MIT Press, 2012.

Slaoui, Moncef and Matthew Hepburn. "Developing Safe and Effective Covid Vaccines—Operation Warp Speed's Strategy and Approach." *New England Journal of Medicine* 383, no. 18 (2020): 1701-1703. https://www.nejm.org/doi/full/10.1056/NEJMp2027405.

Slok, Torsten. *Markus' Academy.* Princeton University Webinar. March 20, 2020. https://www.youtube.com/watch?v=zgxDybynvNM.

Solomon, Erika and Guy Chazan. "'We Need a Real Policy for China': Germany Ponders Post-Merkel Shift." *Financial Times.* January 5, 2021. https://www.ft.com/content/0de447eb-999d-452f-a1c9-d235cc5ea6d9.

Solomon, Erika. "BioNTech Seeks to Develop a More Effective

Malaria Vaccine." *Financial Times.* July 26, 2021. https://www.ft.com/content/e112b318-aced-482b-be4f-ec76f39cdc3f.

Spataro, Jared. "2 Years of Digital Transformation in 2 Months." Microsoft. April 30, 2020. https://www.microsoft.com/en-us/microsoft-365/blog/2020/04/30/2-years-digital-transformation-2-months/.

Spellman, Damian. "Two Newcastle Players Still 'Not Well at All' Following Covid Outbreak, Says Steve Bruce." *The Independent.* December 16, 2020. https://www.independent.co.uk/sport/football/premier-league/newcastle/players-covid-outbreak-who-steve-bruce-b1774816.html.

Spence, Michael. *Markus' Academy.* Princeton University Webinar. July 6, 2020. https://www.youtube.com/watch?v=92-vc238_nI&list=PLPKR-Xs1slgSWqOqaXid_9sQXsPsjV_72&index=6.

Stein, Jeremy. *Markus' Academy.* Princeton University Webinar. May 11, 2020. https://www.youtube.com/watch?v=0iNQNzAUDiw.

Stephen, Bijan. "The Lockdown Live-Streaming Numbers Are Out, and They're Huge." The Verge. May 13, 2020. https://www.theverge.com/2020/5/13/21257227/coronavirus-streamelements-arsenalgg-twitch-youtube-livestream-numbers.

Steverman, Ben. "Harvard's Chetty Finds Economic Carnage in Wealthiest ZIP Codes." Bloomberg. September 24, 2020. https://www.bloomberg.com/news/features/2020-09-24/harvard-economist-raj-chetty-creates-god-s-eye-view-of-pandemic-damage.

Stiglitz, Joseph. *Markus' Academy.* Princeton University Webinar. April 27, 2020. https://www.youtube.com/watch?v=_6SoT97wo3g.

Stock, James. *Markus' Academy.* Princeton University Webinar. January 21, 2021. https://www.youtube.com/watch?v=_7Imhf7t0Co.

Summers, Lawrence. *Markus' Academy.* Princeton University Webinar. May 22, 2020. https://www.youtube.com/watch?v=cZmRtQCR2ns&list=PLPKR-Xs1slgSWqOqaXid_9sQXsPsjV_72&index=17.

Tett, Gillian. "Pandemic Aid Is Exacerbating US Inequality." *Financial Times.* August 6, 2020. https://www.ft.com/

content/8287303f-4062-4808-8ce3-f7fa9f87e185.

The Economist. "India's Giant Second Wave Is a Disaster for It and for the World." April 24, 2021.

The Economist. "'The Covid-19 Pandemic Will Be Over by the End of 2021,' says Bill Gates." August 18, 2020.

https://www.economist.com/international/2020/08/18/the-covid-19-pandemic-will-be-over-by-the-end-of-2021-says-bill-gates.

The Economist. "Are Vaccine Passports a Good Idea?" March 13, 2020. https://www.economist.com/science-and-technology/2021/03/11/are-vaccine-passports-a-good-idea.

The Economist. "Economists Are Rethinking the Numbers on Inequality." November 28, 2019. https://www.economist.com/briefing/2019/11/28/economists-are-rethinking-the-numbers-on-inequality.

The Economist. "How Well Will Vaccines Work?" February 11, 2021. https://www.economist.com/leaders/2021/02/13/how-well-will-vaccines-work.

The Economist. "When Will Office Workers Return?" February 20, 2021. https://www.economist.com/business/2021/02/20/when-will-office-workers-return.

The Guardian. "Big Brother Isn't Just Watching: Workplace Surveillance Can Track Your Every Move." November 6, 2017. https://www.theguardian.com/world/2017/nov/06/workplace-surveillance-big-brother-technology.

The Guardian. "Joe Biden Receives Coronavirus Vaccine" (Video). December 21, 2020. https://www.theguardian.com/us-news/video/2020/dec/21/joe-biden-receives-coronavirus-vaccine-video.

The Renaissance: The Age of Michelangelo and Leonardo da Vinci. Documentary film by DW. April 28, 2019. https://www.youtube.com/watch?v=BmHTQsxxkPk.

The World Bank. "Consumption Expenditure as a Percent of GDP in China." 2021 https://data.worldbank.org/indicator/NE.CON.TOTL.ZS?locations=CN.

The World Bank. "Debt Service Suspension and COVID-19." February 12, 2020. https://www.worldbank.org/en/news/factsheet/2020/05/11/debt-relief-and-covid-19-coronavirus.

Tirole, Jean. "Allons-Nous Enfin Apprendre Notre Leçon?" LinkedIn. April 14, 2020. https://www.linkedin.com/pulse/allons-nous-enfin-apprendre-notre-le%C3%A7on-jean-tirole/.

Titan, Alon, Matthias Doepke, Jane Olmstead-Rumsey, and Michele Tertilt. "The Impact of Covid-19 on Gender Equality." *NBER Working Papers,* no. 27660 (August 2020).

Trading Economics. "Brazil Recorded a Government Budget Deficit Equal to 13.40 Percent of the Country's Gross Domestic Product in 2020." 2021. https://tradingeconomics.com/brazil/government-budget.

Trading Economics. "Sweden GDP Growth Rate." February 26, 2020. https://tradingeconomics.com/sweden/gdp-growth.

Trading Economics. "Taiwan GDP Growth." 2021. https://tradingeconomics.com/taiwan/gdp-growth.

Vegh, Carlos A. "Fiscal Policy in Emerging Markets: Procyclicality and Graduation." NBER. December 2015. https://www.nber.org/reporter/2015number4/fiscal-policy-emerging-markets-procyclicality-and-graduation.

Vissing-Jorgensen, Annette. "The Treasury Market in Spring 2020 and the Response of the Federal Reserve." April 5, 2021. http://faculty.haas.berkeley.edu/vissing/vissing_jorgensen_bonds2020.pdf.

Walsh, David. "Do We Need Coronavirus 'Vaccine Passports' to Get Europe Moving Again? Euronews
Asks the Experts." Euronews. December 11, 2020. https://www.euronews.com/2020/12/11/do-we-need-coronavirus-vaccine-passports-to-get-the-world-moving-again-euronews-asks-the-e.

Wasdani, Kishinchand Poornima and Ajnesh Prasad. "The Impossibility of Social Distancing among the Urban Poor: The Case of an Indian Slum in the Times of COVID-19." *Local Environment* 25, no. 5 (2020): 414-418.

Welt. "Das ist Drostens Plan für den Herbst." August 5, 2020. https://www.welt.de/politik/deutschland/article212941080/Christian-Drosten-Buerger-sollen-Kontakt-Tagebuch-fuehren.html.

Westmaas, Rueben. "World Famous Chicago Skyscraper Sways in Wind." Discovery. August 1, 2019. https://www.discovery.com/exploration/World-Famous-Chicago-Skyscraper-Sway-Wind.

Wharton Research Data Services. "Using the CRSP/Compustat Merged (CCM) Database." 2021. https://wrds-www.wharton.upenn.edu/pages/classroom/using-crspcompustat-merged-database/.

Wheatley, Jonathan. "Debt Dilemma: How to Avoid a Crisis in Emerging Nations." Financial Times. December 20, 2020. https://www.ft.com/content/de43248e-e8eb-4381-9d2f-a539d1f1662c?shareType=nongift.

Wheatley, Jonathan. "Emerging Markets Attract $17bn of Inflows in First Three Weeks of 2021." *Financial Times.* January 22, 2021. https://www.ft.com/content/f9b94ac9-1df1-4d89-b129-5b30ff98e715?shareType=nongift.

Wheatley, Jonathan. "Foreign Investors Dash into Emerging Markets at Swiftest Pace since 2013. *Financial Times.* December 17, 2020. https://www.ft.com/content/e12a1eee-2571-4ae5-bc91-cc17ee7f40d0?shareType=nongift.

Wiegel, Michaela. "Wie Frankreich die Akzeptanz der Corona-Maßnahmen Verspielt." *Frankfurter Allgemeine.* September 24, 2020. https://www.faz.net/aktuell/politik/ausland/wie-frankreich-die-akzeptanz-der-corona-massnahmen-verspielt-16969296.html.

Wigglesworth, Robin, Richard Henderson, and Eric Platt. "The Lockdown Death of a 20-Year-Old Day Trader. *Financial Times.* July 2, 2020. https://www.ft.com/content/45d0a047-360f-4abf-86ee-108f436015a1.

Wikipedia. "Tacoma Narrows Bridge (1940)." https://en.wikipedia.org/wiki/Tacoma_Narrows_Bridge_(1940)#Film_of_collapse.

Wolf, Marin. "How Coronavirus and Race Collide in the US." Bloomberg. August 11, 2020. https://www.bloombergquint.com/quicktakes/how-coronavirus-and-race-collide-in-the-u-s-quicktake.

Xie, Yu and Xiang Zhou. "Income Inequality in Today's China."

Proceedings of the National Academy of Sciences 111, no. 19 (2014): 6928-6933. https://www.pnas.org/content/111/19/6928.short.

Zeckhauser, Richard. *Markus' Academy.* Princeton University Webinar. July 17, 2020. https://www.youtube.com/watch?v=jHTRFizTsFE&list=PLPKR-Xs1slgSWqOqaXid_9sQXsPsjV_72&index=3.

Zhong, Raymond. "How Taiwan Plans to Stay (Mostly) Covid Free." *The New York Times.* January 2, 2021. https://www.nytimes.com/2021/01/02/world/asia/taiwan-coronavirus-health-minister.html.

Index

R

About the Author

Markus K. Brunnermeier is the Edwards S. Sanford Professor at Princeton University and director of Princeton's Bendheim Center for Finance. He is a Fellow of the Econometric Society, a Guggenheim Fellow, a Sloan Research Fellow, a Vice President of the American Finance Association, and a non-resident Fellow at the Peterson Institute for International Economics.